For Joel

FATHER OF ROUTE 66

FATHER OF ROUTE 66

The Story of Cy Avery

SUSAN CROCE KELLY

UNIVERSITY OF OKLAHOMA PRESS : NORMAN

ALSO BY SUSAN CROCE KELLY
Route 66: The Highway and Its People (Norman, Okla., 1988)

Library of Congress Cataloging-in-Publication Data
Kelly, Susan Croce, 1947–
Father of Route 66: the story of Cy Avery / Susan Croce Kelly.
    pages   cm
Includes bibliographical references and index.
ISBN 978-0-8061-4499-3 (cloth)
ISBN 978-0-8061-6473-1 (paper)
1. Avery, Cy (Cyrus Stevens), 1871–1963
2. United States Highway 66—History.
3. Highway planning—United States—History—20th century.
I. Title.
HE356.U55K46 2014
388.1092—dc23
[B]

2014002872

The paper in this book meets the guidelines for permanence and durability of the Committee on Production Guidelines for Book Longevity of the Council on Library Resources, Inc. ∞

Contents

Illustrations

Preface

I first learned of Cy Avery years ago when I was writing *Route 66: The Highway and Its People.* Cy was a charmer, and during my research on the history of U.S. Highway 66, I became intrigued with him. How could one man, in Oklahoma of all places, manage to have an effect on the whole national highway system? Why Cy Avery? Why Oklahoma? How, for heaven's sake, did U.S. 66 become the iconic Route 66?

Years later, when I began to investigate the life of the persuasive highway man from Tulsa, I learned that he and his times were inextricable—and it counted a lot that he was from what then may have been the richest city in the world.

Like many of his contemporaries, Cy started life on a comfortable farm in the settled East and grew up on the frontier. This meant he had a rudimentary understanding of mechanics, how things worked, and how to fix them. From personal experience he recognized that the country was not as big as it seemed and could probably be made smaller. And because he watched a wilderness turn into oil-rich cities, he knew anything was possible. He came of age during a time when the industrial and technological revolutions were giving ordinary men the wherewithal to chart their own courses and change the nation. Telephones, the Panama Canal, steel bridges, skyscrapers, airmail, rural free mail delivery, commercial electric lights, automobiles, and highways—they all happened in his lifetime.

This nation is better, and different, because of men and women who rolled up their sleeves and made things happen, often before the rest of the country knew it was possible. People like Cy Avery.

This book is the story of that man and his time.

Acknowledgments

Many people over many years have provided information, support, and perspectives on Cy Avery and Route 66—and I am deeply indebted to all of them.

Jeanne Kern, especially, has been a counselor, cheerleader, reader, proofreader, and no-holds-barred critic—and even sent me a Route 66 suitcase.

The Avery family, particularly Cy's grandchildren Stevens Avery, Joy Avery, and Bob Berghell, and his grandniece Rose Stauber, have been generous with time, photographs, stories, introductions, and memorabilia. When we met, Joy determined I needed to see Cy's Tulsa and drove me all over the area, from his first farm in northeast Tulsa to Coyote Ranch out by Sand Springs. Rose, a journalist herself, took me on a tour of Spavinaw so I could see Cy's first Oklahoma home and research his later land dealings there. Rose also related stories her grandmother Carrie had told about Cy, and Rose's writing about her great uncle set a high standard for my own endeavors. Stevens counseled, shared his memories, and took time to read and, thankfully, made corrections on the final manuscript.

My former editor, Jay Dew, thought the book was a good idea from the first conversation and was a patient advisor, along with the University of Oklahoma Press staff who have had to deal with me.

Beth Ann Freeman, director of the Oklahoma State University–Tulsa Library, made the Cyrus Stevens Avery Papers freely available to me and helped in dozens of other ways.

Gary Ray Howell at the Oklahoma Department of Transportation (ODOT) found old records and put me in touch with invaluable resources at the Oklahoma State Historical Society, Oklahoma State Library, and ODOT.

Members of the press were also generous with time and materials. Many pre-Internet years ago, Julie DelCour scoured the files of the *Tulsa World* for articles about a then-nearly forgotten road builder. Much more recently Randy Krehbiel took time to tell me about Cy, whom he had gotten to know through reporting on the Greenwood community and other aspects of Tulsa history.

Bob Cullen at the American Association of State Highway and Transportation Officials in Washington, D.C., dropped everything to hunt down old archive material about the national highway movement.

Without the work of Richard Weingroff at the Federal Highway Department (FHWA), this project would have been much, much more difficult. The wonderful FHWA "Highway History" website, www.fhwa.dot.gov/infrastructure/history.cfm, is an amazing resource to anyone interested in how our American road system came into being. Richard, who along with Arthur Krim of the Society for Commercial Archaeology was part of the group of early searchers into the whys and wherefores of U.S. Highway 66, also encouraged my investigation of Cy Avery's life.

Chris Kleemeier, as always, took me in when I visited Washington, D.C., and helped me find my way around the highway history sites there; likewise Jane Wand and U.S. 66 Highway Association sites in Springfield, Missouri.

Paul Stroble, my first and best fan, not only used my first book as a college classroom text but also has been an enthusiastic booster for this project—and sent me a historic U.S. 66 road sign.

Horst Sauer and Hanspeter Shelling opened my eyes to European interest in this quintessentially American highway, and Nobukiko Ozeki, through his marvelous photos and two lovely books about Route 66, showed me a Japanese fan base. Together, they reminded me of the responsibility a Route 66 historian has not only to Americans who grew up with the road but also to those in the rest of the world who see U.S. 66 as the true story of twentieth-century America.

Countless other Route 66 fans have given me their support and encouragement—along with Route 66 earrings, potholders, totes, ash trays, glasses, mugs, coasters, and T-shirts—beginning in the years when photographer Quinta Scott and I traveled the old highway talking with people and uncovering the story of the road that seems to have run though everyone's life.

And then there is my family: Joel, Brendan, Kaylee, Brad, Abi, Franchessa, Wyatt and Pepper, Mary and all the Griffins. Owen, who sent a 66 sign; Leo, who sent the necktie; Lina, and all the cousins in California: you are the best.

Finally, my first knowledge of Route 66 came from my mother, my great-aunt Lucile Morris Upton, and my great-uncle George Morris—I only wish they were still around to watch what has rolled down Route 66 in 2014.

FATHER OF ROUTE 66

ONE

From East to West

"The only object we, of Oklahoma, have had was to have a continuous route number from Chicago to Los Angeles. . . .We assure you that it will be a road . . . the U.S. Government will be proud of."

In that July 1926 letter to E. W. James at the federal Bureau of Public Roads, Cy Avery acknowledged his role in a saga that involved months of maneuvering, weeks of public disputes, meetings with members of Congress, and a day that kept Western Union wires humming minute to minute. No less than the great plan for a national highway system had been at stake. The focus for all the foment was a highway number, and the outcome of those months of contention was not the number Cy had hoped for. Instead, he made a decision to affix the number sixty-six to the still mostly dirt and gravel road that ran between Chicago and Los Angeles. In the years that followed, Cy saw to it that Route 66 held a place on the national stage. What he could not know, however, was that Route 66 would become an American icon.

By the time Cy died in 1963 at the age of ninety-one, his road had been the muse for a Pulitzer Prize–winning novel, a long-running television show, and an ever-popular song. The road that Cy created carried travelers into tree-lined, small-town America then swept them across the vastness of the nation's western spaces, through craggy mountains, across Indian reservations, skirted the Grand Canyon, and charged across the great American desert before it arrived in Hollywood and rolled to a stop on a sandy Pacific beach. Today, visitors from all over the world travel to see what is left of Route 66. Some actually ship historic cars and motorcycles from Europe and Asia to "motor west, on the highway that's the best."[1] Others band together on buses or caravans for the 2,400-mile trip. Still others come alone to soak up a part of the United States that most Americans no longer know.

The highway itself was officially bypassed years ago. The once proud concrete pavement is broken in many places and its black tar joints have shriveled. Today U.S. 66 is more a series of dead ends than a cross-country boulevard. In many instances, it is not even on maps. Yet age and infirmity have only heightened its aura. Against all odds, Route 66—Cy Avery's highway—endures.

The story of Cyrus Stevens Avery and Route 66 is one that could not have happened a decade earlier—the technology to build the road was simply not available, nor was the money. A decade later would have been too late. It probably made a difference that Cy was from Tulsa, a rich little city that was an important source of the nation's petroleum supply. The man, too, was singular. No one else could have accomplished the final sleight of hand that took a bitter loss to the governor of Kentucky and, out of what remained, created a legend.

————

If you had asked Cy, he would have told you his proudest accomplishment was Spavinaw—a dam and fifty-five mile concrete pipeline that brought good drinking water to the thirsty people of his beloved Tulsa in the early 1920s. But if you were to ask anyone else, the answer would be that Cy Avery had everything to do with the national highway system of 1926—especially the road that began in Chicago, took a right turn in Oklahoma, and sliced its way through the great American West.

Cy's world was one that changed from being dependent on man- and horsepower to one that operated on electricity and petroleum. And for a man who was a farmer, teacher, real-estate magnate, and oil producer, it was a time when a person with the right combination of experience, curiosity, motivation, and know-how could achieve heretofore unimaginable things. In this case, Cy's driving enthusiasm for better roads helped change the nation. He had the foresight to join the "Good Roads" bandwagon early in his career. Reared to believe in himself and his abilities, he also had the personality, technical knowledge, passion, and sheer bullheadedness to bring one of the nation's most important east-west highways through Tulsa. And by so doing, he became the Father of Route 66.

His story began in 1871 in Stevensville, Pennsylvania, a small farming community in the Susquehanna River valley, a region of green hillsides, rock outcroppings, and running streams. Small towns and small farms dotted the landscape, and farmers, like young Cy's two grandfathers, grew tobacco, corn, wheat, fruits, vegetables and raised livestock including thoroughbred horses. Stevensville was named for a family that had settled there in colonial times, and, when Cy was born, a hefty part of the population still bore the Stevens name. Among them was Cy's mother, Ruie Rebecca Stevens Avery, a no-nonsense schoolteacher.

Cy's father, Alexander James Avery, generally known as A.J., was a ninth-generation descendant from Christopher Avery, a well-to-do Englishman who arrived in Massachusetts with his son James in the early 1600s. James later moved to Connecticut, and his son eventually settled in Groton, where the Avery descendants still maintain the Avery Memorial Association and receive family members at annual celebrations. Christopher Avery's progeny have been a successful group, counting among their numbers heads of manufacturing companies, professional men, and even John D. Rockefeller, whose wife was an Avery.

Since colonial times, Avery men had been well represented in the military, so when the Civil War erupted A.J., then just shy of twenty years old, signed on with a Pennsylvania volunteer regiment. However, when he traveled to Gettysburg to enter active service, he discovered that the requisite quota of volunteers had already been reached. So A.J. was mustered out, went back home, and never served.[2]

By the time Cy came on the scene a decade later, A.J. was a successful merchant and horse breeder in Stevensville, no doubt benefitting from the fact that his wife and children were related in some way to nearly everyone in the community. A.J. was good-natured, quick-witted, and generally well liked, so he and Ruie Rebecca were surely optimistic about their future and their ability to raise their son and daughters, Caroline (Carrie) and Bertha.[3]

Cy, who was named for his two grandfathers, Cyrus Stevens and Cyrus Avery, spent his first twelve years in the heart of this family community. A small, energetic kid with a boundless curiosity about the world around him and a growing knack for storytelling, he played with his many cousins, attended school, and learned even more in the evenings from his mother. He surely listened to stories about the Avery clan and ancestor Christopher Avery's journey with his young son from England to Gloucester, Massachusetts.

When he was not in school, Cy helped his father and grandfather Stevens on their farms and in various commercial ventures. By the time he was ten years old, he knew the aggravation of driving an oxcart along the rutted lanes of Stevensville to deliver milk, for which he was paid a penny a quart. Much later in life he proudly showed a newspaper reporter the yoke he had used to hitch those milk-hauling oxen of his childhood.

During those Pennsylvania years he also began to acquire the basis for his lifelong political affiliation. His grandfather Avery had been active enough in politics to be appointed postmaster under Democratic presidents Pierce and Buchanan, and his father boasted being part of the only Democratic family in Bradford County. Later, an uncle was a delegate to the National Democratic Convention in St. Louis in 1888 that nominated Grover Cleveland for a second term. Cy was to be active in the party all his life and even took a run at the Oklahoma governor's job when he was in his early sixties.

Close knit and nurturing as his hometown was for Cy, northeastern Pennsylvania was probably not the best place to be born in 1871. Even though the state's economy had grown during the Civil War, Pennsylvania suffered huge losses of men, most especially at the Battle of Gettysburg, which A.J. was lucky enough to have missed. And while the northwest corner of the state was booming, thanks to the discovery of oil near Titusville in 1859, not all was well in Pennsylvania. The move to mechanized farming equipment was causing growing pains for agriculture, and the industrial sector was plagued with strikes by underpaid and long-suffering workers.

Just weeks after Cy turned two, the U.S. economy went into a free fall. The Northern Pacific Railroad declared bankruptcy. Jay Cooke and Company, Northern Pacific's primary creditor and one of the nation's largest commercial banks, suspended operations, and the whole country went down with it. Banks closed, other railroads defaulted, farm prices collapsed, businesses of all sizes failed, and obtaining credit became nearly impossible. Large industrial operations like cotton and iron mills closed, throwing thousands out of work. In New York City, unemployment stood at 25 percent. The agricultural economy foundered, especially out west where nature added her own bite to an already difficult situation: clouds of Rocky Mountain locusts swarmed through croplands, leaving farmers helpless to do anything but watch the destruction of their livelihood by the voracious insects.

When the decade-long depression of 1873 came to Bradford County, A. J. Avery watched his business falter, then fail, and his savings disappear. Over the next six years, he probably spent long hours talking with other impoverished farmers and merchants. Possibly he even got to know soldiers who had fought on the western front in the Civil War or served in the cavalry on the edge of the frontier. A good part of those conversations may have involved talk about better times and speculation about better places.

One place in particular must have come up in those conversations: Indian Territory. By the 1870s, there was talk that Indian lands would soon be legally opened to settlers. In fact, despite treaties and federal laws, non-Indians were already flocking into the region just south of Kansas and west of Missouri and Arkansas. In a new country like that, A.J. may have concluded, an enterprising young man could do well.

Thanks to the fact that most western Indians who fought in the Civil War had signed on with the Confederacy, Washington, D.C., saw no need to support the immutability of their treaties. Among the postwar revisions of those treaties were changes that gave railroad companies the right to build lines through Indian Territory. From there, it was only a short step to white settlement. Especially since some of the fiercest promoters of white settlement were themselves Indians.

A.J. and his friends may have learned about this new opportunity for settlement thanks to a Cherokee attorney and Washington, D.C., lobbyist named Col. Elias C. Boudinot II. A tall, striking man with a flowing mane, Boudinot was the son of a New England mother and a Cherokee newspaperman. Raised and educated in New England, he moved west, become a delegate to the Confederate Congress, and also served as a colonel in the Confederate Army under his Cherokee uncle, Gen. Stand Watie. After the Civil War Boudinot moved to Washington, D.C., where he became a popular figure in social and artistic circles. One of his friends was sculptor Vinnie Ream Hoxie, who created the statue of Abraham Lincoln that stands in the Capitol Rotunda.

Boudinot took part in renegotiating the treaties for the Five Civilized Tribes. He argued that Indians should be made U.S. citizens and that they should hold individual titles to land. This, of course, would give them the right to sell it if they wished. Boudinot further argued that Indian Territory should be made an official U.S. territory. Like much else that goes on in Washington, D.C., Boudinot's labors were not without guile. Even as a member of the Cherokee delegation, he was working closely with railroad lobbyists, who were anxious to lay tracks through Indian Territory. Later, he actually platted a town site so he could benefit from the railroad's arrival.

To assure the success of his various ventures, he penned an article that was published in the *Chicago Times* in February 1879 in which he suggested that two million acres of unoccupied and "unassigned" land in Indian Territory should be considered public domain and open to white settlement. Never mind that these "unassigned" lands had been unwillingly ceded by the Creek and Seminole tribes as part of the Reconstruction treaties and were not then open to whites. Boudinot's article caused a small uproar across the country. It also probably precipitated the arrival of countless illegal "Boomer" homesteaders.[4]

In small, rural Stevensville, it's doubtful that A. J. Avery actually saw a copy of Boudinot's article, but it is very likely that he heard about it. It is also likely that sometime during 1879 or 1880, as the national economy began to improve, A.J. managed to pull together enough resources to make a trip west. Certainly he wasn't living with his family. The 1880 census reports that Ruie Rebecca, Cy, and the two girls were living with Ruie's parents on their Stevensville farm, but A.J. isn't listed.

If he did visit Indian Territory, A.J. probably would have made his way first to St. Louis and then to the far southwest corner of Missouri. He would have heard that just across the state line in Indian Territory people were willing to lease land to white settlers. If he then took time to travel into the Cherokee lands, he would have discovered a country of rugged wooded hills, limestone creeks, and rivers—rougher, but not unlike Bradford County, Pennsylvania. A.J. probably took heart from the similarity of the landscape.

Since 1871, the area closest to Missouri and Arkansas had two through roads of a sort, and thanks to Boudinot, it also had railroads and a town. The two roads ran north to Kansas and south to Texas. One had been developed as a military road; the other was put through to give cattlemen a way to get to railheads in Missouri and Kansas. The Missouri, Kansas and Texas Railway (the Katy) tracks came in from the north in 1871, and Boudinot laid out a town site at what he believed would be the Katy terminus. However, that same year, the Atlantic and Pacific Railroad, soon to become the St. Louis and San Francisco (Frisco), brought track in from the east. The two rail lines crossed and stopped two miles from Boudinot's platted settlement, and it was there that the new town grew up. Perhaps as a consolation prize, Boudinot named the new community. It was Vinita, after sculptor Vinnie Ream Hoxie.

Of course the tracks didn't end in Vinita for long. In the early 1880s, Frisco crews laid sixty more miles of track, stopping this time in Creek territory, near an existing Indian settlement on the Arkansas River. Rail workers erected a tent city there and that community eventually became Tulsa.[5]

Sometime between 1873 and 1880, A.J. became enamored with the idea of Indian Territory and determined to resettle his family there. Like so many other western-bound easterners, he made his move in stages. In 1884, when Cy was thirteen, A.J. loaded his son and most of the family's belongings into a heavy wagon, bid Ruie Rebecca and the two girls goodbye, and set out.[6]

For the trip, A.J. probably chose a Conestoga wagon. Conestogas had been developed in Pennsylvania and were known for size, strength, and the ability to stand up to the trials of American travel. A Conestoga wagon could carry twelve thousand pounds and be counted on to survive river crossings, wheel-deep mud, and heavy going.

Any kind of journey in the United States in those days required time, stamina, and patience, even in the long-settled states east of the Mississippi. Beyond the Mississippi, it was worse: all the through roads were dirt or, if they had been upgraded, dirt and gravel. That was fine for horses and an occasional wagon but not for the heavy loads carried by thousands of settlers moving west. By and large, roads were dusty and rutted in dry weather, frozen and rutted in winter, and muddy quagmires the rest of the time.

Americans had called for good roads since colonial times. Periodically the government responded with funds and plans but the country had neither the technology nor the focus to accomplish much. The Averys' home state of Pennsylvania was one that had taken road building seriously, perhaps because back in the seventeenth century, when white settlers arrived, the roads they found were good ones. The local Indians had created long-distance highways between rivers with different paths for wet and dry seasons and for war parties or peaceful travel.[7] As early as 1700, the Pennsylvania Assembly began authorizing road building, and in the 1790s the assembly commissioned the Lancaster Turnpike, the first macadam road in the United States. By 1830, there were three thousand miles of turnpike roads in Pennsylvania.[8]

The federal government made a foray into national road construction in 1806 when it authorized the Cumberland Road, also known as the National Road, to go from the East Coast to St. Louis, but that road was never finished. Construction stopped in 1839, several miles short of St. Louis, when funding for highways became a lower priority than for canals and railroads. Today Vandalia, Illinois, still celebrates itself as the terminus of the old National Road. In the early 1800s the government also laid out more than twenty thousand miles of military roads across the west, but even that kind of road building stopped almost entirely during the Civil War.

No matter how excited A.J. and Cy were about moving across the country, that long journey from Pennsylvania was a tough one. A wiry, young teen like Cy would have been called on over and over to get off his wagon box and help pull someone's team of horses or oxen through a deep gravel creek, dig wagon wheels out of the mud, or push a wagon through a rough spot. When they left Stevensville, A.J. and Cy probably followed the old National Road all the way to Vandalia. From Vandalia, it was only a short distance to the Mississippi River. They would have crossed the Mississippi at St. Louis, either on a ferry or via the new all-steel Eads Bridge, a combined road and railroad bridge that was a national landmark. Built the year after Cy was born, it was the longest arched bridge in the world, and one of the first to use steel as a primary structural material. It was also a threat to the local ferry operators. Around the time that Cy and A.J. needed to cross the Mississippi, the ferry and the Eads Bridge people were in heavy competition for non-railroad traffic. Wiggins Ferry Company had dropped prices to a nickel to compete with the bridge, while the bridge company offered ice water and free concerts to customers.[9] There is no record as to which our travelers chose.

After a day or two in St. Louis, A.J. and Cy would have set out to the southwest, jostling among farmers, merchants, stagecoaches, and covered wagons as they headed toward Indian Territory. Their route followed the Old Wire Road—later to be part of U.S. 66—to Springfield and on west to Joplin, a raucous mining community. From Joplin, they would have turned south and traveled along the Missouri border to South West City, a jumping-off place for Indian Territory.

About thirty miles into Indian Territory and not far from the little community of Vinita, A.J. brought the wagon to a halt. Despite the railroad, and despite the influx of white settlers, that part of the country was still officially federal land, ruled by U.S. marshals and by Hangin' Judge Isaac Parker's court at Fort Smith, Arkansas. The region had been well known in the East for a half century. In 1832, author Washington Irving visited the area with Judge Henry Ellsworth, one of the commissioners appointed to arrange for the mass Indian relocation into Indian Territory. Three years later, Irving's book, *A Tour on the Prairies*, captivated international attention with tales of his trek into the American West. Geographically, the countryside was a continuation of the Missouri Ozarks, rough hills with outcroppings of limestone, oak forests dissolving into rolling prairies. At the confluence of Brush Creek and Spavinaw Creek, A.J. leased a farm from a local landowner.

Thanks to the two creeks, there was plenty of water for livestock and crops. However there was no house. The property had been the home-stead of Stand Watie, a Cherokee chief, Confederate general, and, as it happened, Elias C. Boudinot's uncle. The original two-story log house burned during the Civil War, leaving only the chimneys that had been at each end. The only real part of Watie's property left on the land was one of the big stone burrs for a gristmill that had once been on Spavi-naw Creek.

The landlord gave A.J. what was known as an "improvement lease" and furnished him with lumber to rebuild a house on the property. Watie's original home had been a dogtrot, that is, two separate buildings under one roof on each side of a breezeway, "where the harness was hung and the dog and cat used as sleeping quarters." The new farmhouse, with no dogtrot, incorporated only one of the chimneys. A.J. and Cy tore down the other one.[10] Probably at the same time they were building the house, Cy and his father rushed to put in at least a small crop. The two worked with industry: Cy later quoted his father as admonishing him to work twice as hard on Saturdays to make up for the fact that no work could be done on Sundays.[11]

Allegedly, they turned the farm into one of the finest properties in the area. They would have put in vegetables and perhaps planted some fruit trees, but with its rolling hills, trees, creeks, and big valleys this was live-stock country. A.J. had been a livestock breeder in Pennsylvania; surely he chose to follow that aspect of farming in his new home. Even today, that part of the country is devoted largely to pasture and rangeland.

During the two or so years that Cy lived with his father in Indian Ter-ritory, he worked on the farm, hunted, fished, and roamed the green hills and valleys. He developed a serious interest in agriculture and grew to love the clear, cool waters of Spavinaw Creek. For the rest of his life, he made a ritual of returning to Spavinaw on his birthday to take a drink of water, kick off his shoes, roll up his pant legs, and go wading. Besides working on the farm, Cy went to school. Even though Ruie Rebecca was still in Pennsylvania, she had instilled in her children such a respect for learning and such an interest in books that Cy attended a nearby Indian Mission School, when time and weather permitted.

About once a month, Cy and his father traveled the thirty miles back to South West City to purchase groceries, pick up mail from those back home, and hear the news.[12] Years later, Cy told a group of law officers, "We never locked our house though we might be gone several days. We didn't lock the smokehouse, and neither men nor women feared hijackers, holdups, petty thievery or any other type of lawlessness."[13]

Two years after the Avery men reached Indian Territory, they sent for the rest of the family. Ruie Rebecca and daughter Bertha joined them right away but older daughter, Carrie, by this time eighteen years old and a schoolteacher, stayed behind in Stevensville. She came west two years later, and, thanks to an uncle who was traveling to St. Louis as a delegate to the 1888 Democratic Convention, she had a chaperone most of the way from Pennsylvania. In St. Louis, Carrie boarded a train to Seneca, a lead mining town in southwest Missouri. At Seneca, she climbed aboard the local mail hack and rode it to South West City, where her family came to meet her.[14]

For the next year or so, the family worked together on the farm. Cy continued his lessons, augmented by his mother's teachings, until he was about sixteen or seventeen, when he enrolled at a county teachers institute in Missouri. He studied there over the next two winters and one summer, leaving home Monday mornings and returning Friday evenings. At the end of that time he had earned what was known as a first-grade teaching certificate, which gave him the credentials to teach elementary school and earn a bit of money, a relatively common way for ambitious young people to amass funds for college.

Sometime around 1890, A.J. purchased a house and farmland in Missouri on a bend of the Elk River and the family left Indian Territory. Ruie Rebecca apparently wanted to live in a more civilized place, one with elections and laws and a post office and commercial establishments. The new farm met those requirements. As soon as they were settled, she and Carrie both began teaching school at South West City. Carrie kept a record of her class and had more than one hundred students in all.

The Elk River farm is still in the Avery family. When A.J. died in 1906, he left a horse to each of his grandchildren and deeded the farm to Cy, who eventually sold the property to Carrie and her husband. Their descendants are still on the property.

With teaching certificate in hand, Cy went to work. He was an engaging young man with a quick wit. He loved people, and his daughter-in-law once described him as "as likely to sit and talk to a boy sitting on a log at the edge of the road as to an oil millionaire."[15]

He taught for three years in South West City. He was popular with students and even had plans with another teacher to start a local academy; however, something—most likely Ruie Rebecca—convinced him he should go back to school himself and earn a college degree. He planned to attend Missouri University in Columbia, but family lore has it that while he was on the train headed in that direction, he met a couple of brothers from the little town of Liberty, near Kansas City. The McClelland brothers piqued Cy's interest with their upbeat talk about their hometown college, William Jewell, and also about their beautiful sister Essie. Avery decided to go home with the McClellands. He visited William Jewell, a four-year all men's Baptist college. He also visited Old Ringo, the McClelland home, an imposing place with four tall Doric columns across the front. Thomas J. McClelland had been a pioneer resident in the area, and the McClellands' was a comfortable, very southern lifestyle in that section of northwest Missouri that had been a Confederate stronghold during the Civil War.[16] After looking around the town and the campus, Cy determined that he quite liked William Jewell. He enrolled as a freshman, in a class made up mostly of Missourians, with a few from Kansas and a smattering of fellow Oklahomans.

A.J. and Ruie loaned Cy $150 to get settled at William Jewell. Beyond that, he supported himself with savings from teaching and by doing odd jobs. According to one source, "He waited on tables, bought some pigs and fed them the scraps from the kitchen table, after which he sold them as hogs at a handsome profit; he managed a lecture course for his college and during the summer vacations traveled for a girls' school for which he solicited students."[17]

Cy's was a busy life, but besides his work and his classes he also managed to take advantage of what William Jewell and the surrounding communities had to offer. He joined Phi Gamma Delta fraternity. He also visited nearby Kansas City to partake of the city's cultural offerings. The society pages of the *Kansas City Star* paid attention to the doings of the William Jewell students, and one report noted that Cy and a group of friends, including the McClellands and their sister Essie, had come to town to attend the theater.

Having taught school himself, Cy was a serious student and focused his efforts on literature, history, and science, all of which became life-long interests. He also took time to study elocution and for the rest of his life was known as an engaging—and persuasive—speaker.

In 1897, at the age of twenty-six, Cy Avery gave his senior oration on Reverence for Authority and was graduated from William Jewell with a bachelor's degree in liberal arts. That summer, he worked as a representative of the Liberty Female College, traveling through Oklahoma to drum up potential students. When he arrived in Pryor, near his old home in Indian Territory, the local newspaper took note. "He resided in Indian Territory when he was a small boy and was well known to this editor. He . . . is a pleasant young gentleman and we predict for him great success."[18]

Cy's decision to attend school in Liberty rather than at Missouri's state university had been fortuitous. He agreed with the McClellands about their college; he must also have agreed with them about their sister because in December, following his graduation, he and Essie were married.

They were a handsome young couple. Cy, though only about five feet eight inches tall, was a good-looking young man with dark wavy hair he parted just off center. His open, intelligent face was augmented by his genuine curiosity and interest in people. Like his father, he was a born storyteller and a good listener, both of which helped him in his insurance and real estate dealings, and later, when he became involved in politics. He also dressed well, a characteristic commented on by his grandchildren many years later. Diminutive Essie McClelland Avery was a good match for Cy, with her soft, dark eyes and masses of dark hair.

The Averys were married at the McClellands' spacious brick home in a settled, eighty-year-old college community. With his college degree and his new wife's family connections, Cy could have stayed comfortably in Missouri, but he had grown up in Indian Territory and Missouri wasn't home. Instead, he chose to make his future in the new land of Oklahoma.

Barely a federal territory in 1897, Oklahoma wouldn't become a state for another decade, but that did not matter to Cy. He took his bride and moved to Oklahoma City. They set up housekeeping in the first high-rise apartment building in a rough, brawling, wide-open town that had been born overnight in one of the biggest land grabs in U.S. history.

White people had been pouring into Oklahoma Territory for decades but they had only been officially welcome there for eight years. In 1889, the U.S. government had thrown up its hands to the pressure for more western land to settle and sponsored an official "land run" on two million acres. Overnight an estimated ten thousand people roared into what became Oklahoma City. By the time the young Averys arrived nine years later, the town's population had more than doubled. It was still largely lawless, dirty, and very much on the frontier, but, for Cy and Essie, it turned out to be a good place to start.

As soon as they landed in Oklahoma City, Cy set about establishing patterns for his lifetime. As an agent for New York Life, he provided a much-needed service to the city's leading citizens and within a few months, he and Essie were welcomed into the highest social circles. The *Daily Oklahoman* carried dozens of articles mentioning card parties, teas, and ladies' luncheons, including one honoring Essie's sister, who was visiting from Liberty. In December 1902 they welcomed another family member, a son named Leighton.

No matter where Cy was, he remained in regular contact with his mother. One letter to Ruie Rebecca during this period shows how close the two were and how much he treasured her counsel and teachings. He wrote: "There should be a good deal of satisfaction to you mother in your every day life to know you have raised three children who though they have never done anything so remarkable have all married happily and are in fair way to build for themselves happy homes. Also they each year realize more and more . . . how untiring you have been in efforts to give them an education and a good Christian training." Less flowery perhaps, but more telling, was his note at the end of the letter: "It is rather hard to live an exemplary life in the world but my early training I find is a good safety-valve to me."[19] Other times, he wrote to her with reports concerning his business progress.

In Oklahoma City it also became clear just how much Cy's book-loving mother had influenced her son's social activities. Always a reader, he played host to poet Fred Emerson Brooks in January 1904, entertaining him at a stag party that garnered about eight inches of newspaper coverage.[20] Brooks was a favorite on the Chautauqua circuit in the Midwest. Billed as "The Man Who Never Disappoints," he was a humorist, orator, and storyteller as well as a ventriloquist and animal imitator.[21] In his career he published a number of books of dreadful poetry and short speeches, including one called "Buttered Toasts," a collection of tributes for weddings and host recognitions.

More than likely, Cy had met Brooks while at William Jewell. At any rate, when Brooks's itinerary brought him to Oklahoma City for a week of performances, Cy rounded up a group of men who might be inclined to listen to a poet and hosted a dinner. This event was an early version of Cy's lifelong favorite way of entertaining: Tom Sawyer–style stag dinners, with Cy pressing his guests into supplying the muscle and know-how to produce the food and drink. In this case, several of his old Phi Gamma Delta fraternity brothers were the "helpers." One even supplied a Chesterfield ham from Virginia as the main part of the buffet meal. Cigars and libations were, of course, part of the evening.

Brooks's work wasn't the only poetry with which Cy was familiar—his mother had seen to that. His lifelong library included serious poetry of all kinds. Essays and biographies were also part of his personal library and his correspondence regularly included quotes by famous men—often Abraham Lincoln.

As much as the Averys seemed to fit into Oklahoma City society and business life, Cy was restless. By the early 1900s, things were happening in the green hills of northeast Oklahoma where he had grown up—things he wanted to be a part of. Before 1904 was out, he and Essie packed up their belongings and moved their little family about 160 miles northeast. He chose Vinita, the little town named by Elias Boudinot, not far from the junction of Spavinaw Creek and Brushy Creek where he and his father had settled half a lifetime before.

By Oklahoma standards, Vinita was an old established city. It was the second oldest city in the territory, the first to have electricity, and a good sight better than Tulsa, one of the small communities Cy and Essie passed through on the dirt road from Oklahoma City. Tulsa, as he told it later, was a muddy little town with pigs running loose in the street.[22]

Vinita had grown and prospered, first because it was a farming center and railroad stop. Corn, wheat, oats, alfalfa, and prairie hay were staple crops here, but the climate and soil were also good for peaches, apples, grapes, and berries. By 1900, Vinita boasted a population of two thousand. It was the seat of the Indian Territory's Northern District Federal Court and a financial center. It seemed to be a perfect place for the Averys to put down roots and enlarge their family. A second son, Gordon, was born there in 1905.

In Vinita, Cy opened another insurance business, and thanks to his history in the area, he also expanded into farm loans. This kept him out in the countryside traveling one difficult, dusty road after another, and put him in touch with the local Indians as well as white farmers. Before long, he was recognized as one of the most savvy and knowledgeable people in the region when it came to land values.

Real estate would be the cornerstone of Cy's livelihood but not right away. Almost as soon as he arrived in Vinita he caught the oil bug, a victim of the oil boom that had begun in 1901 near Tulsa at Red Fork. Cy acquired a number of oil leases when he lived in Vinita and developed relationships with people like William Skelly and Harry Sinclair, another alum of Cy's own Phi Gamma Delta fraternity. With Sinclair as a partner, he formed the Avery Oil and Gas Company.[23] Cy also watched what was happening in that little oil town fifty miles down the road. In Tulsa's back yard, the great Glenn Pool oil field, the country's largest, was belching millions of gallons of oil and was certainly cause for a person to take interest. Beyond that, however, Tulsa was addressing the oil boom differently from most other places. The city fathers there had been quick to seize on the idea that Tulsa should be not just where the oil field was located but that it should also be the city that was the financial, business, and transportation center for those oil fields. Ultimately, that decision was the reason that Tulsa thrived and grew while so many other oil towns just blew away in the Oklahoma dust.

In early 1907, the *Tulsa Tribune* reported that Cy Avery and R. D. Knight of Vinita were in town on their way to visit Tulsa's oilfields.[24] Later that year, just as Oklahoma was becoming a state, Cy was not only visiting Tulsa's oil fields, he was packing up Essie, Leighton, and baby Gordon and making his final move—this time to the little town that soon would be known as the oil capital of the world.

TWO

Tulsan Forever

> Think up something for your town to celebrate. Have a parade. Americans like to parade. We are a parading nation.
>
> —Will Rogers

Tulsa was an interesting place. Originally a Creek Indian town, it was settled sometime around 1830 in the first wave of removal of the Five Civilized Tribes from their ancestral homes in Alabama. After a grueling trip west (what became known as the Trail of Tears), the Lochapoka Clan of the Moscogee Creeks finally ended their journey on the banks of the Arkansas River, where they erected a small cluster of houses and other buildings. They called their new settlement Old Town, or "Tulasi." Within a few years, the community had a trading post and its name had been anglicized to Tulsey Town. In 1879, the name changed again. The federal government designated a post office there, and in a typical bit of bureaucratic misunderstanding, they officially named the village Tulsa. Three years after the post office opened on the banks of the Arkansas River, about the time Cy and his father began farming over by Spavinaw Creek, the Atlantic & Pacific Railroad laid rails from Vinita to Tulsa. With the railhead now in Tulsa, the little frontier town became a shipping center, mostly for cattle.

In 1890, Tulsa boasted 1,390 people. Eleven years later, when oil prospectors hit a gusher on Sue Bland's farm just across the Arkansas River in Red Fork, Tulsa's population exploded. From that day on, Tulsa's growth was tied to the oil fields. Like all boomtowns, the little railroad community soon featured a wide variety of businesses geared to winning the earnings of just-paid oil field workers. What made Tulsa different, though, was that a group of savvy businessmen saw the value in making Tulsa not just an oil town, but the place where oil people did business. It quickly became a banking center and, very soon, claimed the elegant Alcorn Hotel and other commercial establishments worthy of oil barons.

Cy, who was operating his farm loan and oil lease businesses from more staid and settled Vinita, watched what was happening in Tulsa with growing enthusiasm. He took note of the little city's bid to be a business center. He also heard about Tulsa's storied Commercial Club. Organized in 1901 by a handful of city leaders who wanted to lure the Katy Railroad through town, the Commercial Club became the place where Tulsa's moneyed class made decisions and more often than not carried out the business of the thriving little city. It ultimately became the base of Cy's support and his springboard to politics.

The Commercial Club's first venture was an unqualified success. When the members promised free right-of-way and pledged thousands of dollars in bonus payments, the Katy executives scrapped the railroad's planned route between Muskogee and Pawhuska for a new route through Tulsa. Using the same tactics, the Commercial Club managed to bring two more railroads to town by 1904. Before long, the Commercial Club was the de facto city government. Working outside normal channels but headquartered in Tulsa's city hall, the Club was a do-it-now operation, thanks to its many oil-rich members with the will and the resources to put their city on the map. That's the way Tulsa worked. In 1898, the year the city was incorporated, four businessmen had purchased the Presbyterian Mission Day School and held the property until the city could take it over. That school was the beginning of the Tulsa Public School System.[1] In 1904, three private citizens anted up to build the first nonrailroad bridge across the Arkansas River—a project deemed too risky for the city to undertake but necessary in light of the Red Fork oil field.

About that same time, the Commercial Club members decided to make an audacious bid to bring national attention to their rich little city. The members chartered a train, hired a band, brought along Will Rogers to do rope tricks, and sent one hundred enthusiastic businessmen on a 2,500-mile tour around the Midwest to tout the benefits and promise of the big town on the eastern prairie.

While the so-called "smell of money" no doubt spoke loudest to Cy when he made his decision to relocate from Vinita, Tulsa's bent for self-promotion probably also attracted his attention. Even though he was still getting his footing as a farmer, insurance agent, family man, and member of the business community during those early years, he loved showmanship. Later, after he took care of the nuts and bolts of creating U.S. Highway 66, he would become the best and best-known booster of the road that he dubbed "The Main Street of America."

When the Commercial Club sent another train across the country in April 1908 to drum up interest in Tulsa, Cy was on board. As president of the Avery-Roberts Investment Company, he rode with a hundred more Tulsa businessmen through Kansas, Missouri, Iowa, Illinois, Indiana, Kentucky, Ohio, West Virginia, Washington, D.C., and up the East Coast.

In November 1907, when Oklahoma became the forty-sixth state, Tulsa had a population of 21,693. It boasted railroads, banks, hotels, a college, theatres, a growing population, and great wealth. More than one thousand wells had been sunk around the 1905 Glenn Pool discovery, now named "The Richest Little Oil Field in the World."[2]

When Cy, Essie, and the two boys arrived in Tulsa that fall, he hired a local architect to build a comfortable home in the fashionable residential section just south of downtown. Leighton was five, and Gordon not yet two. Part of the move also included Cy's father. After A.J. died in 1907, Cy, who was devoted to his parents, brought the body to Vinita and interred it in a local cemetery. When he moved his family to Tulsa, he had his father's body disinterred and relocated it to a new grave in Tulsa's Rose Hill Cemetery. Years later, Ruie Rebecca, Essie, and also Cy would be buried in the same Avery family plot.

Once he had everyone settled, Cy bought himself a farm. He had grown up on a farm and he missed the cycle of the seasons, the business of planting, and he missed owning livestock. It was a good time to buy land, especially for a young man who had already established himself in rural real estate. Fortuitously for Cy, along with statehood, members of the local Indian tribes received the right to buy and sell their land allotments. Cy, who had grown up among the Indian population by Spavinaw and gotten to know local Indian farmers around Vinita, dealt with several Indian sellers as he put together 1,400 acres about eight miles northeast of town. Within a year, he planted his first crop of Bermuda grass and red clover. Before long he had three hundred acres in alfalfa, timothy, red clover, Kentucky bluegrass, and other meadow grasses on his farm. He also bred Holstein and Ayrshire cattle, Duroc hogs, Shropshire sheep, and Percheron horses.[3] Cy's approach to raising grasses as the underpinning for raising livestock was ahead of its time; certainly he could have been a poster boy for twenty-first-century sustainable farming. He eventually published two monographs on the subject. Within a few years he also became a welcome speaker on the agriculture circuit. His progressive ideas also attracted the attention of the Oklahoma Department of Agriculture, which extended their compliments for his agriculture and stock raising methods.

The farm was a laboratory for Cy, but the farm served another purpose as well. While he was comfortably well-off most of his life, Cy never amassed wealth anywhere close to that of his oil-rich colleagues or even some of his real estate developer cronies. Where A. L. Farmer, a good friend and insurance magnate who later worked with Cy to create Mohawk Park and underwrite the city's municipal airport, built a sprawling Italianate mansion, Cy lived in and raised his children in a pleasant but comparatively unassuming Craftsman-style home on a wooded lot nearby. The white stucco house with its wide verandah had three floors, a sleeping porch across the back, and an apartment over the garage; but it couldn't compare to the ornate villas of his friends and neighbors.

In contrast to his residence, the farm offered Cy a way to entertain business colleagues on his own terms and on his own turf. Because the farm was so close to town, it was easy to get to, and Cy regularly invited friends and colleagues there. On a typical afternoon or evening he would provide a barbecue dinner, and guests would help themselves to, or probably supply, the libations. It was a place they could let their hair down and relax from the high-pressure work of creating a city. Too, the farm was a crucible for many of Cy's projects. He never tired of bringing people there to see the latest results of his agricultural labors, share a barbecue meal, and tell stories far into the night. Or if need be, gently harangue them on various topics. Over time, the Avery farmhouse became something of a showplace, and he regularly hosted Rotary dinners and gatherings for the various fraternal groups of which he was a member. During World War I he used events at the farm to ramp up support for the Tulsa County Bond Drive that he led. The farm was also a family retreat, although neither it nor the ranch that he owned later were ever as dear to town-bred Essie as they were to Cy. In 1912, the *Tulsa World* reported that the Averys hosted a picnic on the farm to celebrate Cy's forty-first birthday.[4]

Cy eventually donated portions of the farm to become part of Tulsa's Mohawk Park and the Tulsa Municipal Airport. More to the point, in the early 1920s he built a gas station, motor court, and café, the Old English Inn, which fronted the gravel road that ran past the edge of the farm. It was surely no accident that in 1926 that gravel road was part of the national highway that was named U.S. 66.

As a large landowner in northeast Tulsa County, Cy became a man to be reckoned with. Besides his farm, he laid out and improved areas into which Tulsa was growing. He also bought and sold lots in Greenwood, Tulsa's highly successful black community that was widely known as the nation's "Black Wall Street." As a result, he got to know many of Tulsa's black citizens and was in a position to offer help after the harrowing devastation of the Tulsa Race Riot in 1921.

When Cy had put together parcels from his farm, he took advantage of offers from local Indian landowners. As other Indian allotment land became available, he also bought up a lot of the hilly, wooded property near his old home at Jay and Spavinaw Creek, including, at one point, the Watie farmhouse where he grew up, although he sold that a few years later.

Land buying was Cy's primary business for the next several years and remained an important aspect of his work most of his life. His years in Indian Territory and his experience in Vinita served him in good stead when he opened his farm loan agency in Tulsa. Known as the "best informed man on farm lands in Northeastern Oklahoma," he had many Indian clients who came to him with land to sell when they needed cash. He built a reputation for fairness and integrity in his business dealings with them.[5]

When he had lived in Vinita, he and Harry Sinclair had started a small oil venture, buying and selling oil leases. Cy later developed a forty-acre lease in Tulsa County's Bird Creek Field, which he drilled successfully in 1905. After that first strike, several others followed, but none were gushers. Once he moved to Tulsa, he built on his relationships in northeast Oklahoma and organized Togo Oil Company with colleagues from the towns of Vinita, Claremore, and Afton.

Cy was seen by the public as one of Tulsa's oil millionaires, which he may well have been during the 1920s. However, he was never successful enough to be placed in the "oil baron" category that included people like Sinclair or other Tulsans like J. Paul Getty, Joshua Cosden, William Skelly, William K. Warren or Robert Galbreath. Cy struck oil on his Tulsa farm in 1916. It was heady business, striking oil, and he commemorated the Tulsa strike in Tulsa style: he commissioned an oil painting by an artist named Alfred Montgomery. According to family lore and the *Tulsa World*, the suddenly rich oilmen loved Montgomery. "It was tradition that as soon as possible after striking oil, these men would get Montgomery to paint a picture for them. . . . Montgomery came and stayed at the Hotel Tulsa when it was the headquarters for oil money and there was a noted Montgomery painting on the mezzanine."[6] It was a quirky sort of tradition. Montgomery, a Kansas native, was known for his paintings of corn. Cy's corn painting depicted a woven basket and burlap bag, both spilling over with ears of ripe yellow corn. He also had another Montgomery painting, this one of barnyard chickens. The fact that these oil-strike paintings inevitably depicted agricultural riches rather than petroleum wealth spoke to the agrarian and midwestern roots of so many of Tulsa's elite. Historians have been quick to point out that Tulsa was never a frontier city in the classic sense; its roots were more Main Street than Wild West, even in those earliest and oiliest days. Harry Sinclair, for example, had been a pharmacist before he found his way to the oil fields, and William Skelly sold newspapers as a boy and later attended one year of business school. This showed in the organization of the Commercial Club and in the community's early focus on building schools and churches.

Once in Tulsa, the same energy that had propelled Cy through normal school two decades before propelled him into leadership circles in the Tulsa community. By 1911 he was a member of the Commercial Club. And while he was to become known as the man who couldn't stop thinking about roads, one of his early Commercial Club ventures was to seek support of his first love—agriculture. He gave his first talk to fellow club members on behalf of the dairy industry. A small man, he was barely tall enough to see over the lectern, but when he launched into a discussion of cows and the commerce of milk and butter, his colleagues sat in rapt attention. A fellow member who heard his presentation reported, "Cy could almost make us . . . see the mammoth cow barns, silos and milk wagons coming to town, while bankers present were already totaling in their minds the several additional millions of dollars this industry would bring to the county."[7]

By late 1912, he was on the club's board of directors, a position he would hold for the next quarter century. It was a useful and interesting group to be a part of and marked him as one of Tulsa's governing elite. For the years he was a board member, Cy would meet and eat lunch with this illustrious group every Wednesday at noon. One of them was William Skelly, who besides being a leading oil man, was an aviation pioneer. Skelly lived in a ten-thousand-square-foot mansion. Another was Eugene Lorton, editor and then publisher of the *Tulsa World*. Robert Galbreath, who had struck the Glenn Pool gusher, was one of several multimillionaire oilmen who put their energy and dollars behind Tulsa progress. A. L. Farmer owned an enormously successful New York Life agency (Farmer & Duran) and became a large landowner. The Mayo brothers, John and Cass, were downtown real estate moguls and proprietors of the world-renowned Mayo Hotel, a center for Tulsa's society events and important gatherings. Cass Mayo, Farmer, and Lorton all became Cy's lifelong friends and collaborators in his various civic ventures. Lorton, in particular, was an important ally in the long fight to bring Spavinaw water to Tulsa.

In 1911, as part of the never-ending campaign to put Tulsa in the national spotlight, the Commercial Club supported Cy's bid to bring the International Dry Farm Congress to Tulsa. As he told his colleagues,

"This is an oil town, but it must not overlook the agricultural resources the surrounding country has."

Dry farming was a system developed in the late nineteenth century to conserve the limited moisture of the Great Plains and boost crop production, mostly wheat. The system involved planting drought-resistant crops, special deep tilling, and mulching to preserve what moisture existed but no use of artificial irrigation. Cy was not a wheat grower, but he was already in a leadership position in the Eastern Oklahoma Agricultural Association and a member of the Dry Farm Congress. More important, the congress would draw an international crowd, something that was very attractive to Tulsa's leaders. American and Canadian bankers, farmers, university professors, politicians, and businessmen would all attend the Dry Farm Congress, as would Swiss financiers and representatives from a host of other wheat-growing countries as far away as China. If Cy could bring this august international body to northeast Oklahoma, it would put a city that already saw itself as the center of the oil world on the international agriculture map as well.

The maneuvering that Cy did to get the Dry Farm Congress to Tulsa is an early example of the way of operating that he would hone to steel-edged effectiveness over the years. First, he raised $15,000 so a delegation from the Commercial Club could join Oklahoma's official mission to the 1912 Congress in Lethbridge, Alberta, Canada. Once on site, he persuaded the Oklahomans to work together to bring the next Dry Farm Congress to their state in 1913. There would be plenty of time later, he told them, to figure it out among themselves which Oklahoma community would be the host city. He also labored behind the scenes to see that a particularly influential Canadian delegate was selected as the conference chair, thereby prohibited from voting in the all-important process of selecting a site for the following year's assembly. Thanks to Cy's maneuvering, the united Oklahomans outvoted everyone else and went home with the prize.

Back on American soil, he won the next round as well: the Tulsa boosters wrested the 1913 convention site away from Oklahoma City. With the international meeting assured, Cy's next step was to rally the Commercial Club to purchase sixteen acres for a new convention center.

Coincidentally, the site was northeast of town, in the area where his real estate business flourished.

In mid-November 1913, Cy welcomed twenty thousand people to Tulsa for the International Dry Farm Congress. They arrived from places as foreign as Russia and Argentina and as familiar as the wheat-growing western plains. Most were American farmers, who came to see dry farming products and machinery and hear lectures from federal and state departments of agriculture, agricultural colleges, economists and bankers. And they all had a chance to see Tulsa.[8] The event was a real coup for Cy.

In 1913 he also made his first foray into state politics. He went with two other Commercial Club members to Oklahoma City to lobby against a 3 percent tax on oil, with instructions to "set up camp" there if necessary.[9]

Cy was a shrewd businessman. He had friends in all the right places. And as a speaker, he was spellbinding. Through his eloquence and his tenacity he was making a name for himself as someone to be reckoned with. He impressed the leading men of Tulsa with his easy manner, his quick wit, and his seemingly boundless energy and curiosity. Cy Avery was fast becoming someone the Commercial Club needed.

Even though the city had plenty of money, most recently pouring in from the colossal 1912 Cushing Oil Field discovery, Tulsa still lacked the basic infrastructure it would need to grow and maintain its position as America's oil city. Especially lacking were good water and good roads. Tulsa lay in the foothills of the limestone and spring-fed Ozarks, yet fresh drinking water was virtually nonexistent. The silty, salty Arkansas River was of no use for drinking. In 1904, Tulsa had built a water-pumping plant, but it failed to control the silt, which ran thick out of city taps, and, anyway, the water's high gypsum and salt content made it unpotable. Wells were not a good answer, either, as they tended to run dry or produce only salty water. Residents resorted to importing drinking water. Water-bottling companies sprang up to serve the Tulsa market from nearby towns, but Tulsans also supplied themselves with water that was trucked in from long distances, like the popular Mountain Valley Spring Water from Hot Springs, Arkansas, almost 250 miles to the southeast. If they were typical of the rest of their neighbors, Cy and Essie's first years in Tulsa included a significant budget outlay for the purchase of bottled water.

Cy, who knew what really good water tasted like, became a vocal proponent of building a pipeline to bring better water to Tulsa. He told his colleagues at the Commercial Club, he talked to his friend Eugene Lorton, who had recently come to town to edit the *Tulsa World*, and he told anyone else who would listen to him. Specifically, as early as 1911, he said he saw no reason the city couldn't tap into Spavinaw Creek and the water he had drunk in the days when he and his father first came to Indian Territory, never mind that Spavinaw was fifty-five miles from Tulsa as the crow flies. Not until 1922 would water finally begin to run clear out of the Tulsa taps, but when it finally happened, it would be Spavinaw water.

Good roads were another problem in Tulsa. In 1887, when places like St. Louis, Kansas City, and even Cy's college town of Liberty could boast brick and gravel streets, Tulsa's three streets were dirt. It wasn't a pretty sight. Besides dust and mud, one old-timer remembered, "We had to dodge roaming hogs, goats and cows when crossing and sometimes wild animals would venture into the middle of town."[10] In 1901, the city was surveyed and more streets, still dirt, were laid out. During this period Tulsa was exploding. Those dirt streets couldn't begin to handle Tulsa's traffic: cattle headed for the railhead, heavy equipment for drilling the next big gusher, building materials for stores, hotels, banks, homes, churches, and thousands of people looking for a new future. As soon as word got around about the Red Fork oil strike those dirt streets filled with every kind of person looking for a new future, never mind the opportunists, drifters, entrepreneurs, and crooks.

In 1903, as one of its first orders of business, the Commercial Club discussed the need for a road department but that idea, as it were, went nowhere. A 1905 census counted 205 cars on Tulsa streets. The next year, First and Second Streets were paved with bricks. That was a beginning, but the brick streets didn't work very well. The brick quickly disappeared below a thick layer of mud.[11] In 1907, while Oklahoma's state constitutional convention was making history over in Guthrie, Tulsa laid down its first asphalt pavements on some of the downtown streets and set a requirement for all men over eighteen and under forty-five—this would have included even new settlers like Cy—to give a day's work to improving the roads or pay a three-dollar tax.[12] In an editorial at that time, the *Tulsa World* commented that "paving is not absolutely essential, but it is absolutely essential if the community would prove itself abreast of the times." Tulsa wanted nothing more than to be considered abreast of the times.

The cars puttering through Tulsa in 1907 were owned by an elite group: oilmen, bankers, doctors, and others who were used to having their voices heard. They were far outnumbered by horse owners, of course, who were clamoring that the noisy and fast-moving mechanical vehicles made them fear for their animals. In a conciliatory move, the town fathers established a speed limit of eight miles per hour for autos, gave horses the right-of-way at intersections, and set a fine of $1,000 or ninety days in jail for violations. Two years later, the city reduced fines and raised the speed limit to twenty miles per hour. This show of support for automobiles was a good move on the part of the city, but it didn't address the sticky, gooey, filthy mud that was still the primary surface material on Tulsa's streets. In 1912 only twelve miles of city streets had any kind of improved surface, and virtually none of the roads outside of town were anything but dirt. Conditions on the county roads were so bad that one resident reported, "It was almost impossible to get five miles from Tulsa during the spring season."[13]

In this situation, Oklahoma was not unique. Road building was still a hit-and-miss proposition over most of the United States. Bricks and asphalt paved many of the nation's eastern city streets, but through roads tended to be much the same as they had been for centuries: mud and gravel with an occasional macadam surface here or there. In Oklahoma, where tribal lands had given way to private ownership, there were other issues. Travel arteries that had once gone through the middle of the country had to be rerouted to follow fences once property lines were established. But the biggest problem was mud. Cars couldn't deal with muddy roads the way a horse could, and the more cars that were manufactured and purchased, the muddier the roads became and the louder the demand for hard surfaces. And coincidentally, fewer horse and ox teams were available to pull them out of the mud.

By the time Cy and Essie and their two sons arrived in Tulsa, the push for good roads in the United States had become a political movement. It was only a matter of time, dollars, and technology before the country would have hard-paved roads through the country to match the automobiles that suddenly seemed to be everywhere.

When Cy was born, paved roads were not even a possibility in the United States. The technology was not yet developed, the government was not interested in building highways, and the population was still recovering from the Civil War and working their way through a devastating depression. However, a serious appeal for better roads began about the time Cy entered the world, and it came from what today seems like a very unlikely source—the nation's growing population of bicycle riders. Invented in Scotland in 1839, bicycles had become widely popular both in Europe and the United States. By the 1870s, American bicyclists, who were a large and relatively elite group, began to make a lot of noise calling for better places to ride. In 1880, East Coast bicyclists organized into the League of American Wheelmen in part to push their agenda for better roads. The group soon went national. The Wheelmen cannily packaged their call for good roads in the guise of helping the less fortunate. Road improvements, contended the Wheelmen, would better the life of farmers and other "isolated" rural residents, an idea, incidentally that became part of the platforms for the Grange, a national advocacy group for farmers, and later for the national Progressive movement.

One part of the Wheelmen's campaign, the idea of free delivery of rural mail, was so popular that in 1890 Congress appropriated $10,000 to look into the practicability of such a luxury. While not explicitly about roads, rural delivery was predicated on the assumption that mail carriers could, in fact, make their rounds in roughly the same amount of time each day and count on getting home at the same time every night. This made the post office a de facto supporter of good roads. The Wheelmen took a major step in 1891 when they published *The Gospel of Good Roads: A Letter to American Farmers*. That polemic went to great lengths to convince rural Americans that their lives were unfulfilled because they lacked dependable thoroughfares. Improvements in the transportation system, said the *Gospel*, would bring social benefits to farmers, lessen isolation, and, most important, improve their economic standing.[14] Cy, by this time a country school teacher in southwest Missouri, may have read *The Gospel of Good Roads*, maybe even giving his allegiance to the movement. It certainly fit with his own political ideals. And since he was living at the Elk River farm, he also surely was a proponent of rural mail delivery.

In 1892 the Wheelmen ramped up their campaign a notch and began publishing *Good Roads Magazine*. *Good Roads* kept readers apprised of the state of road development, road building technology, and road politics across the United States. It was an instant success, and circulation quickly grew to more than a million copies. That same year, more than one thousand bicycle fans braved the "bad roads" to gather in Chicago and organize the National League of Good Roads. They elected Gen. Roy Stone, an engineer and Civil War hero from Ohio, as secretary. Their objective: national road legislation.[15]

During the next few years, while Cy was teaching school and then working his way through William Jewell, pioneering automobile owners joined the bicyclists and farmers in their cries for hard roads. In 1893, at the Chicago World's Columbian Exposition, hundreds of road-hungry individuals, representatives of agricultural colleges, even members of the Board of Trade, and the Agriculture Congress held demonstrations and called on the federal government to do something about roads. By this time, even though the impetus was still bicyclists, the din was becoming too loud to ignore. The secretary of Agriculture, who also oversaw the post office, created an Office of Road Inquiry (ORI) as a first step in figuring out how to build hard-surfaced highways for the country, and named General Stone to head up the new organization.

Stone had been named a brigadier general a few months following the end of the Civil War, primarily for his service during the Battle of Gettysburg. A New York native, he had also fought at Antietam, the Battle of Chancellorsville, and the Battle of the Wilderness. During the Battle of the Wilderness, his horse reared, fell on him, and left him severely injured. Many believed that Stone had been drunk at the time.[16] Whatever the reason for his injuries, he finished the war commanding a prison in Alton, Illinois, near St. Louis. For a New Yorker charged with understanding the nation's road situation, his posting to Alton surely added significantly to his education. Stone's mission as head of the ORI was to evaluate the nation's cross-country roads and investigate the materials and technology needed to build better ones. He began by overseeing the country's first "object lesson" roads—sample stretches of highways featuring different test surfaces, which could later be compared for durability.[17]

The first American-built automobile, the Duryea, had hit the streets in 1893. Three years later, the year the post office began testing rural mail delivery and Stone was in the midst of investigating road surfaces, autos were such a novelty that the Barnum and Bailey Circus ballyhooed an automobile as a major attraction, right along with a fat lady, giant, and elephant. And in Decatur, Illinois, presidential candidate Williams Jennings Bryan actually tried out campaigning in an automobile as he waved to voters from the back of a donated Mueller.

Once the ORI was in place, more road groups formed, some to campaign for good roads and some to develop better road-building techniques. In 1900 many of those groups met together in Chicago to reorganize themselves, this time into the National Good Roads Association.

Even the railroads supported the roads movement in those days. Seeing more freight business in its future if farmers could get produce to the rail lines more easily, the Illinois Central Railroad joined with the Good Roads Association in 1901 to sponsor the first of many Good Roads Trains. These specially equipped trains "toured the country . . . demonstrating road building approaches with equipment borrowed from the manufacturers."[18] A train would pull into a station and unload equipment and men, who would lay down a sample improved road for the local people to look at and drive over. "Improved" still meant sand and gravel, or possibly macadam or a type of bitumen. Nonetheless, the work of the Good Roads Trains gave rural people a taste of what could be.

In 1902 the U.S. Post Office officially began free mail delivery in rural areas throughout the country. It also meant, of course, that post roads would suddenly all be held to a certain standard of passability. President Theodore Roosevelt put his weight behind better roads in 1903. In a flag-waving oration at the Good Roads National Convention in St. Louis, Teddy stirred the crowd into a frenzy. Was Cy at the convention? Probably not, since he was still getting his feet on the ground in Oklahoma City. But he no doubt heard about the president's speech, where Roosevelt had told his cheering audience,

> A few years ago it was a matter of national humiliation that there should be so little attention paid to our roads; . . . I cannot too heartily congratulate our people on the existence of a body such as this . . . having its connections in every State in the country and bent upon the eventual proper work of making the conditions of life easier and better . . . for the people who live in the country districts. . . . We should have a right to ask that this people which has built up a country with a continent for its base, which boasts itself, with truth, as the mightiest Republic that the world has ever seen . . . merely from historic analogy, I say, we should have a right to demand that such a nation build good roads.[19]

Roosevelt's address preceded the Model T by five years, and it preceded the appropriation of serious federal funding for roads by thirteen years. Even by this time, however, support from good roads groups was beginning to make the difference between a politician's winning or losing an election.

One good roads supporter who became an ardent roads-promoting politician was Horatio Earle, a longtime leader of the League of American Wheelmen. Earle, who had grown up on a Michigan farm, owned a variety of businesses with a particular connection to or need for better roads: a bicycle company, bicycle track, a gravel company, the Earle Equipment Company, and the Good Roads Supply Company. A great raconteur known for his homespun "Earlisms," Earle had crossed eyes, which he regularly told audiences gave him occult powers and special insights. He was elected to the Michigan legislature on a good roads platform in 1899. In 1901, he introduced a resolution calling for a state highway commission. Two years later he was appointed the state's first commissioner of highways. His avowed goal: "To conquer the Mighty Monarch Mud." About that same time, Earle also wrote to the federal government proposing a national interstate highway system.[20]

Earle was one of hundreds of individuals who, in those early days, bet their futures on good roads. In Oklahoma, a newspaperman named Sidney Suggs was also one of those people. In Iowa, a young engineer named Thomas MacDonald was one. Another was Frank Sheets, a highway engineer in Illinois. So was Cy Avery. But Cy's most memorable contribution to American roads came more than two decades later.

THREE

Good Roads Man

> The happiness, comfort and prosperity of rural life, and
> the development of the city, are alike conserved by the
> construction of public highways. We, therefore, favor national
> aid in the construction of post roads and roads for military
> purposes.
>
> —1916 Democratic Party Platform

In Oklahoma, Sidney Suggs had been quick to call for better roads, first in his newspaper, the *Daily Ardmoreite*, and later in person. Among other things, he believed roads were "moral agents capable of preserving the virtues of country life threatened by the growth of cities."[1] He was a popular orator on the subject of good roads and eventually became known all over the South. He was also an accordion player and took his instrument with him when he gave talks on road improvement. Five years before Oklahoma became a state, Suggs was among those who supported the formation of a fledgling roads organization. In 1904, in the wake of Teddy Roosevelt's address in St. Louis, the group met in Oklahoma City, named themselves the Oklahoma–Indian Territory Good Roads Association, and played host to a couple of important guests: Martin Dodge, the new director of the Office of Public Road Inquiry in Washington, D.C., and W. H. Moore, president of the National Good Roads Association.[2] In 1906, anticipating statehood, the group changed its name to the Oklahoma Good Roads Association and elected Suggs as their first president. A decade later, they would elect Cy.

Where was Cy during those early years? Likely as not, he was paying close attention. His personal experiences had made him all too aware of the difference better roads could make. His wagon trip west with his father would have shown him the difficulty of cross-county travel. The Indian roads where he grew up had been fairly well maintained, but he also knew the headaches of trying to get a full wagonload of produce from Spavinaw Creek into nearby Jay when horses were knee-deep in mud. As an early day player in the oil business he also saw what happened when wagons hauling heavy pipe and other equipment were sucked down and stuck in roads that could not sustain the weight. He had lived with the red clay streets of Oklahoma City and traveled the farm country of northeast Oklahoma, but he also had experienced the far better roads around Kansas City and Liberty during his college years. It must have been obvious to him that not only time but also money could be saved—and made—if Oklahoma roads could be built to support the traffic. And with his technical interests, it is very likely he was keeping up with the progress being made elsewhere in laying hard-surfaced roads.

Cy was also a joiner and a promoter and roads were a good cause. The Populist philosophy of good roads would have appealed to his egalitarian ideals and as one of the up-and-coming young men of the state, it would also have appealed to his business agenda. He probably had his first involvement with road building while he lived in Vinita and may even have started a Good Roads group there. In 1903, the Vinita Commercial Club appointed an overseer to build roads along the section lines leading out of town. This effort was boosted by the federal government in 1904, when Congress approved $10,000 to open section line roads in Indian Territory and pay damages to farmers whose property and crops would be in the path of the roadways.[3]

In 1906 he probably was a member of the Oklahoma Good Roads Association. He would have supported an unsuccessful Suggs-backed proposal to include a highway department in the new state government. Through his reading, Cy probably also was following the advancement of paving technology as it inched toward a practical answer to Americans' widespread plea for hard-surfaced roads.

Up to the end of the nineteenth century, short of laying individual paving stones as the Romans had done, builders had neither the materials nor the technology to build sturdy, permanent cross-country roads.

During the Industrial Age, an increased understanding of surface materials and the introduction of machines to mine coal and bitumen along with other machines to put down the pavements slowly began to make the whole idea of an interconnected system of good roads sound possible, if not entirely feasible. Developments in Britain during the eighteenth and nineteenth centuries made a significant contribution to America's highway dreams. John Metcalfe, a Scot, developed a system of building roads in three layers, where large stones were covered with excavated road material followed by gravel. Metcalfe's techniques gave his roads a tremendous advantage over others in that they drained during rainy weather. In 1824 in Britain, Joseph Aspdin patented Portland Cement and paved the way for modern road building. Concrete, made from mortar and plaster, was a very old construction material, but Portland cement concrete, as it was first known, was made by burning ground limestone and clay and was much more permanent than concrete. Later in the century, two more Scots, Thomas Telford and John McAdam, were particularly instrumental in developing the technology that eventually paved America. Telford raised the foundation in the center of the road so water would drain off. McAdam used layers of stone in symmetrical tight patterns to build his "macadam roads." Asphalt was the other important road surface material. While the first asphalt roads in the Western world were paved in Paris in the 1820s, it took another half century before Columbia University professor Edward de Smedt developed a maximum-density asphalt that would be used in the United States.

Martin Dodge, who followed General Stone in the Office of Road Inquiry (ORI), opened a roads materials lab in 1900 and hired a Massachusetts highway engineer and geologist named Logan Waller Page to head it. Elsewhere, state engineers undertook similar investigations. The Illinois Road Commission, for example, issued yearly reports on the results of their own tests on road materials and road-building equipment, and Michigan's highway engineers were deeply involved in testing road surfaces in and around Detroit.

In 1904, while the Louisiana Purchase Exposition in St. Louis was showcasing the glory of Portland cement, the federal government estimated that the United States had 108,283 miles of gravel roads, 38,622 miles of composition roads (stone, shell, sand, etc.), and 1,997,908 miles of dirt roads.[4] There was no mention of concrete or any other sure-enough hard surface. By 1905, the ORI had answered its own question as to the value of good roads, and the secretary of Agriculture replaced the ORI with a new Office of Public Roads (OPR), naming testing engineer Logan Page as its head. Page supported the idea of improving local roads that would benefit farmers over transcontinental roadways that would aid car owners and tourists. This was a significant issue, especially since the moneyed automobilists, as they were often called, favored the romantic ideal of cross-country car travel that hearkened back to the pioneers. Agriculture interests and most local road builders believed otherwise. The battle over whether nationally supported roads should be thoroughfares that were useful to local people or cross-country travel routes that connected the East and West Coasts was one that lasted more than two decades. In all actuality, it wasn't resolved until the interstate system was designated to supplement and supersede the national highway system of 1926.

Cy Avery agreed with Page that highways must serve local and regional needs first and took a passionate position on this issue in 1916. Cy's and Page's belief eventually became a federal government policy in the mid-1920s.

Besides being a road-testing scientist, Page saw the value in educating the public firsthand. His office flooded newspapers and magazines with articles about road improvement and maintenance. He also sent his engineers across the country to consult with local officials and build object lesson roads for people to see and try out. As an example, in 1908, the OPR completed a 2,945-foot stretch of asphalt on the Missouri State Fair Grounds in Sedalia, a major railhead during the cattle drives a generation earlier.

By this time, there were about a half million cars and trucks registered in the United States—enough that the clamor for better roads could be heard in Washington, D.C. In 1910, thirty state and national organizations met in the nation's capital to form the American Association for Highway Improvements, soon renamed the American Highway Association. This group became a unifying force for the many local good roads associations and led the charge toward highway construction with the catch phrase "Get the Farmers out of the Mud."[5] In 1909, in Horatio Earle's home state of Michigan, the Wayne County Road Commission built the first rural mile of concrete highway in the nation. For several years, the Michigan Highway Department had experimented with brick, granite, woodblock, and Portland cement surfaces, among others.[6] Concrete won out, and the Wayne County highway became a magnet for aspiring road builders. A half-dozen years later, with a major road bond pending, a Tulsa County delegation headed by Chief County Commissioner Cy Avery visited Wayne County to study the concrete thoroughfare.

In 1914, American highway construction took a big step forward when Page and the federal OPR joined with officials from the various state highway departments to form a national organization. The new group was called the American Association of State Highway Officials, or AASHO. Although they were officially separate from the OPR, the AASHO men depended on and worked closely with Page and his engineers. Oklahoma's Suggs was a charter member of AASHO and a member of its first executive committee. A decade later, Cy was Oklahoma's AASHO member. As a forum, AASHO was a place where members could learn from each other's experience and exchange information. It was also a place where ideas coalesced concerning what type of through roads the country needed. And because AASHO involved men from all parts of the United States, it became a strong and effective lobby seeking federal money to build highways.

In the years between 1910 and 1925, good roads advocates in every part of the country were doing their part to gin up interest and call for Congress to seriously support road building. The need for better roads increased with every car purchase and increased again every time someone cranked an engine.

In Oklahoma, road building had its own story. In 1907, despite the best efforts of the good roads people, the new state's constitution made no mention of a state highway department. Nonetheless, Oklahoma's first governor, Charles Haskell, appointed Suggs inspector of public roads. Suggs was an ideal appointee in that his passion overcame the fact that the job offered neither salary nor budget. He went to work with gusto. Between 1908 and 1911, Suggs worked closely with Page and the OPR engineers. He managed to bring federal engineers into Oklahoma about a half dozen times to oversee road improvements, most along the future route of U.S. 66.

One of those situations where a federal highway engineer came to the rescue occurred during an altercation between two farm towns in the western part of the state. When weather, traffic, and lack of maintenance made two main roads in the area impassable, farmers who normally brought their crops to Watonga took their wagons and their business to nearby Geary instead. A crisis erupted and Suggs brought in a federal engineer to deal with the problem. The engineer surveyed a new route and developed a plan for a sand-clay road to replace the dirt road that had washed out. He also supervised construction although local people, mostly farmers and township officials, actually did the work to build the new road.[7]

In 1909 the Oklahoma legislature took a step toward what they expected would mean better roads and empowered counties to create road improvement districts of their own.[8] This did not turn out to be a very good idea. For the most part counties had neither the money nor the know-how to build many roads. Even in well-to-do places like Tulsa County, there was little money and less technical skill available for roads and bridges. County officials, on the other hand, tended to relish the power that came with control of road jobs and budgets, no matter how small. Even though the state soon realized road building was too big a job to be accomplished locally, it was not easy to pry control out of the hands of the county commissioners. Across the Midwest, county officials challenged state highway departments for years over money, over autonomy, and over control of jobs.

On the state level, Suggs had neither money nor authority to tell counties how or where to build their roads. Instead of fighting the county commissioners, he surveyed the status of Oklahoma's existing roads, perhaps his most important act as commissioner. He reported that Oklahoma's local governments were spending nearly $3 million annually on fifteen thousand miles of public roads—but that these funds were not bringing taxpayers any permanent improvements. He called for a state agency that could collect funds, provide construction, and manage improvements for the state's public roads.

In 1910 Oklahoma could count only twenty-three miles of what were then known as hard-surfaced cross-country roads and ranked last among the states.[9] In response to both the need and the numbers, in 1911 the legislature took a step forward and created a state department of highways with a one-dollar-per-auto fee to finance highway construction and maintenance.

As soon as the new highway law was passed, the state's second governor, Lee Cruce (1911–15), named Suggs as Oklahoma's first highway commissioner. This job promised an annual salary of $2,500 along with an assistant commissioner, highway engineer, and secretary. Unfortunately, the legislation had failed to specify any way to collect the one-dollar-per-car highway tax. Only about 40 percent of the state's automobile owners actually paid the tax, and for more than a year, not enough tax money came in to pay Suggs's full salary or to pay his staff. Finally, he settled on the idea of appointing citizens to collect the car taxes, allowing them to keep part of the total as their fee, a practice still in use in many places even today. Highway department income from automobile taxes was supplemented by financial support from the state's good roads association, of which Cy was an officer. During Suggs's first year and a half as state highway commissioner, his passion for better roads and bridges, his sonorous voice, and probably his accordion took him to sixty-three different gatherings as a featured speaker. He also began an Educational Mile project for schools in which engineers gave high school students rudimentary training in laying out stretches of roadway.[10]

By this time, Cy was building roads in Tulsa County. In his capacity as chief county commissioner, he quickly saw the need for a better-funded source of road construction and maintenance than being dependent on county income. And while some county commissioners would find an answer in higher county taxes, Cy recognized that only a larger political entity, like the state or even the federal government, would be able to make good roads a reality. Suggs felt similarly and came out firmly against allowing local authorities to build and maintain the state's major roads. He also asked the legislature to fund salaries for state highway engineers and urged the construction of intrastate and interstate highways. In 1911, Suggs had written to Pres. Howard Taft, urging his support for road construction. The benefits of good roads would be, he wrote, "that men will be saved from the penitentiary and women from the unmentionable life into which so many are forced by the environments of the city."[11] Suggs judged that it would take six through highways to save the poor souls who resided in rural Oklahoma. Both before and after he was named state highway commissioner he lobbied for five north-south thoroughfares that would cross Oklahoma between Kansas and Texas, and one that would go east and west. A decade later, Cy made them happen.

In 1912, in Tulsa County, Cy was front and center when a Frisco Good Roads train rolled into northeast Oklahoma. The Commercial Club spared no expense in getting people out to see the railcars full of exhibits, hear the lectures, and generally ramp up interest in better roads. Banners and brass bands welcomed the train, and an old-fashioned picnic under the trees attracted hundreds of people from miles around. The train, which had begun its tour in Brownsville, Texas, was on a mission to energize towns and counties to build roads that would bring more farmers and their products to the trains. One railcar featured exhibits of a miniature rock crusher pounding rocks in a small duplicate of a quarry. Another exhibit had a model of a ten-ton steamroller that chugged back and forth over a miniature macadam road. The most memorable of the Frisco exhibits showed a photo collection of a county physician with his buggy stuck deep in the mud, followed by a photo of a hearse also immovable in deep mud. The caption read: "The patient died and the hearse is mired on the way to the cemetery."[12]

Cy, a member of the barbecue committee for the Commercial Club, was also secretary of the Tulsa County Good Roads Association. In that capacity, he welcomed Commissioner Suggs, who came along to eat barbecue and make a speech. Afterward, Suggs termed the gathering as "the best Good Roads meeting ever held in the state."[13] That afternoon, Cy and the other good roads supporters welcomed visitors from as far south as Denison, Texas, and as far north as Caney, Kansas. These particular people had come by special invitation with the idea of joining forces to create a new north-south highway. Later that evening, satiated on barbecue and highway conversation, the good roads throng chose officers for the newly created Mid-Continent Highway Association. That wiry fellow from Tulsa named Cyrus Avery was elected secretary.

The Mid-Continent Highway Association was only the first notch on Cy's road association belt. By this time, Cy was widely regarded as "zealous and liberal in the promotion of good roads."[14] He was also a director of the newly formed Tulsa Automobile Club, an affiliate of the Automobile Association of America (AAA).

Shortly after the Good Roads Train chugged out of town, Cy got his chance to walk the walk on road building. Voters elected him presiding county commissioner for Tulsa County. According to later reports, he did not seek the job and vowed that if nominated he would not campaign.[15] However, as a member of the ruling Commercial Club, his election was probably a foregone conclusion.

During his two terms as county commissioner (1913–16), Cy became a state and regional leader in highway construction. Given the technology of the time, he did what he could to upgrade existing dirt and gravel roads, build new ones, erect bridges, and generally make the act of piloting an automobile a little easier for drivers. He also led the charge to lure road meetings of all kinds and sizes to Tulsa. This had three benefits: it brought always-welcome money and visitors to town, it identified Tulsa's chief county commissioner as a man of growing importance in the road movement, and it helped focus public attention on the cause of good roads. Cy believed that hard-surfaced roads in the United States would never happen without the federal government, and he knew support from Washington, D.C., nearly always depended on voter sentiment. The more people banded together in a given place to demand better roads, the more publicity would be generated, and the more willing politicians would be to support the cause. If these meetings were in Tulsa, so much the better.

Early in his first term as county commissioner, he made one of his regular trips to Missouri to visit his mother and sisters on the Elk River farm. The day he arrived, seemingly everyone in that state was smoothing, straightening, and otherwise hard at work to improve the state's roads. Missouri governor Elliott Major had declared a road holiday and managed to turn out 250,000 people to "Pull Missouri Out of the Mud." An article in *Motor Age* reported, "The 'show me' state has shown a perplexed country an immediate and satisfactory remedy for all road ills. It is work, volunteer but well-organized work. 'A good roads spirit has been kindled in Missouri which will bring rich fruitage for many years,' said Governor Major."[16]

Cy was intrigued. He saw the value of a state-wide road holiday not only in terms of cleaning up existing roads but also in getting voters interested in the possibility of voting for money to build better ones. When he returned to Tulsa, he brought that "good road spirit" with him. He also brought a split-log drag. Invented by a Missourian named D. Ward King in 1907, the split-log drag practically revolutionized road maintenance at the time. A drag was made from logs cut in half lengthwise, held together by chains, and hitched up behind horses, mules, or oxen with the smooth part of the split logs facing forward. The drags were used after rains when road surfaces were still damp. When a team pulled the drag across a muddy or uneven road the drag flattened out ruts, shifted loose dirt to the center to form a crown, and generally improved quality and passability.

Cy hauled that first drag back to his own farm outside Tulsa. Leighton, who was about eleven at the time, remembered working with it. "We'd hook that drag to a Model T truck. The secret of the whole thing was to get in when it was damp but not muddy. We'd tighten the chains a little bit or loosen them so as to change the pressure on the equipment. The trucks in those days had solid tires and they had more traction than anything so you put chains on them and you did fairly well."[17]

In his official capacity as county commissioner, Cy oversaw the fabrication of three split-log drags. He had them delivered to strategically located farmers in Tulsa County who agreed to drag the county's 150 miles of roads after each rain. For this undertaking, the commission paid each farmer one dollar per mile covered.[18] Cy also purchased unhulled sweet clover and had it sown along the county highways to help hold the soil. Decades later, he told a reporter to look and he would still see the clover along many Tulsa County right-of-ways.

Despite his best efforts, by September of his first year in office Cy's experience as a road builder only reinforced what he already believed: for Tulsa to get better roads, it would take an effort that extended well beyond the Tulsa County line. He sounded a call to good roads enthusiasts across northeast Oklahoma and vowed, according to the *Durant Weekly News*, to accomplish in a smaller way what Governor Major and road workers did for the state of Missouri.[19] He tried a "Get Oklahoma out of the Mud Day." He only managed to turn out five counties, but both Cy and the press considered this fledgling effort a great success. From then on he was a point man first on the county level, then state level, and finally as a national player to make his vision of good, year-around cross-county highways a reality.

By this time, Cy was a well-known and welcome public speaker. His enthusiasm carried crowds with him and his passion for his subjects nearly always gave his listeners new information to take back home. He was most often invited to talk about agriculture in those early days, but even then, he could nearly always work highways into the conversation. In 1913, he spoke at an agriculture gathering in Muskogee where he railed against the farmers' high cost of living and encouraged them to do more scientific farming to reap greater harvests, but he also told them to support good roads, which would enable them to get their crops to market more quickly and profitably. It would be a win-win situation for everyone. The roads would be improved and the farmers would make more money.

In 1915, as presiding commissioner of Tulsa County, Cy attended an Oklahoma Good Roads Federation meeting in Oklahoma City to discuss laying out and organizing construction of through roads from one part of the state to another. Attendees were good roads people who represented five different highway groups. The meeting included representatives of the Ozark Trails Association of which Cy was an officer, the Kansas, Oklahoma, Texas, and Gulf Highway Association, Frisco Trails, International Meridian Road Association, and Interstate Postal

Highway Association. All agreed that the state's through roads had to be improved—and all had fought their way to Oklahoma City on the existing roads to make their voices heard and hopefully get something done. During that meeting, Cy was elected president of the Oklahoma Good Roads Federation.

That meeting would also prove memorable for Cy in another way. The state's third governor, Robert Lee Williams, was doing his best to disenfranchise black voters. After a failed attempt to amend the state constitution to prevent illiterates from voting, Williams called a special session of the legislature to find another way to accomplish his goal. He asked Cy to endorse the special session during the Oklahoma Good Roads Federation convention, even promising that the special session would also take up roads. Cy turned the governor down. This was only the first of many times in the years that followed where he would find himself facing off against overt racism in Oklahoma or the Klan.[20]

In December 1915 Cy hosted a statewide highway meeting at the Tulsa Chamber. There, according to the *Tulsa World*, he launched a "gigantic campaign" to improve the state's roads. He envisioned road-building districts throughout the state and subscription memberships in each township. "The only way to build good roads is to get the money, then get out there and build them," he told his audience. The *World* described him as "one of the best practical road builders in Oklahoma and anything he does has a habit of being successful."[21]

In 1915, he also made a political push to move road building to the state level. Cy, along with the Tulsa Chamber, Commissioner Suggs, and state senator Elmer Thomas, had gone to bat for new state highway legislation that would reorganize the Oklahoma State Highway Department and open the way for state control of highway building and federal funding. Thomas, who later served as a congressman and then U.S. senator from Oklahoma, became a key ally of Cy's when he was state highway commissioner and during the creation of the national highway system.

With its passage, the 1915 Oklahoma highway law authorized Commissioner Suggs to establish guidelines for highway construction and maintenance, to work closely with the federal government, and—

probably most important to beleaguered county commissioners like Cy—to provide engineering services for local units of government. As part of the law, counties were instructed to designate at least 10 percent of their roads as state highways. Despite all these progressive steps, no funding mechanism was included in the legislation, so nothing much really changed.[22]

While Cy was county commissioner, Tulsa's city governance evolved a step away from the old boys club that had been running the city. In 1915, just after he was elected for a second term, the Commercial Club joined forces with the Tulsa Automobile Club and several other civic groups and became the Tulsa Chamber of Commerce. Up to this point, the wealthy members of the Commercial Club had called the shots for Tulsa and often provided the money or the muscle to make things happen. Since the new chamber had many of the same members as officers and directors, it continued to be a powerful force in making things happen in Tulsa, but with the wider membership it became more egalitarian. It was also able to muster extensive support for important projects.

The same year that the Commercial Club morphed into the Chamber of Commerce, Cy set out to build a new bridge across the Arkansas River, one that would replace the old toll bridge from Tulsa's earliest days.[23] He asked his friends at the chamber to appoint a Highway Committee to work on behalf of a $200,000 bond issue to build said bridge. The chamber hired a road enthusiast named E. Bee Guthrey to manage the new Highway Committee, gave him a budget, and gave him a mandate to promote roads in eastern Oklahoma and Tulsa's trade area.

Named for two Civil War generals, Jubal Early and Barnard Bee, Guthrey was a lawyer by training, a staunch Democrat, banker, businessman, and newspaperman. He had founded Payne County's first newspaper in 1889 and eventually edited seven others in the state. After practicing law for some years, he turned full time to newspaper and Chamber of Commerce work, after he was attacked and had two fingers shot off by friends of a man he had put in jail. As an active participant in the highway movement, he helped found and later served as president of the White River Trails Association, which promoted a road between Branson through Springfield and Tulsa. In September 1918, Guthrey grabbed local headlines for being the first person to drive a Tulsa-manufactured automobile to the summit of Pike's Peak.

In the chamber, and more specifically, in Cy Avery, Guthrey found his calling. He saw eye to eye with Cy on much that was important to both of them, and for the next twenty years, Guthrey would be around wherever Cy Avery was, promoting highway development, writing articles, running offices, raising money, and doing whatever else was necessary to push their cause forward. Under the auspices of the chamber's Highway Committee, Guthrey went to work. His first-rate promotional efforts, combined with Cy's enthusiasm, and the citizenry's general eagerness for any kind of road improvements made the bridge bond issue a popular one with voters. The bond issue carried easily.

Cy's bridge, which crossed the Arkansas River at Eleventh Street, was completed in the fall of 1916. It was the state's first steel-reinforced concrete bridge and a city showpiece. Eighteen graceful arches extended upward from a concrete base sunk deep in bedrock. Pedestrian walkways extended along both sides of the bridge and initially there was a depressed center lane for the street railway. It was designed by the Kansas City engineering firm of Harrington, Howard and Ash, and built by the Missouri Valley Bridge and Iron Company, and widened during a New Deal public works project about twenty years later.[24] In the 1920s, the bridge was an important part of the decision to route U.S. 66 through downtown Tulsa and today it is preserved as a Route 66 historic site.

Just after the bridge was completed, Cy's county commission called for bids to build the first paved through road in Oklahoma, a twenty-foot concrete ribbon stretching six miles west from the Tulsa City limits to Sapulpa. At the same time, the city of Tulsa agreed to pave five more miles of roads that would continue the hard road through town and lead to and from the new bridge.[25]

Shortly thereafter, Cy proposed a $1,750,000 bond issue for county roads in general. The chamber also financed and managed this campaign, employing a combination of promotion and education and bringing high-level attention to the issue. They began by staging a gala dinner for Governor Williams and the state's highway engineer. According to Cy, "The Governor's address was along the line of good road building and he emphasized the fact he expected Tulsa County to lead the State in this important work."[26]

Next, Cy accompanied the chamber's Highway Committee and the other county commissioners on a jaunt across the United States to assess the state of highway construction. In Washington, D.C., their most important meeting would have been a visit with Logan Waller Page at the (renamed) Bureau of Public Roads. The rest of the trip took them to Albany, New York City, and then to Wayne County, Michigan, where they had a chance to see and ride on the nation's first concrete highway.

The road bond election was held shortly after they returned home. It passed by a ratio of 7:1.[27] It didn't hurt the election's outcome, either, that Tulsa's automobile dealers had donated fifty cars to bring voters to the polls that election day.[28]

This particular project reinforced Cy's growing belief in federal funding of highways. The new roads were to be eighteen feet wide, eight and a half inches thick in the center, and six and a quarter inches thick at the sides. The material was a 1:2:3 mix of cement, crushed limestone, and Arkansas River sand over a prepared base. The whole roadway was between thirty and thirty-two feet wide. When the contracts were let, paving costs were estimated at $17,500 per mile. By the time the contracts were signed, the cost had gone up to $26,000 per mile. By 1921, the cost of building concrete roads had escalated to $35,000 per mile. Even Tulsa County, rich as it was, blanched. Local governments simply could not afford to build all the roads the nation needed.

FOUR

The Do-It-Yourself Highway Movement

> He who lubricates transportation is a world-builder, a
> benefactor of his kind, and will live in the hearts of humanity.
>
> —Elbert Hubbard

All over the country, men like Cy, who held public office and were do-ing everything they could to bring hard pavement to their roads, were frustrated. Never mind that the technology to build hard roads was not much older than the first automobiles. Never mind that the federal government had yet to see the need to provide funding. People wanted better roads and they wanted them NOW. And if the various govern-ments couldn't manage to build roads, then the people would just build the roads themselves.

This aspect of the nation's craze for better roads began to manifest itself around 1912 in a creative push for dozens of virtually "home-made" highways. The 1913 coast-to-coast Lincoln Highway, brainchild of auto racing magnate Carl G. Fisher and a couple of auto manufactur-ing moguls, was one of the most famous. It did not take long, though, before there were dozens of these sponsored roads and then hundreds— all advertising their value as the best route from one part of the coun-try to another. The Interstate Trail ran between Des Moines and Kansas City, the Yellowstone Trail from Massachusetts to Washington state, and the Minnesota-based North-South Trail aimed to stretch from Can-ada to Mexico. Sidney Suggs was personally involved in the Meridian Road that was envisioned to run from Winnipeg, Manitoba, through Oklahoma City, close to his hometown of Ardmore, and eventually to Brownsville, Texas, more or less along the ninety-sixth meridian, eventu-ally becoming U.S. Highway 81. In 1915, Fisher sponsored a second road, the north-south Dixie Highway to Florida. In 1913, Cy added his name to the rolls of the Ozark Trails Highway Association, and in 1919, he founded the Albert Pike Highway Association to promote a road between Hot Springs and Colorado Springs.

By this time, it was already apparent that better roads meant more traffic and more money, so if someone saw potential to create a commercial road between two points, he (or in a few cases, she) would try to sell the idea to communities along the way. If the idea was a good one, the communities would compete to be on the route and would agree to provide funds for advertising and promotion. People in those towns would then join forces to maintain the road, create markers, and help publicize the value of traveling in that direction. Suggs was an early and welcome speaker at gatherings of these "trail" groups across the South. Later, Cy followed suit.

In Oklahoma there were close to a dozen highway organizations at work, largely thanks to the promotional and fund-raising activities of people like Suggs and Avery. Besides the Meridian Road, the Ozarks Trail, and the Albert Pike Highways, there were the Kansas-Oklahoma-Texas (K-O-T) Highway, the Jefferson Highway, the Dallas-Canadian-Denver (D-C-D) Highway, Star Route, Capitol Route, White River Trail, the Postal Highway, and the Bankhead Highway between Washington, D.C., and San Diego.

Years later, after Suggs sold his newspaper and retired, he remained a cheerleader for good roads. He became a fixture at road-paving celebrations and was a special guest at one in his home county in 1924 that celebrated early pavement on what had begun as the Meridian Highway and was to become U.S. 81. As befitted colleagues who had fought a war together, Cy Avery was the person most instrumental in seeing that Suggs's Meridian Highway received a federal highway number. He was also the chair of the Oklahoma State Highway Department in 1924 when the highway was paved near Suggs's hometown.

Decisions as to the exact routing of these homemade highways were fairly arbitrary, made by the executive committees—often the founders—of the various trails associations and often depended on the amount of support and manpower that local jurisdictions were willing to provide. Communities would compete to be on a particular planned route by turning out local citizens to grade and improve the route through their towns. Final selections often caused hard feelings in the towns that were bypassed; on the other hand, towns that chose not to participate were generally left off the promotional maps.

The National Old Trails Road, for example, was envisioned in 1912 as going from Baltimore to California. It took years for the exact route to be set, as town leaders vied to have their towns selected to be included. Eventually, parts of the National Old Trails Road around St. Louis and from Las Vegas, New Mexico, to Los Angeles became part of Route 66, thanks in no small part to Cy.

The idea behind these trails organizations was not only to get better road surfaces but also to get them marked and to get people to travel those roads. Taking a cue from the railroads' famous "See America First" campaign, the highway associations quickly saw the value of making their route sound better than any other. Civic leaders like Cy understood that if they could bring travelers into their towns, those travelers might just spend money or even spend the night. And since better roads benefitted the local community even more than those passing through, the gamble was well worth the time, effort, and money involved.

In northwest Arkansas, a nationally known economist and well-known resort owner named "Coin" Harvey led a movement to develop what he named the Ozark Trails.[1] Initially, Harvey saw the Ozark Trails as a network of highways from St. Louis, Kansas City, Wichita, and Oklahoma City to Monte Ne, his resort. He called an initial meeting for July 1913.

In September 1913, Cy was elected to the Board of Directors of the Commercial Club. As the organization's leading roads man and an unrepentant Tulsa booster, he called for a delegation to attend the organizing Ozark Trails Association (OTA) meeting in Neosho, Missouri, with the purpose of bringing the group's next meeting to Tulsa. He also urged the Commercial Club to send a second delegation to an upcoming U.S. Good Roads Convention in St. Louis with an eye to luring that convention to Tulsa in 1914.[2] His goal in bringing the meetings to Tulsa was twofold. The most obvious was that it would bring business and recognition to the city. More important, though, was his ambition to see that

Tulsa was located on as many national highways as he could lure into town. The starting place for every roads organization was enthusiasm. And during those years, Cy's enthusiasm for highways was rampant.

When Cy arrived in Neosho, he found that three hundred people had braved the muddy, rutted roads to attend the convention. Once the meeting began, Cy was in his element. He spent a lot of time shaking hands, meeting people, telling stories, and making his case for routing the Ozark Trail through Tulsa.

Less than a year later, in May 1914, he was welcoming delegates to Tulsa as chair of the Ozark Trails Association convention.[3] Along with several hundred grass roots good roads men and women, Missouri's governor Major was a special guest. Highway commissioners and engineers had come in from four states. At that meeting Cy helped organize a statewide federation of Oklahoma's various good roads groups and trails association.

Hoopla was a big part of the agenda and Cy saw to it that out of town delegates were well entertained with plenty of parades and parties, but there were also serious items to consider. Final agreement on the route of the Ozarks Trails was a key decision. Other issues included fund-raising, road grading, and signage. Green and white were selected as the colors with a green OT (Ozark Trails) and two green bands to mark the route.

Construction was also part of the purview of the Ozarks Trails Association. Sometime during those early days, the association set specifications for the ideal roadways.

> Our specifications call for a road thirty-two feet wide; a twenty-four foot crown with curvature half an inch to the foot; culverts concrete twenty-four feet wide, same as crown of road; good drainage; above high water; curve turns on radius of not less than 150 feet, outside raised two feet; no grades to exceed five per cent; and hard surface of either sand and clay properly mixed, gravel or crushed rock with clay binder, concrete or other hard surface.[4]

The OTA members further specified that they would "try" never to build the Ozarks Trail through a graveyard.

As far as Cy was concerned, the roads through Tulsa should be significant, national highways and not just regional tracks. During that meeting, he proposed that the Ozark Trail be extended from its current terminus at Oklahoma City into Texas and New Mexico. The delegates agreed to the extension but not the hard work of deciding exactly which towns the route was to pass through.

By the Ozark Trails' meeting in November 1916 in Oklahoma City, Cy was vice president of the OTA and de facto leader, as Coin Harvey reserved the title of president for himself but left Cy in charge. Harvey's original network of trails had become a single route from St. Louis southwest to Las Vegas, New Mexico, via Tulsa. This convention was a very big deal: about ten thousand people from all over the southwest had driven to Oklahoma City to talk roads. The urgency of better roads simply could not be overestimated. Even the weather cooperated to point out the need for better highways. Heavy rains drenched the area and the *Oklahoma City Times* issued a warning about a ferry closure, slippery roads, and the need for chains. It was so bad that some of the delegates who had driven to the convention took a train home, returning to claim their cars after the weather improved.[5]

This meeting was considered the high point of the OTA.

> For two months before the convention the OTA—and the good roads effort in general—had the full support of the Oklahoma City press. Editorials in the *Oklahoma City Times* claimed that good roads would improve education by making it easier for children to get to school and would reduce the cost of food by encouraging a return to the farm. Both the *Oklahoma City Times* and the *Daily Oklahoman* praised the OTA, the Oklahoma City convention and Harvey himself. There were also editorials in favor of a $1,000,000 bond for road building.[6]

The Tulsa chamber delegation rode to the convention in a new seven-passenger automobile purchased specifically for the occasion. Seventeen bands from various OTA towns marched in the parade and the band director from Hobart, Oklahoma, wrote an Ozark Trails march.

One goal of that Oklahoma City meeting was to have delegates decide between three potential routes from Oklahoma City to New Mexico. Cy pushed for the so-called Northern Route, because it would connect to the National Old Trails Road at Las Vegas, New Mexico, thereby giving the Ozark Trails—and Tulsa—a through connection all the way to the West Coast. Although there was much debate by those present, as each group of delegates wanted the Ozarks Trail through their town, Avery, ever the successful salesman, eventually won the day: his northern route prevailed. Ultimately, it would become part of U.S. Highway 66.[7]

Besides the parades, networking, and general ballyhoo, there was also a contest to select the next year's convention location. Again, Cy's personality and way with words got him what he wanted. He also managed to win back some of the goodwill he had lost among those who had pushed for the southern route to New Mexico. In a maneuver that endeared him to the delegates, and one that he would use again in other years, Cy gave a nominating speech for the next convention site. According to the *Daily Oklahoman*,

> A spirited contest for the next convention began . . . between Tulsa and
> Amarillo, Texas, and continued until the last moment of the convention,
> which when Chairman Avery of the Tulsa delegation, after a fifteen min-
> ute speech on Tulsa as a great convention city, nominated as the place for
> the next meeting, the magnificent city of—Amarillo, Texas. This unex-
> pected finale to the splendid address, anticipated only by the speaker and
> three other men, set the convention wild and terminated this remarkable
> meeting by giving to Amarillo the convention, and giving to Tulsa the un-
> stinted praise and loyalty of more than 7,000 delegates at the convention.[8]

Not to mention the personal benefit to Cy.

Later that year, as president of the Oklahoma Good Roads Federation, Cy was the man behind Oklahoma's First Annual Good Roads Week at the University of Oklahoma. This was a chance for local officials and road enthusiasts to learn the fundamentals of road building. Besides Cy, the president of the state's County Commissioners Association promised to be there, along with academics, speakers from state and federal highway departments and road implement and materials companies. H. A. Pressey, who later had a hand in plans for bringing Spavinaw water to

Tulsa, was a consulting engineer from New York City who happened to be in Oklahoma supervising construction of the Oklahoma City dam. Pressey was to speak on the "engineer's control of highway construction." Attendees were promised demonstrations of asphaltic oils and road construction techniques, plus opportunities to visit with road implement companies and watch motion pictures shown by farm machinery businesses. The *Oklahoman* reported that two miles of highway into Norman would be treated with fluid "to show road oil techniques and every aspect of road building will be taken up by Professor J. I. Tucker of the College of Engineering."[9]

The demand for roads in those days was already beyond imagining. The people who flocked to road conventions in those years came from all walks of life, from small businessmen to politicians to farmers to bankers to doctors. They hailed from farms, small towns, and cities; from close by and from hundreds of miles away. And unless they came by railroad, their journeys were not simple. Typical automobile accessories included a large collection of tools, extra tires, a tent and cooking utensils, not to mention an emergency fund that could be used to pay a farmer and team to pull the car out of a ditch, a creek, or deep mud.

Enthusiasm, however, did not bring in enough money for hard pavement. Along with sponsoring massive rallies, canny trails associations regularly petitioned Congress to appropriate funds for highway construction. Until 1916, members of Congress made speeches and made promises but did little to nothing in Washington, D.C. In part, this was because of rivalries over which district and which trail association would be the first to receive funds. The other issue was more long-standing—the philosophical difference over whether federal roads should be veritable interstates that only connected major cities, or "working roads" that connected local communities to larger places and then on to interconnect across the nation. Henry Joy, president of the comparatively well-funded Lincoln Highway Association, concluded that "road building work has always been delayed because politicians couldn't agree."[10] Joy underestimated the pressure those politicians were under.

During Cy's last year in office as Tulsa county commissioner, and while he was leading the Ozark Trails Association, he attended a pivotal good roads convention in Little Rock, accompanied by Guthrey. As he later described the meeting, the Little Rock gathering was one of the places where sentiment coalesced to set American highway policy: "During the early stages of highway organization in the United States, two distinct schools of thought were headed by outstanding leaders. The National Highways Association, headed by Charles Henry Davis of Massachusetts, contended for Congressional legislation authorizing the construction of a system of national highways to be built, maintained and marked at the expense of and under the complete supervision of the Nation, independent of individual states or any municipal sub-division."

The U.S. Highway Association, on the other hand, believed that the states, supported by federal funds, should share responsibility for highway construction with the federal government. Cy and most state and local road officials also shared this position, espoused by road enthusiast Sen. John Hollis Bankhead of Alabama.

At the June 1916 joint meeting of both Davis's National Highways Association and the U.S. Highway Association, delegates passed a resolution that adopted the Bankhead idea. Cy remembered, "Mr. Guthrey was a member of the resolutions committee and cast the deciding vote that brought the majority report of the committee to the floor of the convention for discussion and final adoption."[11]

As far as Cy was concerned that Little Rock meeting was directly responsible for what happened in Washington, D.C., the following November. After years of avoiding the subject, Congress passed the Federal Aid Road Act of 1916, also known as the Bankhead-Shackleford Act. This bill set the country on a course of federal funding for national highways.

Members of the American Association of State Highway Officials, officers of AAA, and a host of others assembled to watch as Pres. Woodrow Wilson, who had campaigned on a good roads platform, signed the bill into law. In essence, the act provided $75 million in matching funds to states for paving up to 6 percent of their highways, with the federal match limited to $10,000 per mile. All plans for state highways were to be submitted to the federal Bureau of Public Roads for approval before being undertaken.

The Federal Aid Act of 1916 was a major step forward but it had two drawbacks. The first was timing because World War I largely stopped any kind of road building in the United States, and the second was the fact that while the law appropriated dollars, it did not offer any kind of direction as to where those dollars were to be used. In other words, paved roads did not have to lead anywhere or necessarily connect with each other. Nonetheless, it was a good start, and for Cy it offered the encouragement he needed to push forward with the Ozark Trails Association and even mastermind another one.

Cy was unable to attend the 1917 convention in Amarillo. He sent a telegram explaining that personal and community affairs would keep him away and such was his reputation that the *Amarillo Daily News* reprinted it with a reminder that it was Avery who had secured the convention for Amarillo.[12] Even without Cy, the Amarillo convention was a blowout. In the darkest days of World War I, when road construction in the United States had almost come to a standstill, six thousand people massed to lend their support, learn something about road building, and urge politicians to pay attention. They mounted a huge automobile parade that stretched far out of town. They listened to speeches and watched road-building demonstrations. They heard from Coin Harvey that the Ozark Trail was now an "official" route to the West Coast.[13] That convention swelled and almost doubled the population of the Texas Panhandle town. To handle the crowd, the city had commandeered nearly all vacant rooms in private residences and erected a tent city that could house thousands more. The newspaper described the city layout as one that would "doubtless resemble other camps 'somewhere in France.'"[14]

Under Cy's leadership, the Ozark Trails Association published a map, and put up green-and-white markers along the way—although the "markers" were as likely to be stripes painted on trees and fences as actual signage.

At home, Cy discussed with other highway enthusiasts in the chamber the possibility of putting another national road through Tulsa. His suggestion was the Albert Pike Highway Association, to be named for a Civil War general and writer. Cannily, because it automatically meant a great deal of support from either end, he set the route between Hot Springs, Arkansas, "the East's favorite winter vacation spot," and Colorado Springs, Colorado, "the West's favorite summer vacation spot."

Years later, Cy reminisced with a group in Fort Smith about his early efforts to gin up interest in the route that eventually became U.S. 64. Sometime after the original Albert Pike Association organizing meeting in January 1917, he recalled,

> Mr. E. Bee Guthrey and myself had occasion to visit Ft. Smith on what was then a very ambitious and almost hopeless vision of a highway from Hot Springs, Arkansas to Colorado Springs, Colorado. The only crossing on the Arkansas River from Oklahoma was the Missouri Pacific toll bridge here in your city. Mr. Guthrey and I had a meeting with some of your citizens, in which I think there was at least a dozen present. We mentioned our plans and explained to your folks that if you wanted to secure the Albert Pike highway you would have to have a free bridge at or near the foot of Garrison Avenue.
>
> . . .
>
> As I look back upon this meeting I am somewhat surprised that we were not thrown out or ordered back to Tulsa. . . . However, someone must have thought that we really had something to deliver, because they arranged a meeting at the Court House for 7:30 that night and that small court room was well filled. That was the beginning of the movement that resulted in building the splendid flanges up Oklahoma and the great State of Arkansas. We had many offers to promote this highway through Poteau and on to the southwest, missing Ft. Smith, but to all of them we turned a deaf ear.[15]

He returned the favor less than a decade later when, as chairman of the Oklahoma Highway Department, he designated the Albert Pike route as State Highway 1.

Since road improvements and signage depended on money donated by towns along the way, it took four years and a lot of legwork to settle the exact route between the three key cities of Hot Springs, Tulsa, and

Colorado Springs. Once the route was fixed, the association tackled the job of establishing permanent markings "so the traveling public can follow the route with the least possible inconvenience." Cy was also anxious to see an Albert Pike group, or at least a representative in each of the counties along the route, who would grade and maintain the road.

"We do not want to wait until every part is hard surfaced before we take up maintenance," he later wrote in *The Nation's Highways*. "It is our desire that this be a 365-day-in-the-year dependable highway. . . . The future holds some wonderful developments for those towns and counties linked together by a permanent highway. Never before was the necessity for motor transportation so great as today."[16]

In January 1919, he and his cronies in the Albert Pike Highway Association were involved in the formation of a national group of trails organizations when delegates from thirty-seven good roads associations held their first nationwide conference. To be a member, an association must have represented a trail at least five hundred miles long that touched at least three states. Dubbed "The Associated Highways of America," or AHA, the group had an express purpose of promulgating "a well defined and connected system of improved highways in order to expedite the distribution of large volumes of foodstuffs, fifty percent of which now are wasted on account of the lack of prompt and adequate highway transportation," and a federally built and maintained national highway system.[17]

In 1922 Cy was elected president of the AHA.

FIVE

Good Roads for the Nation

> We were driving North . . . I think it was, and we could see
> a white streak of hard surfaced road extending for miles and
> miles to the North. To an old timer it was a beautiful sight
> and I realize how much work it took to put through such
> projects.
>
> —C. H. Lamb

The Federal Aid Highway Act of 1916 turned out to be more of a good omen than a means to actually build roads. Only months after the act was signed, war broke out in Europe. Then, in April 1917, the United States declared war on Germany. With that, road building virtually ceased.

Oklahoma, with its petroleum and agricultural resources, became a leading supplier of oil to the military, along with mules, oxen, and draft horses for the battlefront. Oklahoma cotton, which had been shut out of European markets by the German embargo, suddenly was in great demand. Farm prices more than doubled when Americans joined the Allied cause and farmers ramped up production of anything they could raise or grow.

By this time Cy was in his mid-forties and father of one-year-old Helen in addition to two teenage sons. He was well past his soldiering years, but in 1918, he accepted a position as director of Federal Relief in northeastern Oklahoma. He was more than familiar with the region and the farm people there; in 1914 he had been president of the Eastern Oklahoma Agricultural Association and worked with the federal government in placing farm agents in each county.

His tenure was a success: a year after the war ended, Cy received a letter from an assistant secretary of agriculture, "Thanks for the excellent work." The letter went on to point out that his salary was set at one dollar per year and since he had worked only from November 1918 to June 1919, he would be paid a grand total of sixty-three cents.[1]

At that time, and four years later when he was a member of the county water board during the Spavinaw project, one dollar per year was fine for Cy. He even saved a few of those paychecks and the 1919 letter. Later in his life, though, when the oil wells pumped slower and his real estate business had withered, he was still deeply involved in public life—and still on "volunteer" payrolls.

During World War I, Cy also headed the Tulsa County Liberty Loan War Bond campaign through Rotary. His territory was the part of Tulsa County outside the city, a perfect assignment for Cy. To kick off the drive, he hosted ninety fellow Rotarians at his farm for a chicken and possum dinner. As was typical, he enlisted two of his colleagues to help him cook, and as was also typical, they cooked outside. Dinner consisted not so much of possum but of "yellow-legged chickens and hash browns" and probably a good share of sippin' whiskey. After dinner, Cy lined up the champion coon dogs of Owasso Township for a traditional southern coon hunt, one where the people sit around a campfire telling stories and enjoying libations while the dogs are turned loose. The "hunters" follow the hunt and the success of the various dogs by listening to their baying.

As the *Tulsa World* reported the event, "Following a wonderful repast of food cooked out under the forest trees in Avery's famous bluegrass pasture, guests were introduced and among them E. W. Sinclair, who is in charge of raising Tulsa's quota of the war budget . . . said that Oklahoma must raise $1,700,000." Sinclair estimated Tulsa's part of that would be "about 50 percent."[2]

"Farmer Cy" as he was dubbed by the *Tribune*, rang up $742,810 in war bond sales. This averaged $140 per capita and far surpassed his $575,850 quota, as well as the Liberty Bond campaign inside the city limits.

As soon as the war ended, Cy turned his attention back to highways. At the same time, a vast number of other Americans, who couldn't put those hard war years behind them fast enough, were buying cars. Granted, some Americans had owned cars for two decades. But it wasn't until the 1920s that the bulk of the population finally decided to turn their horses out to pasture and "afford a Ford," buy a Chrysler Imperial—"the car of tomorrow"—or purchase one of the General Motors vehicles that was good "for every purse or purpose." In 1900, there had been approximately eight thousand automobiles on U.S. roads. By 1905, there were seventy-seven thousand, and by 1920 there were nearly eight million—one car for every thirteen people in a nation with a population of 106 million. And whether a person was among those who saw cross-country travel as an adventurous re-creation of pioneer covered wagon journeys or was among those who saw their cars as something far more prosaic that could make their daily lives a bit easier, all of those millions of American automobile owners were fomenting for better roads.

Rural people more than city dwellers saw the difference that automobiles and upgraded roads could make in their lives. At least one study has shown that in those days, a higher percentage of automobile owners lived in isolated counties than in more developed places.[3]

Across the United States, especially in the states west of the Appalachian Mountains, men like Cy met that suddenly pressing urgency for roads by staging good roads meetings—often and everywhere. And the people came. These were the years when a farmer, tired after weeks of planting or harvesting, would toss a tent, frying pan, jack, tire repair kit and perhaps a five gallon can of gasoline into the back of his Model T or his Chevy then gentle it across a hundred miles of narrow, rutted, perhaps washed-out roadbeds to join hundreds of other farmers and small businessmen in one of Cy's rallies for better roads.

Even with a fine new vehicle, getting from one place to another was no simple matter, what with cars that broke down and primitive wagon trails that muddied up, but get there they did. A good roads meeting in a small rural town in Missouri or Oklahoma or Indiana or Alabama could draw hundreds of people, not to mention anyone planning to run for office in the coming months.

Time and again over the early years of the twentieth century, hundreds—sometimes thousands—of newly minted automobile owners would converge on small towns and cities furiously united in their conviction that it was past time for this country to build decent cross-country highways. Even the U.S. Army got into the act in 1919 when it sent a caravan cross-country to find the optimal route for a transcontinental highway.

By 1920, as highway construction was picking up again after the war, the men on the ground like Cy could see that the Federal Aid Highway Act of 1916 was too broad to be very effective: it appropriated only a limited amount of dollars and was not specific enough about which roads were to be paved. And so the debate was brought to a head once more, this time over just what sort of national roads the country should have. One faction was still pushing for truly transcontinental highways that would link big cities across the country. This movement ultimately was rewarded with the Interstate Highway Act under Pres. Dwight Eisenhower.

The other faction wanted highways that were utilitarian, linking local communities to one another and then linking to further distant cities. Cy was an outspoken member of this group and he put his organizing talents and oratorical skills to work to achieve that end.

By 1920, the population's hunger for viable roads was finally making true believers of members of Congress. The second Albert Pike Association convention in 1918 had attracted the governor of Arkansas to its meeting in Fort Smith, but by the association's fourth meeting, which took place in Hot Springs in 1920, the mass of road-supporting dignitaries threatened to crush the dais.

The azaleas were in bloom that April as Cy and five hundred Oklahomans joined five thousand other highway-mad Americans in the little resort town. Besides the Albert Pike people, the gathering included delegates from the much larger U.S. Good Roads Association and the Coast-to-Coast Bankhead Highway Association. The Bankhead Highway, the transcontinental route between Washington, D.C., and San Diego, honored pioneer highway booster Sen. John Hollis Bankhead of Alabama, whose name, along with Missouri congressman Dorsey Shackelford, was on the Federal Aid Road Act of 1916. Bankhead had just died a few weeks before the meeting so the urgency for better roads was combined with a widespread sense that the best memorial would be a new highway law.

During the convention sessions, Cy found himself seated on the stage in the company of U.S. vice president Thomas Marshall, a U.S. senator, three governors, and a host of state and national highway officials, not to mention the national press. The most important man invited to the convention was Thomas H. MacDonald, chief of the Federal Bureau of Public Roads. MacDonald was a fearsome figure in the world of highway politics. Taciturn and quite formal, he always wore a coat and tie. He had grown up in a small town in western Iowan, an area where the mud could be so deep that it kept farm families housebound two or three months each year, and had developed a lifelong obsession with road building as a civil engineering student at Iowa State College of Agriculture and Mechanical Arts, later Iowa State University. Upon graduation, he joined the Iowa State Highway Department as an engineer. By the time he was thirty-eight, he was head of the department and president of the American Association of State Highway Officials (AASHO). When the head of the Federal Bureau of Public Roads, Logan Waller Page, died suddenly in 1918, MacDonald's AASHO colleagues nominated him, and the secretary of agriculture appointed him into that job. He asked for, and got, a raise before taking the public roads job and also kept his seat on AASHO's board. A fanatic about improving America's highways, MacDonald lobbied Congress for better laws, assembled a road-focused coalition of civic and business groups to support his cause, made regular radio addresses, and gave hundreds of speeches in all parts of the country. Held in awe by most people he dealt with, MacDonald was widely known simply as "the Chief."[4] His invitation to Hot Springs focused a brighter spotlight and national attention on the good roads convention.

Given the burgeoning interest in all things involving roads, MacDonald was something of a national celebrity. Even though most people might not have been able to identify him on sight, he was known to be a champion for the men and women who lived on rutted country roads. That was why, when a con artist arrived in the small community of Blackwell, Oklahoma, claiming to be the Chief, the town welcomed him with open arms. The city fathers took "MacDonald" on a tour of local highway construction projects, saw to it that he had a hotel room, and even cashed some of his personal checks. When the imposter finally disappeared, the embarrassed community was left with a stack of bad checks and unpaid hotel and meal bills. But the experience showed that even in a remote Oklahoma town, the name T. H. MacDonald was a familiar one, and the potential to entertain such an exalted guest from the all-important Bureau of Public Roads trumped any need to verify his credentials.[5]

In Washington, MacDonald and the AASHO officials were pushing Congress to replace the Federal Aid Highway Act with a new law that would set parameters for a connected system of hard-surfaced roads throughout the country. Just months before the Little Rock meeting, he had made a long and eloquent speech at the American Road Builders Association convention where he called for the country to create a national highway system. First he made a case for federal funding: "It does seem to me that the federal dollar spells a certain opportunity for harmonizing and proceeding with our road program in an orderly manner that the local dollar does not afford." He also plainly showed his preference for a federally managed national system. "If you select the roads of greatest economic need in the states, the chances are that you will be selecting those, which, in general should be parts of a national system," he told the road builders, adding that he had already asked the National Geologic Survey to create basic roadmaps of each state so as to put together a national map from which his men could work.[6]

The 1920 Good Roads meeting in Hot Springs was a next step in MacDonald's push for that national roadmap of highways and before the convention ended, the delegates were united. They enthusiastically supported a resolution asking the federal government for a restricted federal aid highway system. This meant they wanted federal aid dollars to be spent first on primary and then secondary roads. From resolutions like this, surely it was only a short step to a new federal highway law.

The next day, Cy's keynote speech to the Albert Pike Association was an anthem to a national highway system. He asked a boisterous crowd, "Where are the highways of this nation? Since the 'Old National Road' was abandoned over one hundred years ago, unfinished, the Government has not attempted to build a highway. The Federal Aid Act of 1916 was . . . a fine move in the right direction, but it is a move all too slow for this motorized age of undreamed-of development." His rhetoric soared as he continued:

> We should have a master system of highways with Uncle Sam at the head to lead the way—a federal system that will do for the interior states what harbors have done for our lakes and ocean sections, and what the development of our navigable streams has done for those sections tributary to them; a system under a Department of Roads whose business will not be secondary to some other interest of the nation; a system that will be a guide in both the type of road surfaced and the method of construction; and last and most important, one that will establish a permanent system of maintenance that will furnish to ourselves and our posterity, the guaranty of maintenance of this tremendous investment.[7]

As he finished, the crowd thundered their agreement. It was definitely past time to get rural America out of the mud.

For years, Cy would go anywhere and do almost anything to promote highway building. He was charming and gregarious and had useful things to say. He became a familiar figure at road gatherings and took his know-how and influence behind the scenes when necessary. On one typical afternoon he drove seventy-five miles east of Tulsa to eat fried chicken at the White River Trail Association's annual good roads picnic. He slapped backs, he told stories, he stood front and center on platforms and gave rousing speeches about the value of good roads in people's lives. Of course he had a double interest in doing so. The White River Trail had been founded by a good friend, Springfield attorney and real estate developer John Woodruff. More important, the White River Trail was another road to Tulsa. This one came from Springfield by way of Branson and Eureka Springs, Arkansas.

Cy's dogged interest in better roads had put him in touch with like-minded people all over the United States. Like his friend Will Rogers,

Cy never met a man he didn't like, so many of the good roads men also became his friends. One such was Charles E. Thomas. Thomas, mayor of Colorado Springs in 1917, was a well-known architect who had a hand in building many of the fine homes and public buildings in Colorado Springs, including, in the late 1930s, the Will Rogers Shrine of the Sun on the hill overlooking the Broadmoor. Probably he was a friend of Rogers, as was Avery.

Thomas had immediately seen the wisdom in Cy's push to create a Hot Springs–Colorado Springs highway and signed on as a founding member of the Albert Pike Association. He also became a regular at Cy's various get-togethers to raise interest in the road. After one particularly felicitous post–Albert Pike Association meeting, he wrote Cy that he had arrived home safely, presumably having driven from Tulsa. The visit to Spavinaw, Thomas wrote, had been delightful. "It is a beautiful spot and the water is all you claim it to be." However, Thomas finished, "I didn't realize how potent your spicewood brew" was.

Avery long kept a copy of an "oath" signed by Thomas and two others on that trip. It read, "The Sunshine is brighter, water is bluer and clearer, leaves of the trees are greener than anywhere in the wide world and not on account of the fragrant concoction known as Spicewood Tea." Apparently, a good time was had by all.[8]

Over the years, Cy developed a large cadre of friends in Colorado and often went there to vacation and hunt. Because the family was so fond of the area, Cy and Essie held daughter Helen's wedding at the Broadmoor in Colorado Springs more than twenty years later.

In addition to his growing network of colleagues and increasing presence on the national scene, Cy's commitment to highway economics broadened during these years and he built several highway businesses of his own. In 1921, on the edge of Admiral Place, the road that ran past his farm, he opened three of Tulsa's first highway enterprises: a service station, tourist cabins, and a café and tavern that he named the Old English Inn. The prefabricated cabins were made by Tulsa Milling Company and were about twelve feet by sixteen feet square. Cy's son Leighton, who grew up to be a partner in Avery's real estate development business, spent time working there and remembered that the tourist court had about twenty-five one-room cabins with a central bathhouse.

> The tourist court opened in 1921 when I was in high school. . . . We had one family who cared for the place; the husband was a driller and he drilled for oil on the farm and hit oil and gas. We furnished the gas and oil for the houses.
>
> Everybody in each one of the individual units did have a fireplace where they could cook outside, out in front of the doors. They would fix meals and things like that, but they had to go over to a central building that had showers and concrete tubs for laundry. Everyone had to furnish their own linens.   . . .
>
> I worked over at the filling station. I pumped gas but the main thing that I did all during that time was to haul lumber and concrete to build the place. When high school got out my father bought a Model T [truck] and we hauled all the rock, hauled the lumber, everything. We hauled a lot of heavy rocks. They were surface rocks but there were also limestone rocks, so big around [spreading his arms around an imaginary rock] to use on the walls of the station and the cabins.

Avery family cousins also did work at the filling station, "in the summer time, when they could make some extra money," said Leighton. He also remembered he and his cousins taking the family Packard to go to dances in Tulsa on summer evenings. "Father and Mother didn't take the Packard much, except for trips. Father would use it when he took men to show property."[9]

Leighton's wife, Ruth Sigler Avery, who was a child during those years, remembered the place vividly.

> They had a great big farmhouse where the Rotary Club and all of them would have their big picnics. It was quite a showplace. Then, across the way was a place where there was public washing—where people did their wash and hung their clothes out on the line. And then right in the center there was a restaurant that was very, very well attended. They had wonderful food.

The station was a large structure with four or five gas pumps and two grades of gas. The end part was attractive and people would come in, fill up and while their car was being worked on they would go in and have a full meal in the restaurant. They would have marvelous chicken—fried chicken—mashed potatoes, hot biscuits and the whole bit. It wasn't just an ordinary place; it was one of the outstanding places to eat.

Those were the days when cars were new and people traveled for luxury and for excursions. This would be your day's trip and you would eat your meal, get the gas filled up and you would go back home. It was a full adventure.

The recipe for the Old English Inn's yeast dinner rolls even became a popular dinner item in Tulsa homes.[10]

Cy always saw what other people saw in better highways: opportunity. This meant working for the greater good of his nation and his city, but he saw to it that he also took advantage of what the situation offered. He was, after all, a businessman as well as a highway promoter. So it was not surprising that in 1926, when he had a hand in laying out the national highway system, U.S. Highway 66 followed Admiral Place right past the Old English Inn, the tourist court, and the Avery Service Station. The three businesses served him well for quite some time: he had the tourist cabins for about a dozen years and the Old English Inn until 1943, when it was razed to build a traffic circle, but he owned the service station well into the 1950s and possibly until his death in 1963.

Cy loved people and he loved to talk. But he also recognized the value of the printed word and he encouraged his colleague E. Bee Guthrey to found a highways booster magazine. Called *The Nation's Highways*, it debuted in April, 1921. Most issues carried an article with Cy's byline, pieces about him, or stories about one or more of his projects. It was another bully pulpit. In the first issue, one article traced the history of the Tulsa County road system and another focused on the history and potential for the Tulsa-based Albert Pike Highway Association. In that same issue Cy wrote that "Oklahomans are coming to the realization that the ultimate arrival of connected through trunk roads cannot be realized by counties and the federal aid plan, but has to come through the states, assisted by the federal government."[11] His days as a county commissioner had taught him that lesson, but as he was to find out, many of his successors in Oklahoma's county governments did not agree. In another issue, he wrote about his support for the Townsend Bill, championed by Sen. Charles E. Townsend (R-Michigan), which would have created a National Highway Department. "From my point of view, it is the most important piece of road legislation ever to be introduced in Congress."[12] The Townsend Bill failed, but it was further recognition of the swelling tsunami for better roads. A later issue extolled the virtues of the cross-country Lincoln Highway, and reported that in September 1920, 2,500 tourists from outside the state had passed through Salt Lake City on the Lincoln Highway—one-third more than the year before. "The road is not a boulevard but a through, connected and perfectly marked highway."[13] Clearly, a road to emulate.

In 1922, while still deeply involved in the acquisition of land for Tulsa's Spavinaw water project, Cy headed north to Minneapolis to lead the annual meeting of the Associated Highways of America (AHA). It was Cy's good luck that the meeting was where it was; he wound up instead at the Mayo Clinic for an appendectomy.

"Detained in hospital, regret missing convention," he telegrammed H. O. Cooley, general agent of the Yellowstone Trail Association, who was waiting for him in Minneapolis. "Present unsettled transportation situation emphasizes need of heavy and broad national highways. . . . Hope the convention will go on record . . . [with a] resolution asking Congress to increase federal aid."[14] Even an appendectomy couldn't divert his attention for long.

By this time the AHA was a significant part of the good roads movement; representatives from forty-seven different trails organizations were expected at the Minneapolis meeting. The stalwart E. Bee Guthrey, who was attending the AHA convention as president of the White River Trail Association, stepped into the breach and presided in Cy's absence until Cooley was elected the next president.

While Cy recovered from his surgery, he was kept apprised of what was happening not only in the road world, but also back home in Tulsa. One of the things that was happening in Oklahoma was that the Ku

Klux Klan's already significant influence had grown politically and stretched statewide. Among the communications he received while he was recuperating was a letter from attorney Fred Kopplin about Klan doings. "Being a prudent man since the Ku Klux Klan was organized I have done like the oil operators are doing. I have shut down on operations. The Klan took a bunch out here the other night and gave them some treatments."[15]

Cy, already all too familiar with Klan tactics, was probably glad he was still in Minnesota when he read Kopplin's letter. The year before, he had been at home when Tulsa erupted into the country's worst-ever race riot. As one of the people who led in cleaning up after the carnage, Cy kept his reputation as a decent member of the city's white leadership[16] but didn't improve his standing with the reputed three thousand Klan members in Tulsa.

As befitted the oil capital of the United States, Tulsa's black community was a highly successful one. Greenwood, as the thirty-four-square-block neighborhood was called, was home to eleven thousand people and more churches per capita than white Tulsa. The prosperous business area was widely known as the Black Wall Street. Located just north of downtown, it boasted a host of restaurants, grocery stores, banks, physicians, attorneys, two schools, a YMCA, theaters, a library, and two newspapers. One of Greenwood's surgeons was considered by the Mayo brothers as the best black physician in the United States.

In Cy's capacity as an insurance man and developer, he regularly did business with black citizens of Greenwood and had a reputation among them as a man of integrity and fairness.

Despite surface appearances, however, all was not well among Tulsa's black and white races and had not been well for some time. Between 1915 and 1920 the city's population almost tripled to 72,075, and returning World War I veterans, both black and white, often had trouble finding jobs. Farmers, who had seen crop prices plummet following the war, were now suffering through a major drought. Labor unrest was rampant. And, as the *New York Times* pointed out, many of Tulsa's black men had been drafted into service in France during the war and praised for their patriotism, which contributed to racial antagonism when they returned home. All these issues, coupled with an influx of European immigrants with foreign ways and strange religions, fed into the resurgence of the Klan.

Lynchings were not uncommon. Between 1911 and 1921, twenty-three black Oklahomans were lynched. In 1920, Tulsa mobs even lynched a white man—for shooting a white taxi driver. Most troubling about that Tulsa lynching was that the sheriff's office proved to be totally ineffective and both of Tulsa's white newspapers wrote editorials condoning the mob justice. One of the black newspapers, the *Tulsa Star*, quickly saw that if a white man wasn't safe, no black man would ever be safe. It warned that if necessary, the black community should be ready to take matters into their own hands.[17]

Ten months after the white man was lynched, on May 30, 1921, a nineteen-year-old shoe shiner named Dick Rowland, who had been a star halfback at the black high school the year before, fell against or stepped on a seventeen-year-old white elevator operator. The girl, whose name was Sarah Page, screamed that she had been assaulted. The young man was brought in for questioning and then released.

When the next day's *Tulsa Tribune* carried a headline, "Nab Negro for Attacking Girl in Elevator,"[18] the sheriff's office brought Rowland back to the jail for his own protection. Before long, a white mob massed outside the courthouse, followed shortly by members of the black community. People on both sides, were carrying firearms. As the hours passed, more and more people arrived.

Leighton Avery was nineteen and on his way home past the courthouse that evening from his school's Junior-Senior PowWow. He later recalled that when he came to the courthouse, he almost couldn't make his way through the crowd.[19]

Not too surprising, someone in the mob shot a gun. After that, the town went crazy. Over the next eighteen hours, Tulsa's Black Wall Street was destroyed. More than one thousand businesses and homes in the larger black community were looted and then burned. Rumor had it that planes flew over Greenwood dropping bombs.

By the time the National Guard arrived and martial law went into effect, nearly 300 people were dead, and 184 black citizens and 48 white ones were hospitalized. Leighton remembered watching from the roof of Central High School as city trucks drove up and down Tulsa streets filled with dead bodies, both black and white.[20] Tulsa was a disaster. Besides the human tragedy, property damage was estimated at $1.5 million—at least $20 million in 2012 dollars.

Cy and an executive group from the chamber worked with the Red Cross and local authorities to set up camps at the fairgrounds, ballpark, and convention center to house and feed the six thousand black citizens who found themselves suddenly homeless. A finance committee formed to take charge of the victims' financial needs, and a bureau was opened to identify separated family members and collect clothing and household goods. As secretary of the city's relief commission Cy went to bat to procure food and supplies.

Two weeks after the violence, Cy testified before a grand jury. Throughout that summer dozens of cases were filed on behalf of the black community, and the courts continued their investigation into the causes and perpetrators of the riot.

Little to nothing ever came of that effort; certainly justice was never served, and the Klan was never named as having a role in what happened. The elevator operator never filed charges against the shoe shiner, who remained safe in jail during the riot. Supposedly both of the young people left the state.

After the race riot, the Klan consolidated its power across Oklahoma. Over the next decade, Cy clashed several times, mostly unsuccessfully, with the Klan factions in the statehouse in Oklahoma City and the governor's office. In the end, Klan animosity cost him his job as state highway commissioner.

Cy Avery and his mother, Ruie Stevens Avery, in 1907. (Photo courtesy of Bob Berghell.)

Avery family: *(back row from left)* Leighton, Cy, Gordon; *(front row)* Essie and Helen, age eight. (Photo courtesy of Bob Berghell.)

Cy and Essie in later years. (Photo courtesy of Bob Berghell.)

First oil well. Avery farm 1916 —

Cy's first well. (Cyrus Stevens Avery Papers, Department of Special Collections and Archives, Oklahoma State University, Tulsa Campus Library.)

"Muddy" was not a strong enough word for some roads in the early 1900s. (Western History Collections, University of Oklahoma Libraries, Merrill Collection Seminole, Oklahoma, 47.)

Avery home on Owasso Street in Tulsa. (Photo courtesy of Susan Croce Kelly.)

In the early 1920s, Cy built a service station, motor court, and restaurant on the side of the road that became U.S. 66. (Beryl Ford Collection/Rotary Club of Tulsa, Tulsa City-County Library, and Tulsa Historical Society.)

Spavinaw Dam and Lake have been sending water to Tulsa since 1924. (Beryl Ford Collection/Rotary Club of Tulsa, Tulsa City-County Library, and Tulsa Historical Society.)

regarding action taken by the Executive Committee in Chicago, and
in paragraph 3 you will find a statement referring to the subject
of this letter. The members there present were of the opinion
that the numbers 60 and 62 should preferably stand as now proposed,
namely, 60 from Springfield to Newport News, and 62 from Chicago
to Los Angeles, but they believed an alternate proposition to be
feasible to which you and Mr. Piepmeier might agree in case you
absolutely refuse the present proposal. This proposition is to
hold Route 60 as at present from Los Angeles to Springfield, Mo.;
from Springfield, Mo. to Chicago to be changed to 60 North; and
from Springfield, Missouri to Newport News, Virginia to be made
60 East. This will result in no change in your State; will probably be acceptable to Kentucky, according to the advice I have
already had, and will require but little change in Missouri and
Illinois.

I am writing, frankly, to compose the situation and I
trust that you will gratiously accept the existing proposal to
change the Chicago-Los Angeles route to 62, but in case you are
unwilling to do this, the alternate proposal involving 60 North
and 60 East is submitted, and if this is satisfactory to
Mr. Piepmeier and Mr. Sheets it will then be put in the form of
a motion and sent to all of the Executive Committee members,
five of whom including yourself, will then be known to approve the
arrangement. A vote of the Executive Committee will have to be
had on this question before it can be considered as finally
adopted.

I know that you comprehend fully the importance of this
whole work and doubtless realize that unless it is satisfactorily
accomplished now, it will have to be postponed indefinitely.
Apparently this adjustment affecting Kentucky is the only one
left of a serious nature and as soon as we can settle it, we can
proceed with the final map, for which we are having daily demands
from every part of the country.

Kindly write Mr. Markham or me in this matter just as soon
as you can give it consideration.

Very truly yours,

This is why we we took 66 - CSA.

Chief, Division of Design.

This February 20, 1926, letter was what ultimately changed Cy's mind about the
highway numbering situation. Since he didn't select a number for his highway
until April 30, the note must have been written after the fact. (Cyrus Stevens
Avery Papers, Department of Special Collections and Archives, Oklahoma State
University, Tulsa Campus Library.)

THE NATION'S HIGHWAYS

Price, 20 Cents   *September, 1924*

E. Bee Guthrey *(lower left)* and Cy *(center top)* launched *The Nation's Highways* magazine to promote the good roads movement and support Cy's various highway ventures. (Cyrus Stevens Avery Papers, Department of Special Collections and Archives, Oklahoma State University, Tulsa Campus Library.)

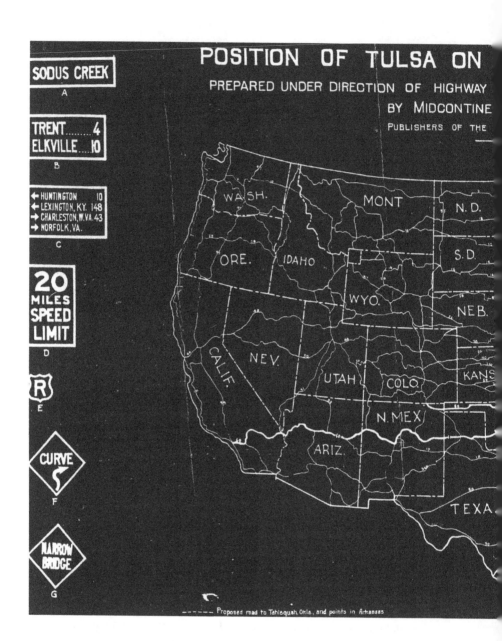

POSITION OF TULSA ON

PREPARED UNDER DIRECTION OF HIGHWAY

BY MIDCONTINE

PUBLISHERS OF THE

SODUS CREEK

A

TRENT.........4
ELKVILLE....10

B

← HUNTINGTON   10
← LEXINGTON, KY. 148
→ CHARLESTON, W.VA. 43
→ NORFOLK, VA.

C

20
MILES
SPEED
LIMIT

D

R

E

CURVE

F

NARROW
BRIDGE

G

Proposed road to Tahlequah, Okla., and points in Arkansas

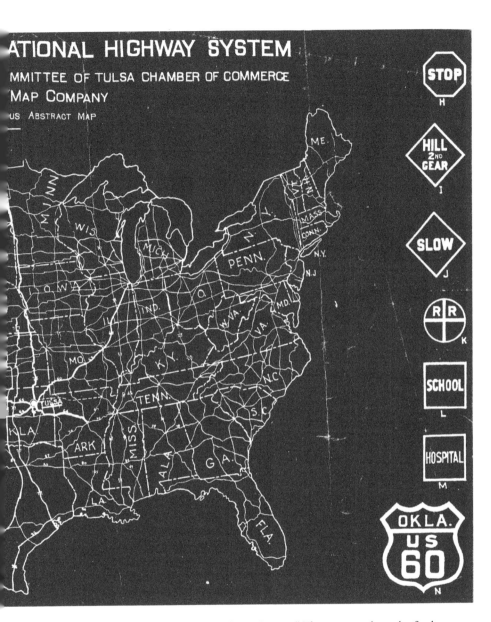

"Position of Tulsa on National Highway System." This map predates the final November 11, 1926, map because the highway route from Los Angeles to Chicago carries the number 60. (Published with permission of the Tulsa Regional Chamber of Commerce.)

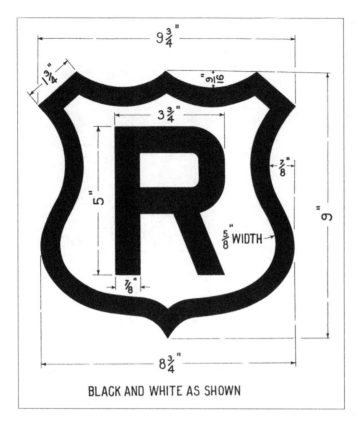

The joint board's early mock-up of a national highway shield.
(Cyrus Stevens Avery Papers, Department of Special Collections
and Archives, Oklahoma State University, Tulsa Campus Library.)

Thomas H. MacDonald, "The Chief," Bureau of Public Roads. (Photo courtesy of the Federal Highway Administration.)

C. C. Pyle's Footrace brochure. (Cyrus Stevens Avery Papers, Department of Special Collections and Archives, Oklahoma State University, Tulsa Campus Library.)

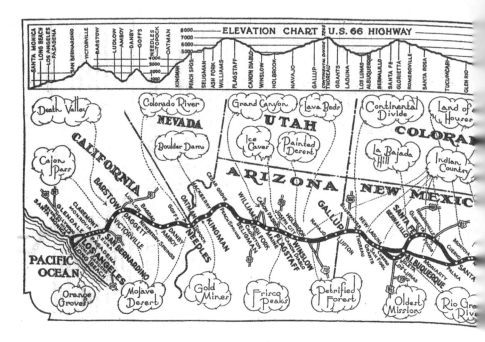

U.S. 66 Highway Association brochure map, circa 1930. (Courtesy National
Archives at College Park, Md., Records of the Bureau of Public Roads 1920–39.)

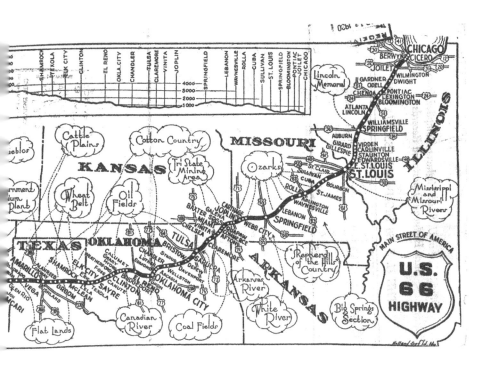

Old U.S. 66 highway sign. Signs like these were taken down as the interstate highways bypassed U.S. 66. (Photo courtesy of Susan Croce Kelly.)

In 1903, Cy was an up-and-coming young businessman in Vinita, Oklahoma. (Photo courtesy of Bob Berghell.)

B. H. Piepmeier, Missouri state highway engineer. (Photo courtesy of Missouri Department of Transportation.)

Laying water pipe for the Spavinaw project. (Cyrus Stevens Avery Papers, Department of Special Collections and Archives, Oklahoma State University, Tulsa Campus Library.)

ELECT
"CY"
TULSA COUNTY'S ORIGINAL
"GOOD ROADS MAN"

CYRUS S. AVERY

DEMOCRAT FOR

County Commissioner
DISTRICT No. 3

 20

(OVER)

In 1944, Cy ran unsuccessfully for his old job as Tulsa County commissioner. (Cyrus Stevens Avery Papers, Department of Special Collections and Archives, Oklahoma State University, Tulsa Campus Library.)

Cy in 1953. (Photo courtesy of Bob Berghell.)

Cy's cabin at his beloved Lucky Ranch. (Cyrus Stevens Avery Papers, Department of Special Collections and Archives, Oklahoma State University, Tulsa Campus Library.)

Tulsa's Avery Memorial Plaza was dedicated in November 2012. (Photo courtesy of Ginger Crichton.)

CHAPTER 6

Water for Tulsa

To the Right Honorable Cyrus Spavinaw Avery

—Address on envelope enclosing letter from
Charles Lamb, May 12, 1957

The early 1920s were perhaps the busiest time in Cy Avery's life. Technology was exploding. Almost every way that Americans had learned to travel, work, communicate, or vacation was being turned on its ear.

Aside from Cy's quest to replace the nation's primitive wagon trails with hard-surfaced highways, he was a key player in another long running saga: the campaign to bring good tap water to Tulsa, a problem that had been festering since before statehood. Today he is remembered for his road building, but it was his involvement in Tulsa's water project that he considered his greatest achievement. It wasn't just any water, either: it was water from Spavinaw Creek, the first water he tasted in Oklahoma.

That day in 1883 or 1884 when Cy and his father pulled into the dilapidated farmstead in Indian Territory and unhooked the tired horses from their heavy wagon was surely a day that Cy never forgot. The house, which had burned, was going to have to be rebuilt, but there was also good news. The property was bounded by two clear Ozark streams—Brushy Creek and Spavinaw Creek. Spavinaw Creek, which is actually a small river, bubbles up out of limestone springs in the Ozark Mountains of northwest Arkansas, and flows southwest into the Grand River, which in turn flows into the Arkansas, although precious little of Spavinaw's clear freshness was ever discernible in the murky Arkansas, which flowed past Tulsa. Mud, silt, salt, and gypsum made the Arkansas River water unpleasant to taste, difficult to filter, and a real threat to Tulsa's growth. As late as 1919, most of the people in town got their water out of bottles—fifty thousand five-gallon bottles of water per week.[1] For years, everyone agreed that something had to be done about Tulsa water. Three years before statehood, the city had built a new pumping station—but it could never filter enough water to make a difference. Another time, voters passed a $100,000 bond issue to dig a series of wells to supply the city's water mains—but within months, the wells ran dry.

Off and on, Cy or someone else would suggest laying a pipeline from Spavinaw or the Grand River, but those ideas were either ignored or scoffed at. Spavinaw was, after all, more than fifty miles away. Like highway construction, the technology to run a pipeline so far was almost out of the realm of possibility in 1910. Also like hard-surfaced highway construction, it wouldn't be impossible for much longer.

In 1913, during Cy's first year as presiding county commissioner, his friend Gene Lorton wrote a series of articles in the *Tulsa World* on insurance rates. In the course of writing the articles, Lorton became concerned that there was not enough water to protect Tulsa against fires. Lorton, who had come to Tulsa from Washington state in 1909 to edit the *World*, was an outspoken Republican. Despite his politics, he and Cy became lifelong friends. They saw eye to eye on the Klan. He shared Cy's passion for good roads and pushed for better highways and licenses for automobile drivers. Lorton was also a member of the Commercial Club and even briefly its president, until pressure from city leaders forced him to resign. He strongly believed the role of a city newspaper was to be an "institution"—a publication that went to bat for what it believed would make the city a better place to live.[2] And after he looked into Spavinaw Creek, he believed passionately that it was the ideal source for Tulsa drinking water. Between 1913 and 1915 Lorton wrote more than six hundred editorials on the subject. He wrote, "What the people want is water. They want it every day and there should be somebody who can devise a system where a man could go to bed at night and be reasonably sure that the water was going to be on tap in the morning."[3] Lorton lamented, "Hundreds have no food because they have to buy water. Hundreds are too poor to buy city water, boil it and partially sterilize it. Hundreds try filters. Hundreds use water from polluted wells. Bottled water is costing Tulsans $250.00 a day."[4] And he went on from there.

In 1914, when Cy ran for his second term as county commissioner, he ran on a highway, and not a water, platform, but by 1915 when he was sworn in, Tulsans were tired of waiting. Water was front and center. That was the year the city and some members of the chamber determined to borrow money to purchase water from nearby Shell Creek in the small town of Sand Springs. An oilman named Charles Page owned the Shell Creek water system and also owned a company that bottled and sold Shell Creek water, mostly to thirsty people in Tulsa. When financing for that deal did not work out, the city moved to hold a bond issue election to pay for the water. The city was supported by some members of the chamber; however, other chamber members like Avery and Lorton saw no future in buying Shell Creek water. Ultimately, the chamber withdrew its support and the election was scuttled.[5]

At this point, Tulsa's two newspapers squared off against each other regarding the best way to solve Tulsa's water problem. In the *World*, Lorton championed Spavinaw water but the *Tulsa Tribune*, which had been purchased by water czar Page, was equally passionate concerning the benefits of Shell Creek water. In the meantime, city officials were still trying to find a solution that involved the Arkansas River. They asked for and got voters to pass a $180,000 bond issue for a new filtration plant with additional settling basins. The plant turned out to be another of the city's many failures: by the time construction was finished, the river channel shifted and the plant's intake line was left high and dry.[6]

In April 1918, a new Tulsa mayor, C. H. Hubbard, was voted into office on the promise that he would actually do something about the city water supply. He duly appointed a nonpartisan committee—endorsed, of course, by the chamber—to conduct a survey of all possible sources for city water. Cy, by now out of office, was named a member of this committee, along with Lorton and chamber president R. M. McFarlin.[7] They hired Harold Pressey, an engineer who had designed Oklahoma City's water system, to conduct the survey.

Pressey compared the Arkansas, other smaller rivers, and the well situation for the amount of water available, quality, cost of implementation and then compared them against each other. He reported back in March 1919 that Spavinaw offered the only viable solution. He estimated that bringing Spavinaw water fifty-five-as-the-crow-flies miles to Tulsa through huge concrete pipes would involve construction of a lake at Spavinaw, two or three intermediate reservoirs, and a city reservoir and pumping station. The cost: $5 million. Cy and Gene Lorton were ecstatic. The city commission set a date for the $5 million bond issue but rather than applauding the results of the survey, the newspapers continued their water wars. Citizens chose sides, wrote letters, and held meetings. The Ozark Sportsmen's Club, a group of Tulsa businessmen with a hunting and fishing lodge on the upper Spavinaw, even hauled in water and passed out Spavinaw samples on downtown streets.

Probably because Tulsans had been burned on water projects so many times before, only four thousand took time to vote. And even though the bond issue carried by an almost three-to-one margin of 818 votes, those who didn't go to the polls actually had the last laugh: the Spavinaw pipeline was not to be. At least not yet. After the votes were counted and project planning begun, it turned out that no one had read the city charter. One section of the charter forbade the city from owning property more than five miles outside the city limits—and the Spavinaw dam would be fifty-five miles away. In an ironic turn of events, the new Taxpayers' Protective League, which Lorton had helped found to support the Spavinaw option, sued to invalidate the election. The case went all the way to the Oklahoma Supreme Court, and on September 14, 1920, the justices ruled that the city charter could not be overruled. The next step, as always, involved the chamber. When the mayor came to discuss the Supreme Court decision with the chamber board, Cy was on hand to hear what he had to say.

By this time, Cy was only peripherally involved in the water wars. As vice president of the Ozark Trails Association, president of the Albert Pike Highway Association, and soon-to-be elected president of the Associated Highways of America he was spending a lot of his time at highway meetings across the Midwest. He was also busy running a lucrative real estate business, managing his farm on the northeast edge of the city, serving as a director of Security State Bank, and was a successful broker in Oklahoma's oil and coal fields.

Despite all that, he couldn't let the promise of Spavinaw water just drain away. He added his vote to the chamber board's unanimous agreement that the Spavinaw project should move forward as soon as possible. The city called an election to change the city charter. Four weeks later, Tulsa voters again went to the polls and again voted to support the city's water plans. They agreed to amend the city charter, empowered city officials to exercise eminent domain and operate utilities regardless of distance from Tulsa, and authorized the mayor to appoint a four-member nonpartisan water commission.[8]

The water commission was appointed in December 1920. The four commissioners were bankers Grant R. McCullough and Earl W. Sinclair and oilmen A. L. Farmer and C. F. Hopkins. One of their first acts was to hire a young city engineer, W. R. Holway, to manage the project. Holway, who had reviewed the Pressey plan, suggested several changes. Most significant was his opinion that water might be brought to Tulsa by gravity flow, eliminating the need for pumping stations.

The water board, who were all members of the chamber, were hesitant to adopt Holway's recommendations so they sought a second opinion—but not just any second opinion. After all, this was Tulsa. Chamber board member Patrick Hurley, later to be Herbert Hoover's secretary of war, had a personal connection with Gen. George Goethals, who had made his reputation through his work on the Panama Canal. And so, in the best Tulsa tradition, the world's preeminent engineer traveled to Tulsa, spent four days with Holway studying the young engineer's recommendations, and on April 4, 1921, pronounced them valid. Shortly thereafter, the project began to move forward.

Sinclair resigned from the commission in September 1921, and Cy was named to take his place. For his work on the water commission, Cy was paid the handsome salary of one dollar per year. For the rest of his life he saved his salary checks from that job.

Because the first bond election had been invalid, and the second election focused on amending the city charter, before much of anything could actually be done about bringing in Spavinaw water to Tulsa, the city had to hold yet another an election to get approval to issue water bonds. By this time, with the project seriously underway, the original estimate for $5 million in bonds was deemed too low and the amount requested was increased to more than $6.8 million. Even though voters had approved the Spavinaw water pipeline project two times already, the potential for $6.8 million dollars indebtedness got people's attention. Once again, sides were drawn, and as soon as this election was announced, the chamber, along with every business group, every labor union, every civic club, and all the women voters held rallies, pro and con.

Because of Cy's connections to land and people around the upper Spavinaw where he had grown up, he was a highly visible target for those who opposed the bond issue. The *Tribune* called for the entire water commission to resign and singled out Cy for specific acrimony. Also, about a week before the election, Cy was among 1,500 people who attended a pro-Spavinaw pep rally at evangelist Billy Sunday's tabernacle. During the rally, a self-described labor organizer charged that water commissioner Avery owned large tracts of land in the Spavinaw area that he was planning to sell to the city for a huge profit. In response, Cy told the audience he would donate $5,000 to charity if the charges proved true. They didn't: within days, Cy's real estate colleagues published a list of owners of record of land near the village of Spavinaw and at the dam site. Cy's name was not listed. He kept his $5,000.

On the day after the rally, the president of the Tulsa Trades and Labor Council made a public statement that his labor group was in total accord with Cy and the water board. This endorsement later stood Cy in good stead when disputes broke out between contractors and the city.[9]

Finally, in a turnout that outdid all previous records for bond issue elections, the people of Tulsa voted more than three-to-one in favor of the Spavinaw bonds. At the time, it was the biggest per capita bond issue that had ever been passed in the United States. And Spavinaw, the biggest-ever water project, had won.

Before it was over, the Spavinaw project would cost $7.5 million. It would involve laying the longest water line ever built in the United States. It would generate a series of disputes between sixty professional engineers and a variety of contractors and this would all happen during a period that produced some of the worst rains the region had ever seen.

One of the biggest parts of the project involved manufacturing and laying the sixty-inch and eight-four-inch concrete pipe. The contractor, Lock Joint Pipe Company, built a temporary pipe fabricating plant near the town of Verdigris about midway along the proposed pipeline, and the water commission built a standard gauge railroad and telephone line to bring pipe, other materials, and supplies to the construction crews. Before the crews could lay the pipe they had to build a series of coffer-dams in the Grand River, tunnel under the Verdigris River, and tunnel through one hill. That was in addition to razing the hamlet of Spavinaw, rebuilding it nearby, and moving a cemetery. Because of the rain and flooding, bridges built for the narrow gauge railroad washed out again and again, and the bridge across the Grand River near the dam was washed out eight times.

Because of Cy's knowledge of land values in the region, his experience in real estate, understanding of eminent domain, and his personal relationships, he headed up the right-of-way acquisition team, a job not unlike what he would be doing two years later as state highway commissioner. The water board also authorized Cy and Farmer to purchase six square miles of land for the pumping station reservoir in Tulsa. As they began buying up land for the Tulsa reservoir, Cy, true to form, got an even better idea: he suggested turning the surrounding land into a city park. According to a report in the *Tulsa Tribune*, "Nary a man who has been out there and visualized the picture which Cy can paint of the future possibilities but has become a raving enthusiast for the project."[10]

Several months after the Spavinaw project was completed, Cy and five other prominent local citizens donated three hundred acres to be the beginning of the park. Their goal was two thousand acres—the largest city park in the United States.[11] Shortly afterward, voters approved bonds to purchase the additional acreage. It was only fitting that the oil capital of the world, with the longest water pipeline and the largest city utility project, also have the largest city park.[12] The park was the easy part. Acquiring the fifty-five miles of land through which Spavinaw water would run—downhill—to Tulsa was more of a challenge.

When it was completed, the Spavinaw Dam raised the water in Spavinaw Creek more than fifty feet—to an elevation of 680 feet above sea level—and impounded 10.3 billion gallons of water. From the newly made lake, water flowed twenty-eight miles through 60-inch reinforced concrete pipe to Tiawah Ridge. There, construction crews built a horseshoe-shaped tunnel to carry the water into a 54-inch conduit that would take it 24.5 more miles to the Mohawk pumping station and reservoir in Tulsa. The Mohawk reservoir, at an elevation of 605 feet, accepted and held 500 million gallons of Spavinaw water. From there, water was pumped four more miles through 30-inch steel pipe into a reinforced-concrete reservoir just northeast of the city limits.

Cy handled the land purchases for the dam, new lake, and the fifty-five-mile right-of-way. Most of the hands-on work was carried out through local attorneys and other real estate men he knew from his business, oil dealings, and his good roads work. One of his allies was J. Howard Langley, a popular Pryor attorney who later ran for and won a position on the Oklahoma Supreme Court. Langley only served as a Supreme Court justice for a few days. Shortly after taking office, he announced he had worn himself out so thoroughly during his campaign that he felt he would be unable to effectively carry out the duties of a Supreme Court Justice.

Under Cy's management, most of the pipeline land was acquired with little difficulty, and even when disputes arose, most were resolved amicably. For the situations when the water commission did have to go to court, the outcomes tended to be expensive. Not surprisingly, jurors were inclined to put higher values on their neighbors' property than the water commission wanted to pay, and as often as not, Cy took the brunt of the criticism for the outcomes. He later lamented "Even a change of venue to the District Court at Vinita in Craig County [where he was well known and had many friends] brought no relief in the tendency of jurors to assess heavy damage against the City of Tulsa in eminent domain cases."[13]

At least two of the land cases went all the way to the Oklahoma Supreme Court. One case involved a land purchase above the planned lake's high-water mark. Cy and the city believed that by owning this land, Tulsa would be able to police the area and guard the lake against pollution. Local landowners, much as they understood Tulsa's need for water, balked at the idea of any nonessential land being sold and sued the water commission. Tulsa eventually won that case. The other supreme court case was a different matter. By far the most interesting of Cy's land acquisition battles, this case involved fifty-five acres of a one-hundred-acre parcel through which the huge water pipes were laid. A bootlegger-turned-hog farmer named William Creekmore owned this disputed land.

Creekmore was not just any bootlegger. He had sold liquor in Indian Territory and then in dry Oklahoma for about two decades, made at least a million dollars, and earned the nickname "King of the Bootleggers." By 1915, he was Oklahoma's largest liquor dealer, apparently working under a distribution agreement with a Kansas City wholesaler. In 1913 he shipped 150 to 200 railroad cars of liquor from Joplin to Enid where it was loaded onto wagons and taken to Tulsa, Sapulpa, Oklahoma City, Muskogee, Miami, Claremore, and other population centers. Needless to say, police in all those places were well paid by Creekmore. He was even said to have paid police to raid his competitors. Eventually, federal investigators, and not those well-paid Oklahoma officers of the law, arrested him. The charge: paying a federal official $20,000 to get a sentence reduced to thirty days in jail.[14]

As his federal trial opened, Creekmore's attorney surprised the court by changing Creekmore's not guilty plea to guilty. He announced, "Creekmore has laid down his arms. He has sold his liquor business and retired forever from 'the game.' He has made up his mind to reform and he will leave the federal prison at the expiration of his sentence with the earnest determination to become a good citizen." Later that day, Creekmore was locked in the county jail with a variety of local bootleggers. He looked over the motley group and spoke, "Have you boys pleaded guilty? You should, it's good for the soul."[15]

By the time of his land wrangle with Cy and the Tulsa Water Commission, Creekmore had served his time in Leavenworth Federal Penitentiary for the above crime and theoretically changed his ways, although there are suggestions that he was still trading in illegal alcohol until the end of Prohibition.

Cy and the Tulsa Water Commission began condemnation proceedings against Creekmore on July 5, 1923. Before it was over, there were three trials, several retrials, and a change of venue. There was also some indication that Creekmore had tried to bribe at least one of the jurors. In the end, although three juries sided with him against the water commission, the Oklahoma Supreme Court ultimately upheld Tulsa's right to purchase the Creekmore land. However, the high court split the difference on the jury awards—two of the juries had recommended $10,000 and one had recommended $15,500 for the fifty-five acres—and ruled that Creekmore be paid $12,000 for his land, more than $218 per acre.[16] Cy, knowing the area's land values as he did, bitterly lamented that decision: Creekmore, Cy said, had originally purchased that land for only ten dollars per acre.[17]

Although his "job" was land buyer, Cy played a significant role throughout the Spavinaw project. At one point toward the end when labor issues with contract management engineers threatened to stop construction, Cy was summoned to help sort things out. Along with Holway and Lock Joint president A. M. Hirsch, he traveled to Baltimore to consult with officials of the bonding company for the project, where they determined the city would take over management of the work. Soon thereafter, the state district court in Mayes County issued a restraining order preventing the removal of machinery from the site and directed the companies to surrender the project to the city. Late that afternoon, Cy, Farmer, and other water commission members, along with the local sheriff's department, took control of the equipment. They also rehired most of the contract workers as water commission employees so construction could continue. It was during this period that he began his personal dealings with Lock Joint Pipe, a subcontractor with whom he would have a lasting relationship.[18]

On November 1, 1924, three years after Cy had joined the water board, the pipeline was completed and the celebrations began. The first ceremonial event took place at the new Spavinaw Dam. Cy, two other water commissioners, and project engineer Holway stood together and turned the cranks that opened one of the floodgates then watched as Spavinaw water began to pour into the giant pipes below. Cy leaned over, cocked his head, and announced, "That's the sweetest music I ever heard in my life."[19] About forty-four hours after Cy and the project team opened the dam, Spavinaw water rushed into the Mohawk pumping station en route to the new Tulsa reservoir.

Then the people of Tulsa waited for two weeks for their party to start. On November 17, 1924, according to a story spread by the Chamber of Commerce, Pres. Calvin Coolidge pressed a button in Washington, D.C., to open the reservoir flow into city mains. In Tulsa, Gov. M. E. Trapp turned a tap that filled a golden cup with fresh, clear water from Spavinaw Creek. He took a long draught. With that, the city of Tulsa began to celebrate. Cy, however, wasn't part of the festivities because by the time the partying started, Cy wasn't even in Oklahoma. As soon as the Spavinaw water began to flow toward Tulsa, he had packed his bag and left for San Francisco to attend his first annual meeting of the American Association of State Highway Officials.

The saga of Cy and the national highway system was about to begin, but the saga of Tulsa's water system wasn't quite over. It took time before old caked mud was flushed out of city pipes, new city water mains could be added, and other issues could be taken care of. Several lawsuits still had to be worked through. Finally, it took another bond issue, this one for $700,000 to complete the system, followed by yet another, highly controversial, $500,000 bond issue to pay off all the debts. Although it did eventually pass, voters were so distraught over the $500,000 bond issue that Lorton and the *World* totally withdrew support from the project and rancorously accused Avery of wrongdoing.[20] Lorton was so lathered up he wrote in the *World* that the Spavinaw project had been a colossal failure and that the Tulsa Water Commission should resign. Further, he said the water commission was a one-man agency that could not or would not transact any business without Cyrus Avery's presence. The paper even demanded that Cy resign from his new position as chairman of the Oklahoma Highway Commission, a job he had assumed on February 15, 1924.

That was not about to happen. When Governor Trapp originally asked Cy about the highway job, Cy had agreed only on the condition it would not interfere with his work on Spavinaw. He also talked to his lawyer. His attorney assured him that holding the two positions—member of the Tulsa Water Commission and state highway commissioner—was neither unlawful nor incompatible. Since one job paid only one dollar per year and the other only a per diem and expenses, he certainly wouldn't get rich.[21]

For the next several months, the *World* continued its vitriol against all things Spavinaw in such a foment that on July 7, 1925, the Chamber of Commerce passed a resolution expressing outrage at the way Tulsa's water had been libeled and calling for a vote of thanks for the water commission.[22] That didn't even slow Lorton down. Another month later, he and the *World* branded Farmer and Cy as "speculators who were using their positions of trust to advance their own private interests" and praised the Tulsa mayor, who had refused to approve payment of a $2,500 expenditure by the "Avery crowd" in certain activities involved with developing Mohawk Park.

Even as Tulsans were enjoying their new water system, Lorton's assault continued. He accused commissioners Avery and Farmer, along with another realtor and a local farmer, of developing a six-hundred-acre tract just south of Mohawk Park for financial gain. (That at least was partially true: Cy built a golf course near the park, which his son Leighton ran for a time.) Further, according to the *World*, Cyrus Avery was a "Trapp Machine Politician."[23] Eventually Lorton threw in the towel and patched things up with Cy. He had always been a staunch supporter of Cy's highway work, and the two renewed their friendship. Years later, after Lorton's death, Cy was the person chosen to present the Tulsa Historical Society with an oil portrait of the newspaperman.

For Tulsa, Spavinaw water came just in the nick of time. In 1925, Cy's good friend Cass Mayo and his brother John opened the luxurious Mayo Hotel. Built in the latest Louis Sullivan style with an art deco interior, the Mayo, the tallest and most opulent building in Tulsa, was the ideal place for VIP oil barons and their even more important oil customers. When it opened it had six hundred rooms. It also had Tulsa's first running—clear running—ice water.

In April 1926, Tulsa held one last election on Spavinaw. This time, there was no controversy; voters agreed to officially decommission the Tulsa Water Board and turn the city water system over to elected officials.

Cy believed his role in the Spavinaw project was the most rewarding of his life, but his feelings may have had more to do with the fact that it was about Spavinaw than that it was about Tulsa's water system. Years later he wrote,

> To me it is interesting that I was one of the four members of the water board who had charge of the construction of the first Spavinaw project and it is also interesting to me that I represented the City of Tulsa in purchasing most of the land for the upper Spavinaw lake, which included the Stand Watie homestead.
>
> It is also interesting to me that I was Chairman of the State Highway Commission that laid out and improved State Highway #10 that runs from Miami to Grove, to Jay, to Tahlequah and on South through the Cookson Hills [all the country around Spavinaw].[24]

No matter what he thought, getting northeast Oklahoma out of the mud seemed to be the clarion call of Cy's life. By the time Tulsa's water system was out of the mud, he was back at work in his nearly lifelong effort to do the same for automobiles.

SEVEN

Highway Commissioner

The time has arrived in the development of our State when we should have a State Highway System in fact. The development of motor-driven traffic has been so rapid that our dual system of road construction and maintenance has proven entirely unsatisfactory, and, in my judgment, our counties should be relieved of the enormous burden of building and maintaining inter-county highways.

—Martin Trapp, governor of Oklahoma

While Cy was sorting out the drinking water situation in Tulsa, Oklahoma's highway department was floundering. Until 1915, Sidney Suggs had brought vision, if not funds and technology, to the goal of creating a state highway system, but after Suggs left office, the highway department came untethered.

Late in 1922, the Bureau of Public Roads' (BPR) chief engineer for the region that included Oklahoma, Louisiana, Arkansas, and Texas was a man named A. R. Losh. Distraught over the situation in Oklahoma, Losh wrote to the bureau's chief, MacDonald, that despite the existence of a state highway department, Oklahoma's road-building program was a shambles. Oklahoma, still needed a central agency with the power to insure proper care for bridges and highways, Losh said. Things in the forty-sixth state were "completely unsatisfactory."[1]

Back in 1915, while Cy was presiding commissioner in Tulsa County and the last year of Sidney Suggs's term as state highway commissioner, Oklahoma passed a new road law that appropriated $2 million for highway construction, $1 million for 1918 and $1 million for 1919, but offered no sure way to see that roads actually got built with the money. Under the law, counties had to match the state funds on a fifty-fifty basis, but after that the counties were pretty much on their own. The state highway department had authority to approve the counties' plans but no authority to oversee construction or maintenance. In Tulsa County where Cy was in charge, the system worked fairly well. Elsewhere, due to the lack of construction oversight or financial controls—or greed—most of the counties treated the road funds as a political bonanza. Road projects would be begun then abandoned. Corruption was rampant. For Oklahomans with automobiles—by now approaching two hundred thousand—the situation became so dire, and voters so angry, that four years into the new road law, many county commissioners wisely chose not to run again. Of incumbents who did seek reelection in 1920, more than half were voted out of office.[2]

In Oklahoma City, the largely powerless highway department racked up an equally bad reputation. In the years after Suggs stepped down and before Cy took over, the state highway commissioner's office was known for infighting, patronage abuses, and generally unprofessional behavior.

Meanwhile, in Washington, D.C., lobbying by the various good roads factions, road construction companies, auto manufacturers, by Mac-Donald from the BPR, and by American Association of State Highway Officials (AASHO), combined with the explosion of automobile owners and the general frustration over the unsatisfactory 1916 Federal Aid Highway Act finally convinced Congress to pass a new national road law. This law, the Federal Aid Highway Act of 1921, divided the nation's through highways into two categories—primary and secondary. Further, it specified that 7 percent of the mileage of those primary and secondary roads, as designated by each state, would be eligible for federal funds, up to $20,000 per mile.[3] Expenditure of the funds would be subject to approval by the BPR, and all construction contracts and plans were to be carried out under the direct supervision of state highway departments. The law further set specifications for these through highways. Among other requirements, the federally funded roads were to be at least eighteen feet wide. The 7 Percent Law, as it was called, was an important step toward consolidating road building at the state, rather than local, level. It was this legislation that finally took road funds—and jobs—out from under the direct control of inept and corrupt county commissioners. Most important, the 7 Percent Law explicitly stated that states had to have highway departments and that those departments were to have teeth: power for direct supervision and approval of all construction contracts and plans.

The law meant that Oklahoma had to change the way it worked. While most states did have highway departments by 1921, many were like Oklahoma's, with power only to administer grants. Local entities still had charge of the actual construction and road improvements. Oklahoma might have rocked along for some time before facing up to the requirements of the 7 Percent Law except for a series of only-in-Oklahoma events that turned the state government inside out and brought Cy into his own as a highway builder.

In 1921, 201,000 motor vehicle tags were sold in Oklahoma, enough to make automobile owners a loud voice in calling for hard roads. In 1922, the statewide elections ultimately led to a vast improvement in the highway department and a spurt of highway construction, but not until after the new governor was impeached, the lieutenant governor was sworn in, and the legislature was convinced to pass a serious new highway law.

The election of 1922, in many ways, was about the power of the Klan in Oklahoma. John C. Walton, a strong anti-Klansman and former mayor of Oklahoma City, was elected governor on the Democratic ticket. One of the state's shortest-serving governors, he had made a name for himself during his mayoral term when he saw to it that food was supplied to workers on strike against the local meatpacking industry. This made him a hero to the state's liberal factions. Later, when he was nominated by a Progressive coalition aptly named the Farm-Labor League, Walton allowed he wasn't sure what the league stood for but "I'm for it all the way." His flashy campaign often included a jazz band. Because Walton was a Democrat, and strongly anti-Klan, Cy had been one of his many ardent backers.

Walton beat out a KKK-backed candidate in the Democratic primary, which was the only race of any consequence in those days, and was sworn in as Oklahoma's fifth governor in January 1923. When Walton took office, he threw a party that befitted someone who had won on a Progressive platform. He canvassed the state, and Oklahoma communities provided meat for a grand barbecue: venison, buffalo, bear, antelope, beef, pork, rabbit, squirrel, chicken, and even opossum. The rest of the party included a parade, ball, fiddlers contest, and a clog-dancing contest.[4] His grand beginning notwithstanding, Walton's anti-Klan politics were bound to make his governorship difficult. He added to his difficulties, though, almost as soon as he took office, by making enemies in other places.

Cy saw Walton's election as an opportunity for better highway legislation. He was convinced that it was past time to consolidate control of construction at the state level and that one answer would be a three-person highway department. As much as his duties with the Tulsa Water Board allowed, he and the ever-present E. Bee Guthrey went to work for new legislation. It was not to be, at least not yet, and in no small part because the governor was not on his side.

By late March, Cy had all but given up. His friend John Hayden, was sympathetic, writing to Cy:

> I see by the *World* that both you and Guthrey are having one devil of a time with the Legislature over your Highway program, but I am not surprised. What can you expect from a bunch of moss back Democratic wampuses? . . . That Bill of yours providing for three Highway Commissioners was a splendid measure, and its defect [*sic*] by Gov. Walton should forever condemn him for another pubic office, and every Good Roads man in the State should be ever and always against him. . . . If we must be eternally afflicted with Democrat Governors, I hereby nominate you for the job.[5]

Walton seemed to be focused on self-destruction. Besides his failure to support road building, he fired the president of Oklahoma A&M University and was in the process of doing the same at the University of Oklahoma when the OU president left to assume the presidency of Missouri University. As part of his fight with the Klan, he called for a complete ouster and replacement of Tulsa's city and county officials just as the city was playing host to the International Petroleum Exposition and Congress. And he placed Okmulgee County, just south of Tulsa, and then Tulsa under martial law and suspended the writ of habeas corpus in Tulsa so as to investigate Klan activities in those two areas.

When an Oklahoma City grand jury was convened to investigate

Walton's administration, he put the whole state under martial law and sent National Guardsmen with machine guns to seal the courthouse doors. Next, he had National Guardsmen turn away legislators at bayonet point after they returned from a recess. In October, the legislature called for a special impeachment session and state government essentially shut down to focus on the trial. Over in the highway department, things were dire. In Washington, D.C., the BPR was so concerned over the lack of action by the legislature that BPR officials threatened to stop sending funds to Oklahoma. Without federal funds and the approval of the bureau, the Oklahoma Highway Department could not continue to build roads.

On October 23, 1923, the Oklahoma house adopted twenty-two articles of impeachment against the governor, and suspended him from office. On November 19 he was convicted on eleven counts, including general incompetence, by the senate. Lieutenant Governor Martin Trapp, also anti-Klan, but a party regular and staunch good roads man, was sworn in as Oklahoma's sixth governor. Trapp had been Oklahoma's first state auditor and was a three-term lieutenant governor. Far more conservative than his predecessor, he became a widely respected governor. During his term, he increased efficiency of the state's bureaucracy, trimmed unnecessary operations, and left the state treasury with a surplus. More to the point, he made road building a central focus of his administration. Trapp already was well acquainted with the feisty highway man from Tulsa. They had no doubt spent many hours—possibly at Cy's farm or one of his family's Spavinaw cabins—talking about ways to fix the state highway department.

In early October, when it became apparent that the lieutenant governor was in fact the governor-in-waiting, Trapp had contacted Cy to ask if he would consider becoming state highway commissioner. Cy demurred, noting his duties to the Tulsa Water Board. Only after Cy's attorney assured him that there would be no conflict of interest did he tell Trapp that he would take the job, provided that (1) it would not interfere with finishing the Spavinaw project and (2) the state's highway laws would be revised so that the department could actually accomplish something.

Trapp agreed to Avery's conditions, and in his first state of the state address in January 1924, Governor Trapp called on the legislature to pass laws that would reform the highway department and create a three-man commission. The elected representatives met in special session to consider highway legislation. Representative R. A. Singletary, an officer of the Oklahoma Good Roads Association and a crony of Cy's, was one of the champions of the new law. The primary opposition, not surprisingly, came from those who said the legislation would reduce the power of local authorities. Over the next several weeks, the legislators debated the pros and cons of the highway legislation. Even in light of Washington's mandate regarding control of highway construction, it still took a good deal of jockeying and horse-trading, but the bill finally passed. In mid-March, just as the Spavinaw project was coming to an end, Governor Trapp signed the Oklahoma Highway Law of 1924 and presented Cy with the pen he had used.

Avery's fingerprints, it was suggested, were all over the new law. First and foremost, the legislation concentrated state highway construction and maintenance responsibilities in the state highway department. Following the lead of Oregon, which had initiated the country's first gasoline tax in 1919, the law raised Oklahoma's 1-cent-per-gallon gasoline tax to 2.5 cents. The first cent and a half was to support the new reorganized highway department; the other penny was to go back to the counties for local road improvements.

The law also called for a three-member Oklahoma State Highway Commission with no more than two members to be from the same party. Perhaps to assure that they remained citizen-statesmen, the commissioners were to serve only on a per diem basis. An appointed secretary was to be the department's executive. The new law gave the commission complete responsibility for the state highway system and empowered the commissioners to plan, construct, and maintain roads designated as part of the state highway network. The commission was also authorized to employ engineers, purchase equipment, hire laborers, and oversee a highway construction and maintenance fund. All taxes earmarked for road improvements would be deposited into this account and would be used for state projects and to match federal subsidies. The commissioners had authority to exercise the right of eminent domain to acquire rights of way and were charged to "take whatever steps may be necessary to cause said state highway system to be constructed at the earliest possible time."[6]

The new law meant that, a decade after the Oklahoma State Highway Department was put in place, it finally had the wherewithal to build roads. It also brought Oklahoma back into the good graces of the BPR and Chief MacDonald. And it established the state highway department on firm footing for the future.

The 1924 highway act also designated seven major thoroughfares to be the official state highway system. The general routes described in the law followed some of the most popular Trails Association highways. Two of them were Avery's. One was to be named OK-7. This ran southwest from Kansas through Miami to Altus then into the Texas panhandle— essentially the Ozark Trail. The other was OK-11, which followed the Albert Pike Highway west from Arkansas via Choteau to Boise City in the far western Oklahoma panhandle.

Shortly after the highway bill became a state law, Governor Trapp appointed and the legislature confirmed Cy Avery of Tulsa as chair of Oklahoma's new state highway commission. F. J. "French" Gentry of Enid and Roy M. Johnson were named as the other two commissioners. E. Bee Guthrey, Avery's sidekick from Tulsa and editor of *The Nation's Highways* magazine, was hired as secretary. At the time, Trapp said he considered Avery and Gentry the best road men in the state. Avery, of course, was well known because of his county and trails experience plus his leadership in the Oklahoma Good Roads Federation. Gentry, a wealthy auto dealer, lumberman, and longtime highway promoter himself, was a director of the Meridian Highway Association. The Meridian Highway ran through the Great Plains from Winnipeg, Manitoba, through the Dakotas, Nebraska, Kansas, Oklahoma, and Texas to Mexico. In Oklahoma it went through downtown Enid on the north and Sidney Suggs's town of Ardmore on the south. It eventually became U.S. Highway 81.

Johnson, also wealthy and a longtime road booster, was a staunchly Republican newspaperman and oil magnate from Ardmore. Like Cy, he was a former county commissioner.[7]

Cy brought a new level of professionalism to the department. Before his tenure, legislators and friends of the governor would send requests and recommendations—nearly always honored—regarding employment of constituents or friends. Cy, for the most part, tried to hire people with training and experience to do the jobs in the highway department.

One of the first things Cy did when he took office was to establish a policy of holding weekly meetings. Most of the time, they met in Oklahoma City, but as often as they could, the commissioners would assemble in other towns and cities across the state. This gave the Avery, Gentry, and Johnson good visibility, but it also enabled them to know firsthand the needs and priorities of each county and determine which would be state funded and which would be federal aid projects.

From the day he took office, Cy labored to bring Oklahoma roads and bridges up to national standards. In its first year, the highway department completed 347 miles of highway upgrades and surveyed about 330 more. Of those, only 227.42 miles were concrete, 4.06 miles were brick, and 63.52 miles were asphalt. Many of the new highways were sand and gravel, but the communities were so eager for any kind of better roads that bond issues were being passed almost as fast as towns and counties could hold elections.

Highway and bridge construction were not Cy's only concerns, however. He was also responsible for maintaining the five thousand miles of mostly dirt roads that already crisscrossed Oklahoma. He hired his old ally Sidney Suggs to oversee collection of auto license fees across the state and he published Oklahoma's first highway map.

Years later, Johnson sent Cy a telegram inviting him to a dinner for newly installed governor Johnston Murray. "I would be especially honored if you could be present. I particularly want you, Cy, to remind this illustrious assemblage of the great work you did laying out Oklahoma's highway system."[8]

Overall, Cy's time as head of Oklahoma highways was a good one. He gained a reputation for solid work and fairness in his dealings. He hired professionals. He was successful in planning and expanding the state's main thoroughfares. And as soon as he became Oklahoma's highway commissioner, he became a member of the AASHO, a position that gave him the wherewithal eventually to create U.S. Highway 66.

AASHO membership put him in touch with his counterparts in other states, but it also brought him into closer contact with the officials at the BPR in Washington, D.C. The AASHO-BPR link was a productive one. AASHO and BPR cooperated in lobbying Congress on highway issues, and the BPR served as a federal resource to the states. Regional BPR offices provided the states with professional engineering support, oversaw use of federal funds, and offered other resources to state highway departments as well. In Fort Worth, A. R. Losh and his colleagues were particularly important to Avery, Johnson, and Gentry as they sought to set up a functioning highway department. Conversely, Losh was delighted with the turn of events that had put three knowledgeable highway men and dedicated public servants in charge of Oklahoma's road construction.

Early in his term, Cy established a good relationship with the BPR. He wrote to Chief MacDonald, "We always had the highest confidence in the Bureau of Public Roads and look to them for guidance. Your Mr. Losh is a personal friend of mine and I learned to respect his ability and judgment several years ago."[9]

Under Cy's leadership, the whole organization of the Oklahoma Highway Department was rearranged. He hired John Marshall Page from the BPR office in Fort Worth to be State Highway Engineer. And though Avery, Johnson, and Gentry did not earn a salary, they paid Page the princely sum of $5,000. Because he already had been working with Oklahoma roads, Page was familiar with the conditions there, knew many of the people, and was in a perfect position to begin moving forward right away.

Cy also set up divisions for bridge building, for plans and surveys, and for tests and materials. Later, he carved a Construction Division out of the Plans and Surveys Division. Under his leadership, highway width was increased from eighteen to twenty feet, a change which increased the cost per foot but improved safety.

The key, he said later, was speed. Not automobile speed, but speed in getting the roads located and surfaced. The twists, turns, and steep grades of early roads reflected the need for haste. It wasn't that the engineers and highway departments didn't know better, it was just that the counties controlled rights-of-way, and blasting hillsides or removing other obstructions would take time and more money than the department had to spend.[10]

He grouped his field organization into twenty-six geographic divisions, each headed by an engineer responsible for ongoing construction. And he hired a single state maintenance engineer to oversee upkeep of state roads in all the districts across Oklahoma. Even though he had owned large automobiles and pickups since their earliest days, Cy's initial solution to highway maintenance was not mechanized trucks but individuals with teams and blade graders. He told reporters that "one man with a team and blade grader comes nearer to being the perfect system on which to depend for maintenance than any internal combustion engine."[11]

In Cy's highway department, maintenance workers furnished and cared for their own draft animals, wagons, and hand tools. The state provided plows and Fresnos—open-ended U-shaped scrapers that allowed workers to pick up dirt and dump it in specific spots. A maintenance man would patrol as few as eight miles of unimproved dirt road up to as many as thirty miles of paved highway. One of the department's maintenance men in those days was Ross Venable. Venable patrolled twelve miles of state roads around Forgan, Oklahoma, on what became U.S. 64. The state gave him a road grader to use and Venable contributed six horses and a metal washtub to the job. He used the horses to pull the road grader, and he put the washtub over his head to stay dry when it rained or hailed. After a storm, he would drive his team across his twelve miles to drain low places on the dirt roads. His pay was six dollars per day, which included two dollars for horse feed.[12] Of course, despite Avery's preference for mules and horses, the more hard pavement that was created, the more mechanized maintenance vehicles were pressed into service.

In 1924 when Cy took office, the state had only 290 miles of hard-surfaced roads.[13] Under Cy's direction, the state adopted an official highway numbering plan, a system that brought order from chaos as far as drivers were concerned. The idea of using numbers to identify roads, rather than the trail associations' slashes on trees or painted stripes on fence posts, was a welcome change, and workers soon were erecting uniform signposts along the roads. Old habits being what they are, those early highway crews also stenciled the road numbers on bridges, culverts, rocks, trees, and utility poles. The idea of identifying highways by number had originated in Wisconsin a few years earlier. Avery not only adopted numbering for Oklahoma's state highways, but over the course of the next two years he would play a role in seeing to it that all the nation's major roads were identified that way. Besides making it easier for drivers, numbers also allowed for the first real highway maps to be published.

That first year, Cy's department contracted for $5,748,000 in new construction. By 1928, the state could boast more than 1,100 miles of pavement. However, the commission soon found that the 2.5-cent tax wasn't enough to do everything that the state needed. In January 1925 Cy asked for help from the BPR in assessing the best way to increase Oklahoma's highway revenues. L. E. Boykin from the BPR Division of Road Economics met with Avery, Johnson, and Gentry. As Boykin wrote to T. H. MacDonald, "They were interested in devising ways and means for obtaining more funds for the State Highway Department." The commissioners were trying to decide whether to increase the gasoline tax to three cents for the state and another half cent for the counties or to change the auto license tax from a graduated scale to a flat fee of five dollars or ten dollars—all of which would go to the state—and allow the counties to assess an ad valorem tax on the car values. Boykin met with the commission in Oklahoma City on the evening of January 26, and near the end of the meeting, at about ten thirty, the group adjourned to the room in the Skirvan Hotel, where the governor had been meeting with members of the state senate.

The next evening, as was Cy's style, he convened a dinner of his own, with Boykin, H. K. Bishop, Losh, state highway engineer Page, Governor Trapp, the chair of the House Committee on Roads, the president of the Oklahoma State Senate, the speaker of the Oklahoma House of Representatives, and two more state senators. The group uniformly agreed on the need for more highway funds but differed on whether to issue bonds, raise taxes, or institute a license fee. At this point, even with the taxes levied under the 1924 Oklahoma highway law, the state's highway income was less than required by the Federal Highway Act of 1921. The bureau had written to then-governor James Robertson in 1922 and Jack Walton during his brief term in 1923 urging an increase in Oklahoma's highway taxes. The dinner and discussion lasted until almost midnight. By the evening's end, the politician-heavy group had agreed that a gas tax increase to 3.5 cents was the most feasible. Boykin wrote MacDonald, "It was largely a question of what could be gotten through the legislature. There was not very much real help which either I or other Bureau representatives present could give. . . . I believe that they will work out a plan which will give the State Highway Department ample funds both for construction and maintenance purposes."[14]

As a result of Cy's canny advance planning, the 3.5-cent tax was passed by the legislature. That tax was the primary source of new highway construction funds throughout his term, supplemented by registration fees from the increasing numbers of motor vehicles on Oklahoma's roads. In 1926, the state collected registration fees on more than a half-million motor vehicles. Between 1924 and 1933 the highway department was self-sustaining, thanks to the gasoline tax revenue and also funds from a portion of the state's vehicle registration.

However, the more successful Cy was at consolidating and professionalizing road building in Oklahoma and the more identifiable his successes to automobile owners, the more difficulties he faced from the old county commission faction. Cy came under attack by a member of the legislature shortly after his strategy meeting with Boykin in early 1925, most probably as a result of his move to increase the gasoline tax and further consolidate highway building at the state level. The subject of the attack in this instance was *The Nation's Highways*, which Cy and E. Bee Guthrey had brought into the state highway department as an official publication. Representative W. I. Cunningham of Creek County charged Avery and the highway department with misappropriating public funds in the amount of $624 to pay for 312 magazine subscriptions, a use of state monies that the irate legislator deemed inappropriate. The state auditor had already disallowed another $720, which would have paid for subscriptions for the state's county commissioners. Cunningham stated that at no time had the county commissioners subscribed to the magazine and also protested the fact that the magazine included advertising by companies that did business with the highway department. Cunningham called for an official investigation.

Cunningham's vendetta against Avery was a big enough deal that it even made the *New York Times*. The *Times* saw the story for what it was, but perhaps because of similar unrest in many other states between local and state road men, it chose to make this one a national story. On reporting the accusation and upcoming investigation, the *Times* noted that "the Highway Commission, composed of Chairman Avery, Roy Johnson oil operator of Ardmore, and Frank Gentry, motor car dealer of Enid, has made important strides in road building in less than two years. Criticism heretofore have come principally from County Commissioners who declined to make the necessary financial arrangements for upkeep of state highways and from counties where aid not being contracted for, the State Commission has changed routes of state highways to suit their convenience as well as the convenience of the Federal Department of Highways." The article further added that some "disappointed road contracting concerns" had paid a newsboy to yell out about a highway scandal as he sold newspapers.[15]

On February 18 Losh telegrammed Washington, D.C., that he had been requested to go to Oklahoma City and testify before the legislative investigating committee. Like the *Times*, it was Losh's feeling that the uproar was actually about the county commissioners' ire over losing control of highway funds and highway jobs. In another communication, this one to head BPR engineer captain Philip St. John Wilson, Boykin wrote, "Apparently it has been brought to a head by the County Commissioners' Association as a means of combating the move to pass a bill giving the highway department funds for the construction and maintenance of the State Highway System."[16] What was happening in Oklahoma may have been extreme, but it was far from unusual. Across the Midwest, county commissions, trying desperately to hang onto control of road-building money and jobs, were at war with their state highway departments.

Other things that happened in Oklahoma were unlike anything else, anywhere. One such event was an outgrowth of Cy's efficiency and vision. Besides centralizing state highway building, Cy also set about eliminating toll bridges on the state highway system, a far from simple task. As with the first bridge across the Arkansas River at Tulsa, local governments often lacked money to pay for bridges, so private citizens had regularly stepped up and built many of the state's bridges themselves, making their investments back by levying tolls on travelers. As soon as Cy was running a solvent highway department, he decided it was time to replace the toll spans, and the department made plans to build new free bridges or acquire the existing toll bridges. Priority was given to the Red River, which flowed under nineteen different toll bridges between Oklahoma and Texas. Needless to say, owners and operators of the spans were not necessarily in agreement with the highway department's plans.

By the end of 1926, the state had purchased the Red River bridge between Frederick, Oklahoma, and Vernon, Texas, and Cy's commission had financed two new bridges jointly with the Texas State Highway Department, these linking Hugo, Oklahoma, with Paris, Texas, and Randlette, Oklahoma, with Burkburnett, Texas. In 1929 more joint construction agreements were negotiated between Oklahoma and Texas's highway departments.[17] Then, in 1931, as Oklahoma and Texas completed one of their many jointly financed free Red River bridges, the Oklahoma bridge program begun by Cy Avery in 1926 made international headlines. Just before the new bridge between Durant, Oklahoma, and Denison, Texas, was to open, officials of the Red River Bridge Company, which owned the existing toll bridge, obtained an injunction against the Texas Highway Commission that effectively banned traffic on the new free bridge. For his part, Texas governor Ross Sterling decided that the best way to honor the injunction was to barricade the new bridge from the Texas end.

On the north, Oklahoma governor William "Alfalfa Bill" Murray opined that Oklahoma owned both ends of the bridge as a result of the Louisiana Purchase of 1803. He sent Oklahoma crews to destroy the barricades. Governor Sterling retaliated by sending three Texas Rangers to take charge of the situation and Texas Highway Commission workers to the bridge site to rebuild the barricade. The next day, Governor Murray ordered Oklahoma Highway Department crews to demolish the Oklahoma approach to the toll bridge. A few days later he declared martial law and sent in two companies of Oklahoma National Guard to open the free bridge. Murray also showed up at the site packing a revolver—until a Muskogee, Oklahoma, court issued an injunction against him for blocking the toll bridge's northern approach. Finally on August 6, a federal judge lifted the original injunction against the free bridge. Governor Murray ended martial law in Oklahoma and Governor Sterling called off the three Texas Rangers.

Today part of that first free bridge is a historical attraction in a park in Colbert, Oklahoma, but in the late summer of 1931, the great Red River Bridge War kept the nation captivated. With events like this one demanding their attention, it is no wonder that communications from the BPR field office to Washington, D.C., regularly referred to "the Oklahoma situation." Except for Cy's tenure, the highway department in those years was a revolving door of new commissioners and one new highway law after another.

In 1927 Governor Trapp spent a good part of his third, and final, state of the state address to the legislature in praise of Avery and the highway department, telling legislators:

> The Oklahoma State Highway Commission has, for the past two years, been recognized throughout the nation as a most efficient and model institution. It has inaugurated a policy of highway maintenance and construction, which has been carried on with economy and rapidity to the extent that it has been complimented and admired by experts in highway construction everywhere. Its accomplishments are the pride of the people of our State and the 6,000 miles of wonderful highways throughout the length and breadth of the State constitute a lasting monument to the great work performed.[18]

During the three years Trapp served as governor, the state highway department had connected all seventy-seven of the county seats and all major traffic routes. In May 1926, the state highway system's 5,148 miles of roadways included 634 miles of pavement, 832 miles of gravel roads, and 3,682 miles of graded dirt road. Cy had established a practice of using patrols for road maintenance, had erected highway route markers throughout the state, and had adopted Wisconsin's system of numbering roads. A 1924 map issued by the state shows a "preliminary designation of the state highway system" with numbered routes designated. Much of Oklahoma State 7, which appears on that map, became U.S. 66.

Another thing Cy did was to adopt national road building standards in Oklahoma. Under his direction, Oklahoma's highway roadbeds became thirty feet wide—eighteen feet of pavement and twelve feet of shoulders. The 1921 Federal Aid law had made funding available to states to pay for paving 7 percent of the total road mileage and in Oklahoma, that meant Cy's crews could make six hundred more miles of highways ready for paving. To stretch their dollars and keep the public convinced that road progress was being made, he had his crews grade, build drainage, and cover roadbeds with gravel until further funds were made available.

He sent out four survey teams to develop the exact routes for the state's highway system and to plan for shortening and straightening existing roadways where appropriate. His maintenance crews rebuilt many square corners to make them easier-to-drive curves, eliminated railroad crossings, flattened grades, and improved drainage. His highway-testing laboratory improved on the materials that were being used and generally brought down the cost of highway construction in Oklahoma. By emphasizing the routes between population centers, he provided solid support for the road-building approach promoted by Chief MacDonald and the BPR. After a great deal of study, MacDonald had concluded that the heaviest highway use would be by local people on short trips between population centers, and he urged that the nation's highways be developed accordingly, a position strongly shared by Cy.

In the meantime, probably Cy's greatest success from his term as state highway commissioner was through his AASHO membership and the role he played in creating the national highway system. Out of that project came U.S. Highway 66.

EIGHT

Building a National Highway System

> Highways of the United States have been numbered. . . .
> Principal roads are designated with units and tens, such as
> 10–20–30, etc. for east and west roads, and 1–11–21, etc. for
> north and south roads.
>
> —"Highways of the Nation Are Now Numbered," 1925

When Cy joined the American Association of State Highway Officials (AASHO), he became part of a brotherhood of like-minded men. He already knew many of them. Some he had known through his good roads work or from various trails associations. Others, like B. H. Piepmeier of Missouri, Frank Sheets of Illinois, and C. M. Babcock of Minnesota, he knew from the Mississippi Valley Highway Association, a group of state officials who met together periodically to handle common issues in the central part of the country. He also knew Sheets by reputation as a practical pioneer in testing road surface materials.

AASHO's executive secretary W. C. Markham was another old colleague of Cy's. Like Cy, Markham was a staunch good roads man. As a former Kansas postmaster, Markham had spent years wrestling with the issue of post roads and pavement. In 1912, he had been an initiator of the Kansas City–centered move to develop the National Old Trail highway between Baltimore and Santa Fe. (A subsequent National Old Trail president was a former Jackson County commissioner named Harry Truman.) And Markham had been Kansas's first highway commissioner. So when he joined the AASHO staff at the end of 1922 to help open a Washington, D.C., office, he was already conversant with the players, knowledgeable about the issues, and passionate about highway building. He was also a longtime newspaperman and well acquainted with the national press corps. He remained AASHO's executive secretary for twenty-two years.

Cy, in his capacity as Oklahoma's highway commissioner, saw AASHO as the most logical conduit to securing a national highway system. Since it had opened its Washington, D.C., office, AASHO had become a strong lobby for safer, higher-quality roads across the country. It did not hurt matters, either, that former AASHO president T. H. MacDonald was now leading the federal Bureau of Public Roads (BPR).

Laying down hard pavement on the nation's highways was dependent on four things: the perfection of concrete as a road building material, a cadre of technically savvy highway builders, available federal funding, and a critical mass of strident automobile owners. Although car ownership had been growing since the 1890s, it was not until the end of World War I and the subsequent "return to normalcy" that the majority of Americans turned out their horses and put dollars down on automobiles. Once they had cars they climbed on the good roads bandwagon in force.

Cy arrived on the federal scene just as the next logical step was falling into place: knitting together a national system of paved, marked—and safe—U.S. highways. By 1924, the main streets in most cities and some of the cross-country roads on the East Coast were hard surfaced, but that was as far as it went. Most roads still were full of ruts, washed out, ran with mud, or were otherwise unpredictable. Coincidentally, as more and more Americans traded their horses for automobiles, trucks, and tractors, there were fewer and fewer teams that could be called on to pull stalled and mired cars out of ditches and mud holes.

Safety was a growing problem. In 1899, twenty-six people were killed in vehicle accidents. By 1910, there were 1,599 road fatalities involving automobiles. Just over a decade later, in 1921, with nearly eight million automobiles on the road, the country saw more than eight times as many fatal accidents—13,253—plus more than a million and a half nonfatal but serious accidents. In Oklahoma, 122 people died in automobile accidents in 1921 and many more were injured.[1] The first great hope for highway safety was higher-quality roads, which could only be assured by federal involvement and federal dollars. Uniform signage was almost as important: without readily identifiable stop, yield, caution, and railroad crossing signs, for example, drivers had no idea what would be around a blind corner. Without speed limit signs, traffic was unmanageable. And without some sort of consistent highway identification, thousands of drivers were regularly getting lost.

In an otherwise laudatory article, the *Literary Digest* had lamented the difficulty of finding one's way across the country, pointing out that "unfortunately a great deal of confusion and in some cases deliberate misrepresentation exists. In many cases even nationally known highways coincide for a distance, tending to confuse the tourist who attempts to follow the markers; and in other cases, owing to sectional disputes or road construction, the exact routing is uncertain."[2] Something clearly had to be done, but men like Cy and his AASHO colleagues, who were on the ground doing their best to accommodate their states' needs for improved roads, faced some major obstacles. One, amazingly enough in the no-holds-barred twenties, was Pres. Calvin Coolidge. In his first annual address to Congress on December 6, 1923, President Coolidge had confirmed his support for highway building. "Everyone is anxious for good highways. I have made a liberal proposal in the budget for the continuing payment to the States . . . for this necessary public improvement. No expenditure of public money contributes so much to the national wealth as for building good roads."[3]

Only a few weeks later, Silent Cal did an about-face and sounded off squarely against higher taxes and federal aid. He called the system a "double burden of taxation—Federal taxation . . . which the government donates to the states, and state taxation . . . to meet the extravagances of state expenditures which are tempted by Federal donations."[4] By all accounts, the president remained committed to building highways. His concern was with federal aid itself, whether for highways, education, or other state/local needs. What the road-building world heard, however, was that federal aid dollars for highway building were about to be eliminated. That would effectively end any hope for a national system of paved roads.

Without federal matching dollars, hard-surfaced roads would be difficult to come by, especially in the western states. And for the state highway officials, building roads was still their primary focus even as they worried about safety and interstate and intrastate linkages. In Congress, members weighed in. When Ohio senator Simeon D. Fess (R), a known good roads supporter, called the Bureau of Public Roads program "hit-or-miss," BPR chief MacDonald reacted vehemently, reminding the senator that the federal aid program was restricted by the 1921 federal highway law to not more than 7 percent of the total national road mileage. As a result, federally funded construction was necessarily limited and being done in stages, which varied depending on the part of the country. In the Northeast, which had plenty of already-improved roads, the highway departments were surfacing roads with either asphalt or cement. Further west, the federal funds went to more basic needs like grading dirt roads, building culverts, and constructing bridges.

In Oklahoma, Cy's highway department spent the year of 1924 working toward the eventuality of hard-surfaced highways by preparing roadbeds and erecting bridges. His ever-more-professional teams built bridges over the Canadian River, Salt Fork of the Arkansas and the Chikaskia. In all, Cy's department spent more than $5 million in federal and state funds for bridges on the federal aid highways in Oklahoma in 1924.[5] These bridges were particularly important, as they would later play a significant role in the politics of determining which roads would be part of the national highway system. Like Oklahoma, other states in the Midwest and West were approaching highway construction as a series of steps. In some places, just getting a road graded and perhaps graveled was a great feat. Then would come bridges and culverts. The actual hard surfacing could not take place until those other things had been completed first.

When Chief MacDonald wrote back to Senator Fess, he included a map and pointed out to the senator that the nation had 174,350 miles of federal aid roads, that is, roads eligible to be paved with federal aid matching funds, but that the federally supported work was being done on only about 9,000 miles per year.[6] Given the demand, 9,000 miles was nothing.

In the run-up to the 1925 national election, both the Democratic and Republican platforms supported federal aid financing for road construction. Never mind Coolidge, the party leaders understood the voting public's priorities: better roads and as fast and as soon as they could be built.

In Oklahoma, even as Cy garnered accolades for the professionalism of his department and the success of road projects, he still found his efforts hampered by opposition from various county commissioners, including one from his own Tulsa County. Conflicts between local politicians and state highway departments were not limited to Oklahoma. State highway departments across the Midwest were under constant criticism from local and county office holders who wanted to recapture control of road jobs and road dollars. Counties, after all, were where votes were counted. In Washington, D.C., MacDonald was more than a little concerned.

That was the situation in mid-November 1924, when Cy skipped out on Tulsa's Spavinaw celebration to travel to San Francisco for his first AASHO annual meeting. Despite ongoing impediments thrown up by the counties, he had high hopes that he could find a way to connect Oklahoma's highways to others across the country. Or at the very least, that the influential federal/state association could guarantee that he and his department could keep control of highway construction inside the state.

He brought two colleagues from Oklahoma to the AASHO meeting: bridge engineer Walter Burnham and state highway engineer John M. Page. Page, whom Cy had hired away from the Bureau of Public Roads' regional office in Fort Worth, was well acquainted with most of the AASHO members and the large cadre of BPR staff who attended the meeting. When the Oklahoma group arrived in San Francisco, they joined Piepmeier and Sheets in representing the midwestern states.

Despite worries about the president's opposition to federal aid funding, the AASHO men spent their time in San Francisco looking toward what they could do to make the nation's roads better and safer. When it was BPR chief MacDonald's turn to speak, he stressed the urgent need for safety measures on America's roads, especially national signage. The chief also called for a sorting out of the nation's roadways so that drivers could find their way from one population center to another.

He was, of course, preaching to the choir. In response to his presentation, the AASHO members passed one resolution calling for uniform highway markings and warning signs, and a second resolution to ask Secretary of Agriculture Howard Gore to appoint a committee of state highway officials to organize a national highway system. This committee was not to be about paving, which was already defined in the 1921 highway act. AASHO's idea was that the committee would map out a national system from already-existing federal aid roads, and by linking the roads together between states, automobile drivers would be able to travel from one side of the country to the other without getting lost or finding themselves at a dead end.

From their own day-to-day turf battles, the AASHO men well knew that getting the country to adopt matching road signs for every state and every county might not be a simple matter, but they also understood that something as badly needed as good signage probably could be accomplished. On the other hand, given their collective engineering and political experience, they saw all too clearly that the national highway map could be a nightmare. Roads were so important to so many people and so many government entities that Cy, Sheets, Piepmeier, and the rest knew up front that everyone who owned an automobile would have an opinion about which roads should be selected and how the roads should be linked. Besides that, there was the issue of the existing non-government roads community—the men and women of the trails associations who had worked for years and laid much of the groundwork for a national system. By 1924 there were about 250 trails groups of various types, and each one was highly political. They had carried out the delicate negotiations to fix exactly what towns would be on what routes. Beyond the obvious, a lot of the trails' executive directors derived a good part of their incomes from their association work and wouldn't give up their livelihoods without a fight.

Since Cy and several other AASHO members were trails entrepreneurs themselves, they well understood the politics of these booster road groups. Probably because of that, the AASHO members agreed up front that the trails system would not be the route to America's highway future. While they concurred that many trail associations had done an exemplary job in promoting the cause of U.S. highways, they also knew the trails were confusing, costly, and often not worth the money, time, or effort expended. The AASHO resolution pulled no punches: "Many individuals have sought to capitalize on the popular demand for inter-state or cross-country routes by organizing trails, collecting large sums of money and giving practically no service in return with resulting dis-credit to the reputable trails associations which have rendered a distinct public service by stimulating highway improvements, maintenance and marking."[7] The state highway officials further decided that "reputable trails associations"—presumably including the Albert Pike, Ozarks Trail, White River Trail, Meridian Highway, and other members of the Associ-ated Highways of America (AHA)—be allowed to continue with their markings until the new system was put in place, but they ordered that no new trail routes were to be established.

Because they were so concerned about partisanship, the AASHO members made it scrupulously clear that membership on the secretary of agriculture's joint board be divided equally among state officials from the various parts of the country and that it not include AASHO execu-tive committee members, perhaps in case they needed to be called on to sort out any turf-related problems that might develop. By the time Cy raised his hand to vote for the resolution, he may have already set his sights on becoming a member of the joint board. It would be his chance to work on a national level, but even better, it would be a golden oppor-tunity to bring more highways through Tulsa. He had only been an AASHO member since midyear, but he knew many people, had been front and center at the meeting, and even led a discussion on highway legislation for public land states, something that as an Oklahoman he had to contend with.

In all probability everyone went home from San Francisco with a share of exuberance, hope—and concern. Road safety desperately needed to be addressed. Likewise, it was past time for something to be done to cement a system of national roads, and the AASHO members were the people who had to do it. All that was left was to get the secretary of agri-culture on board and hope the president didn't get in the way.

As if to underscore the signage issue, only a few weeks after the

AASHO meeting, Secretary of Commerce Herbert Hoover hosted representatives of state highway commissions, along with police, insurance companies, labor unions, women's clubs, automobile associations, and manufacturers, at the First National Conference on Street and Highway Safety. This broad-based group agreed with AASHO: "Signs should be uniform for a given purpose throughout the United States."[8]

Immediately following the conference, newly elected AASHO president Frank Rogers of Michigan wrote a letter to Secretary Gore in which he shared the highway officials' resolutions from San Francisco. Gore was in total support: "I believe there is a desire among a very large number of citizens in every part of our country for such a systematic designation of highways as provided by the resolution. This desire has been shown in many ways and civic organizations have on their own responsibility expended considerable sums in making unofficial designations. . . . Practically all the State Highway Departments have recognized the need of indicating for the benefit of the traveling public main market roads and other roads of primary importance within their respective States."

The secretary agreed that it was time to consolidate highway issues in one place. He pointed out that automobile traffic was constantly on the increase and concluded with an endorsement of AASHO's plan. "I believe the State Highway Departments, all of which are cooperating with the Department of Agriculture in cooperative road construction under the Federal Highway Act, are as a matter of course the logical agencies for carrying out the plan proposed by the resolution of the Association which voices their opinion."[9]

With that solid endorsement, Rogers put together a potential list of who should be named to the joint board. Bureau of Public Roads chief MacDonald would chair the group, BPR chief of design E. W. James would be secretary, and BPR consulting highway traffic engineer A. B. Fletcher would also be involved. AASHO's Markham would coordinate the activities of the various AASHO members.

Even though Cy was relatively new to AASHO, Rogers put his name on the original list to represent the region that included Arkansas, Louisiana, Texas, Oklahoma, Kansas, Nebraska, and Iowa. It was a shrewd choice. Cy came from the state that had supplied a third of the U.S. oil in World War I and was at that time producing more oil than either Texas or California, and he was from a city that had fifty millionaires on the finance committee of its chamber of commerce. Oklahoma had a lot to gain from good highways and the state highway official from Tulsa could wield a lot of clout should the need arise.

Cy, however, nearly missed his opportunity to participate. On January 24, 1925, he received a frantic telegram from Markham. "Wrote you January 12 asking if you would accept appointment from Secretary of Agriculture on Joint Board to Number Highways. Have had no reply. Necessary he know at once. Please wire me your answer." Cy answered immediately in the affirmative. Apparently the letter had been delayed, but he assured Markham, "Will be pleased to accept appointment from Secretary of Agriculture as suggested by you."[10] Once he heard from Cy, Markham wrote to Rogers acknowledging he had "the last telegram of acceptance from men chosen by you to be appointed by Secretary of Agriculture as the Representatives of the AASHO on the Joint Board to number and mark the highways of interstate character."

That original list had fourteen names plus a space for someone from Texas. Markham wrote, "You will note I have . . . left Texas blank, as the personnel of the Department in that state is still unsettled." Given the vagaries of elections and political appointments, highway departments in those days were nothing if not fluid.[11] On January 28, Rogers dispatched a somewhat longer list of names to Secretary Gore and shortly thereafter Gore mailed letters of appointment to the men who would create the national highway system. As it turned out, this was one of the secretary's last official acts before he departed Washington, D.C., to become governor of West Virginia, where he became such an unwavering supporter of road construction that he earned the nickname "road building governor."

The original appointees to the joint board included twenty-one state highway commissioners and state highway engineers. That number remained constant throughout the project although the makeup of the group changed as members lost jobs or rotated out of office. Cy, his AHA friend Babcock of Minnesota, O. A. Brown (later replaced by I. J. Moe) of

North Dakota, and Piepmeier of Missouri were the appointees named to represent the eleven states of the Mississippi Valley. The eleven western states' representatives were James Allen of Washington (shortly to be replaced by Roy A. Klein of Oregon), Preston Peterson of Utah, Robert Morton, state highway engineer from California, and James A. French from New Mexico, one of AASHO's founding members. The Great Lakes region was represented by Rogers, W. O. Hotchkiss of Wisconsin, Lou A. Boulay of Ohio, and A. H. Hinkle of Indiana. Selected from the nine southern states were C. P. Fortney of West Virginia, H. C. Dietzer of Mississippi, Henry Shirley of Virginia, and Charles Moorefield of South Carolina. F. S. Greene of New York, and William Sloan of New Jersey were named from the five North Atlantic States. William F. Williams of Massachusetts and John A. MacDonald of Connecticut, no relation to the chief, came from the six states of New England.[12]

The original list did not include Frank Sheets of Illinois, who was the newly elected AASHO vice president. However, things changed midstream when Cornelius Miller, the superintendent of public works for Illinois, protested to Chief MacDonald that Sheets had been left off the joint board. AASHO's Markham wrote to Frank Rogers in Michigan explaining the situation: since Illinois was certain to carry several of the direct highways and "has been very active in the organization [AASHO] and Mr. Sheets has given a great deal of thought to the subject," Superintendent Miller insisted that Sheets be included as a member of the joint board. Chief MacDonald then spent quite some time with Miller, explaining in detail how the joint board was formed, and that except for Rogers, members of AASHO's executive committee and officers had been deliberately omitted from the list. This did not satisfy Miller. He came back with another letter to MacDonald still insisting that Sheets be appointed. With a great sigh (surely), Markham finished his letter to Rogers: "Mr. MacDonald seems to feel that under the circumstances it will be necessary to recommend . . . the addition of Mr. Sheets."

For his part, Rogers countered with a suggestion to wait until an upcoming retirement of one of the joint board members in a few months and then appoint Sheets "on account of his long acquaintance with the highway problems of this country," but the pressure on MacDonald was too great. Sheets was invited to join the joint board by telegram and made it to Washington, D.C., for the group's first meeting on April 20, 1925.[13] This meant that Sheets of Illinois, Piepmeier of Missouri, and Avery of Oklahoma were all members of the joint board. The team that would create Route 66 was in place.

Sheets was a positive addition to the group. About twenty years younger than Avery, he had joined the Illinois Highway Department at the age of seventeen, leaving only to earn a degree in highway engineering from the University of Illinois. In 1916 he was promoted to assistant maintenance engineer and in one of those coincidences common among the small fraternity of early highway men, his boss was Piepmeier, who would later become Missouri's chief highway engineer. From 1920 until 1932 Sheets was head of the Illinois Division of Highways. Under his leadership, the state perfected Portland Cement concrete as a paving material and went to work hard surfacing Illinois's roads. Thanks to Sheets, when the national highway act was passed in 1926, Illinois would be the only one of the seven Route 66 states with pavement from one end to the other.[14]

Cy probably also knew Sheets as a contributor to *The Nation's Highways*. In 1922, Sheets had authored an article on how to select satisfactory road locations. A few years in the future, when Cy was out promoting the Main Street of America, Pres. Herbert Hoover would send Sheets, along with Chief MacDonald, Babcock of Minnesota, and various government dignitaries to the second Pan American Road Congress in Rio de Janeiro.

So how did the joint board turn 7 percent of 1,826,197 miles of "certified" federal aid roads into a national highway system? In the first place, the national highway system was not necessarily tied to the roads identified by their states as federal aid roads under the 7 Percent Law. The federal aid roads were about money, and states had begun designating those roads when the law was passed in 1921. As fast as local and state funds could be raised to match the federal funding for the 7 percent roads, state highway departments were building bridges, grading, and paving. In most states, the only issue was how fast the primary roads could be selected and approved by the BPR so the work could begin.

In Oklahoma, Cy's highway department had all but finished selecting the state's primary federal aid roads by early April 1925. He had construction projects underway all over the state when he left Gentry, Johnson, and John Page to continue the hard work of highway building and made his way to Washington, D.C., for the joint board's first meeting. Before he arrived on April 20, Cy and the other board members had been contacted by BPR's James, who sent a national map divided into regions and asked whether they had any particular recommendations concerning the task ahead. Cy said he believed regional meetings would be a good idea and named Kansas City and St. Louis as likely sites. Piepmeier declared that the interstate highways should be confined to the primary federal aid highways and agreed that regional meetings were a good idea. He also suggested that his state of Missouri should have four major north-south highways, three east-west highways and "one diagonal from St. Louis to Springfield." Lou Boulay of Ohio asked for a full board meeting at a central point like Chicago to keep things organized. C. P. Fortney of West Virginia contended that the same highway numbers should be continued regardless of state lines. John A. Macdonald of Connecticut was emphatic. "We must approach the work with an absolutely open mind, and with the thought that a uniform system must result from our work."[15]

All veteran road builders, the men on the joint board were used to dealing with county governments, legislators, automobile associations, and trails groups. They were well aware of the potential for chaos that hung over their assignment. Given that there were more than 250 trails associations, hundreds of towns, and thousands of state, county, and federal elected officials, they could foresee the possibility of endless hearings and having to answer complaints for years to come.

With all that in mind, the members of the board made several important decisions before they got to the real meat of their April meeting. They agreed unanimously that publicity and public hearings would lead only to gridlock and failure, so one of their first decisions was that while they would hold regional meetings, there would be no open-to-the-public discussions and there would be no prepublicity— reports of the meetings would only be distributed afterward. They also decided that most of the roads selected would be federal aid highways, but that it might be necessary to go out of the system to make logical connections.

The joint board also set a goal to complete their work before the year was out. To do this, they scheduled six meetings to be held between mid-May and the end of June in the various regions already established when the board was created. The idea was that joint board members would attend the meeting in their region along with other AASHO members and state officials. Together attendees at each regional meeting would rough out the national highway map for their own section of the country. Once all six meetings were completed, the board would gather again in Washington, D.C., to iron out details, with an ultimate goal of issuing an official map of the national highway system in the fall.

This tight schedule proved to be a good thing on several counts. With President Coolidge's growing attacks on federal aid and money, it was certainly best that the board get on with their task. And since, like Cy, every one of the members had a state highway department job, the less time away the better it would be.

Several other significant decisions were also made at that first two-day meeting. The members unanimously decided that the national highways should carry numbers. Lou Boulay suggested that the highway routes be selected first and numbered later. He added that the official U.S. shield with "USA" and a number on it would make a good marker. He then moved to have the group adopt "a uniform system of through route marking for the United States" and that a "uniform shape and type of route marker, to be adopted later, be selected for the marking of these routes through the different states."[16] The board voted in favor of Boulay's motion.

Hotchkiss of Wisconsin urged that the main routes be direct connections between population and commercial centers with alternate routes chosen to disperse traffic. The board also agreed to his suggestions to set 1 percent of a state's mileage as most important, 1 percent of secondary importance, and 1 percent as third in importance. This decision would become significant when numbering decisions were made.

That day the board also went a step beyond Boulay's suggestion and adopted the federal highway shield for the national highway signs.

BPR's James, who sat next to AASHO president Rogers, later wrote about the meeting: "As we discussed a possible distinctive and unique marker . . . he [Rogers] doodled and produced a sort of shield. He handed it to me. I think I improved on his design by drawing a picture of our present shield. He took it back, presented it to the Board as just what was wanted, and that was that." After Rogers showed his drawing of the federal highway shield to the assembled group, they approved unanimously and voted to send copies of the design to all the state highway departments for their consideration.[17]

Also at the meeting, each of the regional board members highlighted their preliminary choices as to which roads would become national highways with the idea that routes would be finalized after the regional meetings. Immediately following the meeting, James sent a new regional map to each board member marked with the federal aid routes already chosen by the various states to be national highways. These maps would serve as a starting place for the mapmaking at the regional meetings.

The first regional meeting was held on May 15 in San Francisco for the West region and went off without a hitch. It included board members from the West plus James. None of the other state highway departments were represented in person although several submitted letters and several individuals from three states were invited to testify. There were no representatives of the trails organizations or other name routes either, but a group from the California Automobile Association did attend part of the meeting to talk about signage. Once the meeting ended, the western delegation of the board finalized their selection of roads for the national highway system, making sure it was no more than 7 percent of the total western federal aid roads. And then they went home.

The second meeting, twelve days later at the Baltimore Hotel in Kansas City, was a little different. Besides Avery and Piepmeier, Brown of North Dakota and Babcock of Minnesota were present from the board with James serving as secretary. They had invited eighteen guests, including four from Oklahoma: French Gentry and Roy Johnson, plus maintenance engineer W. H. Rhodes, and state highway engineer John Page.

Taking advantage of the wealth of highway people in Kansas City for the meeting, AASHO's Markham had put together a ten-state Conference of Mississippi Valley Highway Officials in a nearby hotel for the same day. Markham had also invited representatives from Wyoming and Colorado to the Mississippi Valley meeting to discuss progress of highway construction in their states. Since the two hotels were just a few blocks apart, several of the men, including Piepmeier and Oklahoma's Johnson managed to attend part of both meetings.

The board had not invited outsiders but by the time of the Kansas City regional meeting, word had spread. About fifty or sixty trails association people descended on the Baltimore Hotel, all concerned that a national highway system meant they were about to lose their identities and, in many cases, their incomes. Both, of course, were true. They made their stand at the Kansas City meeting.

As the Joint Board's host state member, Piepmeier explained to the throng of trails people that the meeting was not open to the public. Nonetheless, the trails people demanded to be heard and refused to leave. Finally, given that they were, after all, highway supporters and that most of them were acquainted with one or more of the AASHO members, the board relented.

Cy and James met with the trails association people in another part of the hotel. Once everyone was settled, they explained the board's plans. They answered questions. They also showed the trails representatives the routes selected so far and explained what the uniform markings would look like. By the time the informal meeting ended, the trails people seemed to be on board and voted to accept the work to date. Later James wrote, "On the whole the Trail organizations so far appear to be taking a very sensible and broad attitude toward the work of the board."[18]

It is interesting that, with Cy so involved in three trails organizations himself, this was the meeting where the trails groups demanded to be heard. On the other hand, so many of the trails rolled through the Mississippi Valley states that this meeting was an obvious one to attend. The question of how they all knew to converge in Kansas City on May 27, however, still remains open.

Cy must have been comfortable with the day's events because he left the meeting early to attend a William Jewell alumni dinner in nearby Liberty. After he left, James and the others stayed on into the evening to mark up the map with their Mississippi Valley highway choices for the national system. The next morning, when Cy saw the map, he was aghast. He later told a group of highway supporters, "I found that our secretary, Mr. James of Washington, D.C., and the man who represented the Bureau of Public Roads, had designated U.S. 64 from Conway, Arkansas, a point which had been previously agreed upon by us, to Tulsa. On looking over the new map I immediately asked him why this road had not been continued on west through the panhandle, and his reply was that it was unnecessary; that anyone going to the Rocky Mountains or Colorado could go north at Ft. Smith and go through Kansas, or go north at Tulsa and go through Kansas to the Rocky Mountain region." James's logic may have been sound, but he had failed to factor in that what had been left off the national map was the western end of the Albert Pike Highway—the trail that Cy himself had designed and promoted—and that he had effectively put Tulsa at a dead end.

Cy continued: "I then proceeded to deliver him a thirty minute lecture on the greatness of the Arkansas valley and the panhandle of Oklahoma, showing the difference in the type of soil, climatic conditions, etc., for a route leading to the Rocky Mountains, from a scenic standpoint as well as from the standpoint of serving the State of Oklahoma and connecting New Mexico up with the States of Oklahoma, Arkansas and on to Tennessee."[19] James changed the map.

Another national highway route mapped at the Kansas City meeting apparently received little to no discussion. That was the joining together of roads that linked Chicago and Los Angeles by way of Springfield, Missouri, and Tulsa. It was not until later, when the subject of highway numbers was addressed, that this highway would come under scrutiny.

Cy went home from the Kansas City meeting extremely pleased with himself. He announced to anyone who would listen, and especially to the *Tulsa Tribune*, that Oklahoma State Highway 7—the road between Tulsa and Joplin—was tentatively selected to be one of the new U.S. national highways. "Whether it will be the number One coast-to-coast highway remains to be thrashed out at an August meeting," he told the *Tribune*, adding that only twelve highways would cross the mountains and desert to the Pacific Coast. Only twelve, therefore could be marked with an unvarying number from coast to coast. He pointed out that the road from Los Angeles split at Albuquerque with one leg following the old Santa Fe Trail through Colorado and Kansas while the other came on to Amarillo and thence to Oklahoma. The *Tribune* reported that "the fight will be between these two as to which will carry the numeral through from the Pacific Coast. Kansas will fight for the Santa Fe Trail, but Avery will stand up for the road passing through Tulsa." The fact that there was no Kansas representative on the joint board certainly tilted the map in Cy's favor.

Cy described this road—his road—to the reporter with some of the soaring rhetoric that was so familiar to his fellow Tulsans. "This road of ours is the shortest . . . to Southern California. There is already a tremendous traffic volume and it will increase rapidly when the national highways are designated. Auto tourists will say take National Highway XX in the east and follow it all the way: there will be no chance of getting lost. Naturally it will be the best road . . . it will get the business." Cy also made a comment about the meeting that suggested he was not particularly concerned about where the highway went after it left Oklahoma to the northeast. "We purposely, at that time, stopped the road at Conway [Missouri] for the reason that there were too many difficulties in the way of un-completed bridges and highway, to make it feasible for a U.S. designation."[20]

The board's next meeting took place June 3 in Chicago. Sheets, as a representative of the Great Lakes region, attended. James recorded that like the San Francisco gathering, the meeting was held in "entire harmony."[21] Atlanta on June 8 was another success. Four of the board members were there with James. They invited fourteen others, including six from Georgia. Later James reported that as in the West and Midwest, there was an inclination to fill and add roads to the primary map, but overall, he said, it was a good meeting.

At the Atlantic States meeting in New York City, only F. S. Greene of New York and James were there from the board along with two other AASHO members. The general feeling among this group was decidedly different from the others. They felt that too many roads had already been selected. Greene wanted to reduce the mileage of primary roads in New York and also suggested that the board eliminate a large number of alternate routes, short cuts and cross roads, "which could not be considered as of transcontinental significance or even of major interstate importance."[22]

The New England meeting in Massachusetts on June 18 followed in a similar vein and James later wrote that again everything was in harmony. There was a general feel that more routes had been introduced than should be adopted, but to give parity to New England they did adopt some of them.[23]

After the New England meeting, James went back to Washington, D.C., to consolidate the results of the meetings and get ready for the board meeting on August 3 that would finalize the highway map.

Cy, back at work in Oklahoma, spent a lot of time considering the efforts of the board. Excited as he was about the prospect for national highways to run though Oklahoma, he saw no reason why his state couldn't also supply the signs to mark those highways. Following the meeting where the board had agreed to the national shield for highway signs, Cy got in touch with his friend William Key, a military man who was then serving as warden of the Oklahoma State Penitentiary, to find out if the crew who turned out license plates could also make highway signs. In mid-June, Cy sent James a sample federal highway marker made at the penitentiary, which he said could be manufactured for about twenty-five cents each.[24]

Back on the job at home, Cy, Gentry, and Johnson continued the tedious work of determining which of Oklahoma's federal aid highways to list next to be funded for paving. By this time many of their decisions had more to do with making politicians happy than with where the roads went. Requests for minute changes to move a federal aid–designated road only a few miles—or feet—one way or another were submitted to the highway department and had to be dealt with. Towns and counties that had passed bond issues to match federal aid funds were suddenly urging the highway department to "get on with it" and upgrade their roads. And since federal dollars were involved in nearly every case, BPR engineer A. R. Losh was there, working closely with the three highway commissioners. Losh made sure his higher-ups were kept informed in detail about his work, and sometimes the local quibbles found their way to Washington, D.C.

In May 1925, for example, Losh wrote to Chief MacDonald that the Oklahoma Commission had discussed designating an east-west Oklahoma highway as a primary federal aid road. The road would run about seventy miles south of Oklahoma City from Healdton via the towns of Loco, Comanche, and Walters, to Frederick. Apparently, Cy's department had promised the Comanche town officials that if they could pass a bond issue, the Oklahoma Highway Department would route the road through Comanche.

About a month later, Losh wrote again. The highway department had, in fact, designated the route in question through Comanche, Losh's letter said, but despite that, "Bids were received in Oklahoma City yesterday for the construction of nine miles of highway east of Duncan [a town ten miles north of Comanche]. . . .We are reciting these facts to you in order that you may realize the complicated situation which exists and I believe you will concur with us that the present plan proposed by the state in view of existing conditions is not going to satisfactorily solve the situation."[25]

Another month later, the Duncan city fathers sent a series of telegrams to Washington, D.C., seeking a revision because the previous designation was unacceptable. The BPR, in its wisdom, wired back that they should take up the issue with their state highway departments.[26]

When the situation was personally important, Cy took care of it, as he did when he set the routing of what became U.S. 64 through western Oklahoma along the route of his old Albert Pike Highway.[27]

And then there were the cases that involved elected officials. In March 1926 after the federal aid roads supposedly had been settled, Oklahoma senator J. W. Harreld contacted BPR chief MacDonald over a particular section of highway between Shawnee and Harrah, east of Oklahoma City. It seems the road in question had been slated to go behind the Catholic University (now St. Gregory's) in Shawnee rather than in front of it. No doubt they called on God first, but university officials also contacted Senator Harreld for help. By the time Chief MacDonald was brought in, the Oklahoma Highway Department had worked with the university and moved the road. MacDonald assured the senator that the issue had been settled peaceably.[28] And so it went.

Because Oklahoma had only been a state for seventeen years, there were fewer already-existing roads than in other states, so there may have been more nit-picking over the map. But the road complaints were more or less the same in every state. Until the hard pavement was down and signs were posted, towns would compete to be on the soon-to-be-paved routes. Every community saw the federal aid highways as the keys to a better economy, to more children in school, and even to higher church attendance. For the politicians, it was a case of keeping voters happy. And this was just to get pavement.

For the state highway departments' and the BPR's field staff, the national highway system could not come fast enough. There was ongoing pressure from inside the states, but there was also uncertainty about funding, thanks to the president's continuing assaults on the federal aid system. Back in May, while the joint board began holding their regional meetings, President Coolidge had set the already concerned road-building community on its ear. In a Memorial Day address at Arlington National Cemetery, he spoke about federal matching funds and contended that "we may go on yet for a time with the easy assumption that 'if the states *will not*, the nation *must*.' But that way lies trouble. When the National Treasury contributes half, there is temptation to extravagance by the state. We have seen some examples in connection with the Federal contributions to road building. . . . Yet there are constant demands for more Federal contributions."[29]

For Cy, who was already under attack at home for usurping tax dollars, the president's speech must have been bad news. It would have made his difficult political situation even more problematic, but it was tempered by the fact that Oklahoma was heavily Democratic—and Coolidge was a Republican—and by the fact that across Oklahoma, roads were finally being paved.

In Washington, D.C., AASHO members and Markham worked to support BPR and counter Coolidge's denigration of federal aid. They wrote articles, sent out news releases on highway construction, button-holed members of Congress, and made speeches. By August, however, news of the president's speech had become a major political issue for the roads community.

While James was shepherding the joint board toward a national highway map, Chief MacDonald spent most of that summer on the road, reviewing federal aid highway projects in the Midwest and West. At the end of that trip, he sent a call of alarm to his new boss, Agriculture secretary William M. Jardine, a Kansan who had replaced Gore. He told the secretary that the state highway people saw Coolidge's Memorial Day address as evidence that the president would oppose a continuation of the federal aid highway program.

"The road program now underway is the very life-blood of the Western States," the chief wrote to Jardine. In the Midwest, he said, the Federal Aid Highway Act's requirement for state highway departments to control highway expenditures was the only thing that prevented county government coalitions from taking over.

In Kansas, he reported, the county-state highway strife was particularly bad. The county governments there were waging a battle to keep the income from automobile license and gasoline taxes in local coffers. "No State can build a State highway system unless it creates an adequate State highway department and places within the control of this department the adequate support funds. . . . The highway authorities in the United States who have been the most careful to protect both the Federal and State treasuries, are the men who have supported the plan of Federal cooperation with the States in the building of highways."

Further, MacDonald pointed out to Secretary Jardine, as he had to Senator Fess a year earlier, in every state, auto license and gasoline taxes more than paid the state's share of the federal/state road paving costs. Plus, in many states, voters added extra funds to make paving happen more quickly, with an end result that the federal government paid for only about 20 percent of the ongoing road improvements instead of half. The chief noted also that it wasn't just midwesterners and westerners who were in turmoil over roads and needed federal dollars to continue their work. Even in the eastern United States, state highway departments needed both federal funds and federal engineering expertise to upgrade and put down hard surfaces on existing roads. Then,

MacDonald repeated the obvious: "The old roads are not adequate to withstand the present day heavy traffic."[30]

Over the next year, Coolidge continued his attacks. In the media and the halls of Congress the war over federal aid raged. In the meantime, members of the joint board carried on, working to develop a coherent system of national highways.

In early July, Cy, with the regional meetings over and the highway commission under control, invited Losh to join him and several others on a Colorado hunting trip at the end of the month. Typical of Cy, the trip was planned to combine entertainment with politics. He would be presiding at a meeting of his cherished Albert Pike Highway Association, but he rarely went to Colorado without a hunting trip thrown in. And because he had made so many friends in Colorado Springs over the years, he also planned to bring Essie and ten-year-old Helen. By this time sons Leighton, at twenty-two, and Gordon, at age nineteen, were busy elsewhere.

When Losh wrote to Washington, D.C., seeking permission to spend bureau funds for the trip, he noted that Oklahoma's Governor Trapp, who would also be a member of the party, had made a special request that Losh be there. Expenses, he said, would be about fifty dollars.[31]

In Cy's planning for Colorado he had overlooked only one thing: the joint board was to reconvene August 3. In a panic, he wrote to James at the BPR office in Washington, D.C., that because of the Albert Pike convention he probably would be unable to make the meeting and asked James to change the meeting date. "This date is practically an impossible one for me owing to the fact of previous arrangements to be in Colorado Springs on the 29th and 30th of July. I could hardly reach Washington even by leaving there on the night of the 30th in time for the meeting. . . . The Governor of our State and several other State officials are going along and this is the annual meeting of the Albert Pike Association of which I am president."[32] His plea was about three months too late. Whether he remembered or not, the meeting date had been set in April. Invitation letters had already gone out. James suggested that Cy would have to figure out what to do.[33]

Faced with no alternatives, Cy made it to both meetings—but he probably didn't get in much hunting. He left Colorado in a rush after the Albert Pike convention and arrived in Washington, D.C., midday on August 3. The joint board had not waited for him and had already been in session for a half day.

The part of the meeting that he did attend turned out to be exceptionally important for Cy, for two reasons. On the one hand, during that day and a half, the group made decisions on what were to become key parts of the national highway system. On the other hand, it was at that meeting that the highway numbering committee was appointed.

One of the issues covered by the board in those quick two days involved yet another discussion of just what the national highway system should be—national roads or interconnected local roads—and whether the country would be better off with many or fewer highways in the system. Once more, the decision was made to connect the towns and cities, but the call for limited access transcontinental highways did not go away.

Another question was how the numbering would work. Hotchkiss of Wisconsin suggested the lowest numbers be given to the longest, most important roads with higher numbers for the connecting routes. Hinkle of Indiana recommended numbering be consistent across state lines and AASHO president Rogers announced that Michigan had adopted the "Wisconsin Plan" for identifying routes by number "and have not regretted it."[34] Cy most certainly agreed with Rogers. Sometime before, he, Johnson, and Gentry had also adopted a numbering system for Oklahoma's federal aid highways, despite his and Gentry's personal devotion to their trails associations. In fact, his early adoption of both numbers and trail names for Oklahoma roads may have foretold his amazing ability, three years later, to imbue the number "66" with a character and mystique that ultimately transcended even national boundaries.

Cy took special note of a motion by Babcock of Minnesota that the chair of the joint board appoint a committee of five to come up with a numbering scheme for the designated national highways.[35]

He was on hand to vote with the board to accept the sign committee's recommendations for signs and safety devices. They agreed on the final design of the federal highway shield—with state names included. They also voted on the safety signage, including round railroad signs, octagonal stop signs, yellow diamond-shaped caution signs, directional signs, rectangular speed limit signs, and various others. These signs would be vastly important in curbing traffic accidents and highway deaths and have remained little changed in the years since. One exception was the octagonal "stop" sign: it began as a yellow sign but soon was changed to red.

The board then recessed to take one more look at their national highway map, drawn with input from all the states and over the course of the five regional meetings. They made a few changes but overall were pleased with the results. One issue that had been left hanging was whether to designate the Old Santa Fe Trail or the New Santa Fe Trail through Kansas. The Kansas Highway Commission had pushed for the Old Santa Fe Trail but Cy pointed out that Secretary of Agriculture Jardine was a Kansan and favored the New Santa Fe Trail. After some conversation, the board left the map as it was, with the Old Santa Fe Trail route.[36] At this point the map showed 50,100 miles of national highways. Over the next fourteen months, before final acceptance by the states, the designated highways on the national map would increase by more than 50 percent.

Next, the board voted to formally adopt the Wisconsin model for highway identification. This meant that the new soon-to-be-designated interstate highways would carry numbers and not names. True to Babcock's motion, the chair then appointed a committee of five of those present to come up with a numbering system for the highways. Cy was one of the five. Two of the other four were Sheets and Piepmeier. The others were Roy Klein of Oregon and Charles Moorefield of South Carolina. The committee's marching orders were that the highway numbers should be no more than two digits and that the state and national signs should not be the same.

Interestingly, Richard Weingroff of the Federal Highway Administration Office of Engineering and author of the FHWA's comprehensive history of American highways later speculated that if Cy had, indeed, been unable to get to Washington, D.C., for the August meeting, as he had maintained to James, and stayed in Colorado, things might have turned out very differently. "Would a Chicago-to-Los Angeles route have been linked up and given the number 60? After all, Avery would not have been on the numbering committee. We'll never know."[37]

The numbering committee went to work on what was considered pretty much a pro forma project. The big job, the one fraught with emotion, had been the actual selection of the highways themselves. How much difficulty could there be in doling out numbers? Not much, initially. At the end of the second day of that August meeting, the committee of five reported they had come up with a system designating eight primary east-west highways and ten running north and south that would be numbered and considered most important. They also agreed they would give numbers to fourteen secondary, but also important, roads. After their report, the rest of the board gave them the go-ahead to work with James on a final numbering system and report back.

Before they adjourned and went home to oversee state highway construction, the board also gave each of their regional groups the authority to finalize the map with their constituents once it was completed.[38]

In the weeks immediately following that meeting, James recommended a tiered system of highway numbering. He later recalled, "With north-south roads numbered odd from east to west, and east-west roads numbered even from north to south, you at once start a simple, systematic complete expansible pattern for a long time development." He suggested for the most important east-west roads a number ending in zero. The main north-south roads were double-digit numbers ending in one or five.[39]

On September 15, Cy traveled to St. Louis to meet with the committee of five at the old Jefferson Hotel. They approved James's numbering method, and by that evening they had a map filled in with a grid of highways beginning with U.S. Highway 1, along the east coast, and U.S. Highway 10, which stretched between Detroit and Seattle as the northernmost transcontinental route.

As James had suggested, important north-south routes ended in one and important, but secondary, north-south routes ended in five. Important east-west routes ended in zero. Two-digit numbers were used for alternates, cutoffs, and connecting routes. As laid out, the system was for the most part consistent—with one glaring exception. The committee had labeled a sweeping curve of a road linking Chicago, Tulsa, and Los Angeles as U.S. 60. And while the meeting report does not suggest any collusion, it is worth noting again that Avery, Piepmeier, and Sheets were on the committee.

When the committee had completed their task, they had given seventy-six numbers to what would become the major U.S. highways. Only twenty-four single or double-digit numbers were left. One of those unused numbers was sixty-six.[40]

Right on schedule, in late October the joint board was finished. They sent a packet to Secretary Jardine that included a national map with 75,884 miles of numbered highways and examples of their final choices for signs and highway markings. They also sent a thick document that delineated the towns on each numbered highway—for example, U.S. Route 1 would run between Miami, Florida, and Fort Kent, Maine, and a list of all the towns along the way. They asked the secretary for his comments and suggested he send the packet on to the states for their individual approval.

A short two weeks later the secretary responded to AASHO. He thanked them for their diligence and concurred with the highway system, signage, and marking plans. "It is gratifying to have the States on their own initiative originate a plan of such broad national aspect and value."[41] He added the obvious: that the success of this planned national highway system would be up to the state highway officials themselves. Finally, he thanked the joint board members and terminated their appointments.

Cy must have been satisfied. He had managed to number seven national highways through Oklahoma, including three through Tulsa. These three were north-south U.S. Highway 75, from the Canadian border near St. Vincent, Minnesota, to Galveston; east-west U.S. Highway 64, the Albert Pike Highway; and diagonal U.S. Highway 60, which was partly the old Ozark Trail. Back at home he returned his attention to building highways and bridges in Oklahoma.

When he attended the AASHO annual meeting in Detroit on November 18–21, 1925, everyone must have been in a positive mood, at least as far as the national highways were concerned, although the president's attack on federal aid was still causing problems. The joint board's report and map had been sent to each of the states. By and large, there was general agreement the job had been well-done.

At that Detroit meeting, Cy had another bit of luck. He was elected to the AASHO executive committee to fill a vacancy caused by the death of the W. S. Keller of Alabama. Sheets, as AASHO's vice president, was also on the executive committee. Since the joint board had been dissolved by the secretary of agriculture, AASHO members passed a resolution calling on the executive committee to deal with the individual states and handle any changes in the national highway system that were still left hanging. E. W. James, who had provided such invaluable assistance to the joint board, was asked to again cooperate with Markham regarding future work on highway numbering, if any, and help in getting the directional and safety signs erected.

A highlight of the Detroit meeting was a detailed presentation made by James to the AASHO membership regarding the work of the joint board. He expressly thanked the joint board members for "the willingness, the hearty cooperation, the harmony and the careful thought they have displayed continually. The task has been full of pitfalls and might very easily at a number of points have been seriously embarrassed had we had any other than the most unselfish and broad attitude of mind among the members." James went on to describe the national highway project in glowing terms.

> The conflicting demands of the Forty-eight States have been met on a broad gauge basis. The Middle Western States have secured the larger mileage, which undoubtedly is required in that region. The Eastern States, which strongly favored a skeleton system of roads of comparatively limited mileage, have been satisfied to accept the soundness of the reasons for an amplified system in the Missouri Valley. The Western Land States have recognized the difficulties that would be raised and the weaknesses that would characterize a system of paper roads where construction could not be effected for financial reasons until relatively far in the future. All groups have viewed the general situation with vision and tolerance and have given their suggestions and advance in a fullness of comprehension and harmony

of purpose that leave no room for a charge of narrowness or lack of vision. The conditions of the problem required open-handed treatment, and the Board's whole action has been consistent with that idea.[42]

Cy and his fellow joint board members had done well. They took their compliments and sat back to enjoy the fellowship of the rest of the conference. When the AASHO convention ended, it was with a good feeling that a large and important task had been accomplished and that any loose ends would easily be tied up in short order.

A year later, at the AASHO annual meeting in Pinehurst, North Carolina, James made another address to the members. It is clear from his second report that most of the high-mindedness of the joint committee's original work had been left behind in the squabble over highway numbering.

NINE

The Fight over Highway Numbers

The absurd part of this thing to me is that one State after the map is made up and has been accepted by forty-eight states wishes to make a change affecting every State from the Atlantic to the Pacifica [*sic*] coast along Route 60. . . .

I think the position is that we should stand pat on giving them 62 from Springfield East.

—Cyrus S. Avery to Roy M. Johnson, March 19, 1926

When Cy arrived at Chicago's Congress Hotel for the American Association of State Highway Officials (AASHO) executive committee meeting on January 14, 1926 he and his colleagues were confronted with nearly one hundred requests to change either highway routes or numbering. The petitions came from bypassed towns, from trails associations that had lost their identity, from individuals, and from state officials who felt their states had been shortchanged when numbers were handed out.

In the months after AASHO secretary Markham sent the first national highway maps to state officials, the highways with numbers ending in one, five, and zero quickly took on an aura of their own. A community that could boast one of those numbers would be a place that would draw people and business. It would be a community set apart. Every town wanted to be on those numbered roads and those that were not, asked for changes to be made. The executive committee dealt with seventy-nine of the appeals during that one-day meeting. Others that were not so straightforward were held over for a later time, and one became so contentious that it threatened to undo all of the joint board's work of the past year.

Even the safety signs raised issues. New Mexico's highway commissioner, James A. French, for one, had contacted Bureau of Public Roads' (BPR) James in early December, objecting to the cost of installing stop signs for New Mexico. "In this state we have no intersecting roads both carrying enough travel to require the octagonal stop sign."[1] Time, of course, solved that problem.

Representatives from Maryland and Pennsylvania, who had not even attended the regional meeting the year before, decided they didn't like anything that had been done by the joint board and threatened not to endorse the map. F. S. Greene from New York continued to believe there were simply too many roads. He even told the *New York Times* that as an example to other states, he would work to eliminate a road from New York City to Albany that ran on the west side of the Hudson River.[2]

The Kansas people were still at loggerheads over the Old and New Santa Fe Trails and over a numbering switch just past Manhattan, Kansas, in what had been the cross-country Victory Highway. That latter even elicited a telegram from the secretary of agriculture. To address the Victory Highway issue the executive committee split U.S. 40 into U.S. 40 North and U.S. 40 South. They turned U.S. 50 into U.S. 50 North and U.S. 50 South for the two Santa Fe Trails. Neither decision turned out to be the right one, and the issue festered for years.

The biggest wrangle, though, came out of Kentucky. Gov. William J. Fields, a former congressman and longtime highway booster, was beside himself that in all the road numbering, Kentucky had not been given even one prestigious single-digit or zero-ending number on any of her primary federal aid highways.

Fields was having trouble back in Kentucky anyway. He had planned the centerpiece of his administration to be a $75 million highway-focused bond issue, but thanks to strong opposition from his own Democratic party he almost didn't get the proposal through the legislature. As it was, he had a long, difficult fight, not an auspicious way to begin a term as governor. Then when it came to getting the bond issue approved by the public, voters rejected it by ninety thousand votes. So besides state pride, Fields had something to prove when he complained about being slighted by the joint board.

First Fields announced that Kentucky would simply ignore the U.S. numbers. That was in December. In January, he went to Chicago to attend the executive committee meeting. There, he told the AASHO leaders what he had already pointed out in writing: the major east-west routes divided around Kentucky, with U.S. Highways 20, 30, 40, and 50 bypassing his state on the north and U.S. Highways 70, 80, and 90 running to the south. It was more than clear to Fields that, since U.S. 60 went from Springfield, Missouri, to Chicago, and not east through Kentucky as any sensible person would expect, a Chicago faction was in control of the mapping. Likewise, he said, the famous Dixie Highway, which had many "detours" through Kentucky anyway, had been split in Kentucky into U.S. 31 from Mobile, Alabama, to Mackinac, Michigan, and U.S. 25 between Toledo, Ohio, and Augusta, Georgia. And then there was his personal favorite, which had also been dismembered. "I particularly object to the obliteration of my idol, my dream, the Midland Trail, running from Ashland to Lexington and to Louisville. I have worked hard for this great road."[3] It did not help the governor's case that Kentucky's state highway engineer, E. N. Todd, had assented to the numbering plan or that Kentucky had not paid its $200 annual AASHO dues, which meant that Todd could not have voted on a change anyway.

By the time the executive committee met, Piepmeier had already given his opinion to the BPR's James: "The fellows from Kentucky think we should change some of our main roads through Missouri. I will not agree with this as they have had their opportunity to be heard and are now trying to upset the plan that had been worked out by the Joint Board." James, for his part, saw the hands of the trails associations at work in the Kentucky protest.[4]

At this juncture, Cy did not seem nearly as concerned as his friend Piepmeier. At the Chicago meeting he said that he did not really care whether the number of "his" route was 60 or 62, just so long as it was a consistent number from Chicago to Los Angeles.

Before the meeting ended, the executive committee voted to keep 60 for Cy's road. They also assigned the single number 62 to the road from Springfield, Missouri, to Newport News, Virginia. If Kentucky objected, the committee agreed, they would switch the two numbers.[5]

Not only did Kentucky object, but as soon as Governor Fields found out what the executive committee had decided, he stormed to Washington, D.C. He rounded up his state's whole congressional delegation and paid a heated visit to Chief MacDonald on January 25. There, the Kentuckians pointed out that their state, alone of all the states in the Mississippi Valley, did not have a road designated with a zero ending.

At that point—seeking the path of least resistance—MacDonald and James changed the numbers. They made U.S. 60 the highway from Springfield to Newport News and renamed Avery's route U.S. 62. As they were to soon discover, that was not the easy way out. Cy was furious. He telegrammed his friend and Oklahoma congressman Elmer Thomas in Washington: "Bureau of Roads attempting to change U.S. route number sixty from Chicago to Oklahoma City to Los Angeles. . . . This change without notice to us effects [sic] Missouri, Oklahoma and other states. We have had most of our numbers made and ready to put up. Kansas and Kentucky are the states asking for this change. . . . See MacDonald and insist on this being left as it was agreed on in Chicago. Wire me collect results of your interview."[6] Just as Governor Fields had been sure that the Chicago mob was behind the decision not to grant Kentucky a zero highway number, Cy was at least suspicious that disgruntled Santa-Fe Trail Kansans were working against Oklahoma.

Avery and Piepmeier both sent scathing telegrams to Markham expressing their dissatisfaction with the choice of number sixty-two, Cy in part because he had not been party to the final decision making. On February 9 he telegrammed Markham: "If routes are to be changed this way without any notice to States or to Executive Committee, you are making a joke of the interstate highway. I can think of nothing more unfair to the original marking committee or to the members of the Executive Committee." Cy also made note of the fact that Oklahoma had signs and literature in the works that carried the number 60.[7]

In response to Cy's biting telegram, Markham sent his own relatively scalding letter back: "I have been in this work too long and have been too careful in my management of affairs to deserve the telegram which you sent. The item to which you refer of the change of 60 to begin at the East Coast of the country was arranged by Mr. MacDonald and Mr. James with the congressional delegation of Kentucky, subject, of course, to the approval of the Executive Committee." Finally, Markham pointed out that at the January executive committee meeting Cy had declared that he was not so much interested in whether the road was 60 or 62 so long as the entire distance between Los Angeles and Chicago carried the same number. He told Cy that AASHO president Frank Page would be in town the following week to attend congressional hearings, and Markham would talk with him at that time about contacting the executive committee for final decisions on this and other pending road-numbering situations. In closing, Markham said: "The selection of the interstate system of highways, while it was more or less contentious, was nothing in comparison to the contention that is going on between the States in reference to this numbering system."[8]

On February 10, Cy got back in touch with Congressman Thomas. While he admitted that "prior to final action in Chicago I did suggest that the number was immaterial" he added that the penitentiary was close to completing work on the U.S. 60 signs for Oklahoma and that "the change would delay our marking for this summer. This vitally effects [*sic*] Oklahoma and I feel it would be a rank injustice to make the change at this time."[9] That same day, he telegrammed Chief MacDonald. "Strenuously object to this change at this late hour without notice to us. . . . I did suggest in Chicago that it was immaterial to me as to the number but later in the Executive session we acted on the number definitely and when I came home I considered it settled."[10]

Four hours later MacDonald wired Avery: "If this arrangement is not acceptable to you and Piepmeier, Kentucky will accept U.S. Route 60 . . . U.S. 60 North to Chicago and U.S. 60 South to Newport News. We have been endeavoring to compose situations all over the country in order to prevent attempt to upset whole plan. Expect your cooperation."[11]

An hour and twenty-four minutes later, Avery sent a wire to James: "We are very much surprised at change in Number of Route 60 . . . vigorously opposed . . . have wired Markham and MacDonald."[12] Almost immediately Avery contacted Oklahoma's senator William B. Pine and his friend Elmer Thomas. They, in turn contacted the Bureau of Public Roads.

Two days later, on February 12, a frustrated MacDonald wrote to Avery: "I do not quite understand why you have thought it necessary to take the matter up with Sen. Pine and others of the Congressional delegation, as these are not political matters. . . . Unless all the States cooperate fully in this matter it is hopeless to expect to accomplish anything, and appealing to members of Congress only makes the whole work more difficult."[13]

Because they had to rely on the U.S. Postal Service for the most part, some of the communications were a bit jumbled. Piepmeier had posted a letter on February 13 to Cy—four days after Cy's telegram—that observed, "It seems that North Carolina and Kentucky are making a very strenuous fight for the through routing of No. 60. We cannot afford to lose Route 60. In fact, I will have it marked very shortly."

Piepmeier also leaned on Cy for leadership: "I hope you will keep after this situation, as I do not understand what authority the Bureau has to change route numbers without proper procedure. Mr. Sheets agrees to our numbering. I think if we three stand pat we will mark No. 60 through to Chicago." He enclosed a new road map—one of six hundred thousand already printed by the Missouri Highway Department—identifying the road from just west of Joplin to the Mississippi River via Springfield and St. Louis as U.S. Highway 60.[14]

Two days later, Piepmeier telegrammed Avery: "Object seriously to using sixty north and sixty south. Our road is too big to become a part of something else. We should insist on Route sixty as originally assigned."[15] Piepmeier followed that telegram with a letter. This time around, he waxed eloquent. "In my judgement this is one of the biggest highways in the country. There is more travel between Los Angeles and Chicago, or in that vicinity, than any other transcontinental route. There will not be one vehicle out of fifty which reaches Springfield, Missouri, that will want to go east over the route which our friends are contending for in Kentucky. . . . You know our plan was to designate all of the big roads with zero numbers. I am ready to oppose to the limit a different designation."[16]

The BPR was involved in many things: materials testing, bridge building, advising Congress on highway matters, consulting with highway engineers across the nation, and developing road locations. But in February and March 1926, it appears that the whole focus of the Washington, D.C., office was on the dispute between Kentucky and Oklahoma.

In mid-February, when several members of the executive committee found themselves in Washington, D.C., they held an impromptu meeting in Chief MacDonald's office to dispense with the large and continuing stream of requests for changes and pending disputes from the states. Those present included AASHO president Frank Page of North Carolina, who had been elected at the Detroit meeting, F. R. White of Iowa, J. N. Mackall of Maryland, Markham, James, and MacDonald—but not C. S. Avery of Oklahoma or B. H. Piepmeier of Missouri.

During that meeting, the AASHO and BPR officials dealt with a protest, involving Utah and Wyoming over U.S. 30, by changing a division in the highway originally named 30 North to U.S. 530 and renaming 30 South as U.S. 630. They satisfied another complaint from Wyoming by changing what had been named U.S. 87 East and West to U.S. 87 and U.S. 187. They added several roads in North Carolina. They discussed but did not act on the question of extending U.S. 54 from Dodge City, Kansas, to Tucumcari, New Mexico. They assented to most of Kentucky's other requests for additional roads. On the biggest Kentucky concern, they sided against Avery and Piepmeier. They agreed that Kentucky should have some zero-ending highway and let stand the most recent designation of U.S. 60 as the highway from Springfield to Newport News. But given that they had just changed two other east/west and north/south designations to straight numbers, they made a curious decision that may have had more to do with a reluctance to finalize their actions than any question about the outcome. They agreed that before submitting the matter in the form of a motion they would find out whether Mr. Piepmeier and Mr. Avery might prefer 60 East from Springfield to Newport News and 60 North to Chicago rather than 62 to Chicago.[17]

On February 18, Cy wrote another letter to Chief MacDonald, defending his reasons for contacting the Oklahoma congressional delegation.

It was the only way he had, he said, to protect Oklahoma against the onslaught from Kentucky. Then he continued:

> Mr. Piepmeier of Missouri strenuously objects to any change of Number 60 and is not in favor of using 60 North and 60 South. The U.S. Route 60 runs as near east and west as practically any of the routes until it gets to St. Louis. Illinois, Missouri and Oklahoma consider this route along the line of travel in these three states and where the traffic will go regardless of the number, therefore we feel that this route is of enough National importance that it should not be confused with any other number. . . . We do not see why Kentucky should be insistent upon taking a number of a route that never at any time touched their state. . . . Our numbers are all ordered and we expect to start putting them up in a few weeks.
>
> I have spent many years in cooperation for the benefit of highways and am willing at all times to use my best efforts to harmonize any situation, but we do not feel in Oklahoma at this time that we are justified at all in consenting to change the Number 60 at this late date.[18]

On February 20, James wrote to Cy outlining the situation regarding Governor Fields, the congressional delegation visit, and the highway numbering protest. In three long, single-spaced pages, James recapped the story of the various meetings, the Kentucky governor's concerns, and the situation as it stood. "The burden of their appeal was that Kentucky had been discriminated against in that no through East and West Route had been given to that State."

He continued, "It was believed this adjustment would be satisfactory to you as it essentially met the conditions which you were understood to have indicated as acceptable. Mr. Piepmeier was not present at the meeting in Chicago and the matter was presented to him for his concurrence. As you know, he has objected, and objection has also been received from you."

At the end of the letter, James made a personal appeal to Cy: "I know that you comprehend fully the importance of this whole work and doubtless realize that unless it is satisfactorily accomplished now, it will have to be postponed indefinitely. Apparently this adjustment affecting Kentucky is the only one left of a serious nature and as soon as we can settle it we will proceed with the final map, for which we are having daily demands from every part of the country."[19]

The bureau was in a tough spot, but that did not seem to bother Cy. His usually upbeat demeanor was already being put to a test at home, where he was facing corruption charges for misusing road funds. The charges proved to be without foundation, but throughout 1926 the attacks continued. Most could be traced to the ongoing battles with the county commissioners over road funds and patronage jobs. In Oklahoma, of course, he had more supporters than distractors, and Johnson, Gentry, and Guthrey were there to defend the state highway commission. As far as the national issue was concerned, it was Cy's fight.

Two days after receiving James's letter, Cy wrote again to Oklahoma congressman Thomas and copied MacDonald, the AASHO officers and executive committee, enclosing a copy of James's letter and his response. He wrote to Thomas that the entire Kentucky delegation, including the governor, was insisting on the change, despite the fact that until now Kentucky had not raised an objection, and furthermore the executive committee had

> granted them everything they wanted except U.S. Number 60.
>
> The people of Oklahoma do not buy goods, do their banking nor trading with men in Tennessee, Kentucky, North Carolina or even Arkansas. . . . U.S. 60 is going to be one of the greatest traffic lines in the United States. It is on the most direct and easiest line following along where there is the greatest wealth and is headed both East and West along the direct [*sic*] of business interest. This Route will connect up with the entire oil field of Oklahoma, the oil field of New Mexico and Amarillo, Texas, and Oklahoma City will become the diversion point for all traffic going West and Southwest.

He concluded his letter to Thomas with good wishes and an offer of support for the congressman's upcoming campaign for the U.S. Senate. He also added an apology—of sorts: "This letter is rather lengthy but the Route is too."[20]

Despite his passionate letter to Thomas, Cy actually did pay attention to James's letter of February 20. Like all the correspondence from that period, he saved it, and sometime later he wrote a note in blue ink next to James's signature: "This is why we took 66—CSA."[21]

In the meantime, the standoff continued. Five days after mailing his letter to Congressman Thomas, Cy wrote another litany of complaints to James. "I thought we settled the matter and made 62 a continuous route from Springfield east to Newport News. . . . The first intimation I had of any change came in a roundabout way. Our markers have been ordered. . . . I cannot see why one State has the right to discommode five or six States. I am not willing at this time to consent to change 62 from Chicago to LA. I did not understand the motion made in Chicago was to give Mr. MacDonald or anyone else the authority to change a Route across the United States."[22]

The letters and telegrams between Oklahoma and Washington, D.C., continued at a furious pace. More than one also found its way to Frank Page in North Carolina. On March 4, Piepmeier wrote to Page, rehashing the executive committee meeting in Chicago, then said, "Missouri protests very seriously to any changes in the numbering system . . . for no other purpose than to satisfy a few fellows who are making a lot of noise, or who represent some trail associations" and also pointed out that the various north and south designations in Kansas "are not making a big hit."[23]

Page forwarded Piepmeier's letter to Markham in Washington, D.C., with a note. "As I recall, everyone affected by this change—except Mr. Piepmeier—was pleased." Cy, apparently, was seen as someone caught in the middle even though his protests were as loud as his Missouri colleague's.[24] Presumably because of his long involvement with the trails associations and his national stature he was also better known to Markham, Page, James, MacDonald, and the others.

The Kansas problem referred to in Piepmeier's letter to Page, in fact, had also elicited a communication that involved Cy. In the midst of the Kentucky-Oklahoma-Missouri disagreement, the Good Roads chair in Kansas wrote to Page in North Carolina concerning the disposition of U.S. 54 on a route across Kansas then southwest through the Oklahoma panhandle into Texas and New Mexico. The writer assured Page that the highway commissions of Missouri, Kansas, Texas, and New Mexico were for the change but that Oklahoma had not signed on, "for the very obvious reason, as we see it, that they are fearful that the development of U.S. Route No. 54 will detract from U.S. No. 60." His hoped-for U.S. 54 mostly followed the old Atlantic-Pacific Highway and was, he said, the shortest route to Los Angeles.

In his pique, the Good Roads man from Kansas had to add an observation that he was afraid had been overlooked by the officials in Washington, D.C.: "U.S. Route No. 60 is an arbitrary route, placed on the map by Mr. Avery, who was a member of the Federal Joint Board. It has never been recognized as a tourist route, and was *created* at the instance [*sic*] of Mr. Avery who wanted an east and west route through his home city of Tulsa and Oklahoma City, the state capital." Further, the Good Roads man noted, Avery had made a point of turning down requests from the towns in northwestern Oklahoma that he support the U.S. Route 54 designation. Finally and perhaps most important, he contended that Cy was ignoring the potential for U.S. 54 "to maintain prominence for U.S. No. 60 to the very great disadvantage of Kansas and the territory served by No. 54."[25]

The jockeying for highway number preeminence continued. In a show of support for Kentucky's bid, Frank Dunn of the Lexington Auto Club invited James to present the keynote speech at a convention of the Appalachian Way, one of the several trails through Kentucky. Dunn promised ten governors and several highway officials would be in attendance.

Ever conciliatory, James replied that he was trying to work out his schedule but added a note that was probably of more concern to Dunn than any speech: "We are still endeavoring to secure agreement regarding the Kentucky situation but so far have been unable to do so." He added a message to Governor Fields and the Kentucky Highway Commission: "If Kentucky would accept U.S. 62 there would be no difficulty whatever. The map of the U.S. is being held up pending this adjustment and I regret we will be unable to give Mr. Todd the numbers for his state until this detail has been adjusted."[26]

On March 10, James wrote again to Avery. As secretary to the joint board, charged with shepherding the project to completion, James was desperately trying to sort out the problem and save the national highway system. He asked Cy again about the 60 North and 60 East designations from Springfield, and pointed out, as MacDonald already had, "This matter is giving us considerable difficulty."[27]

It was not as if there were not plenty of other matters demanding attention. Besides his work on the national highway project, James was also MacDonald's second, filling in whenever the chief was away from Washington, D.C. Avery and Piepmeier were supervising engineers and construction projects in Oklahoma and Missouri. In Kentucky, Governor Fields was still at odds with his legislature and a sizeable portion of the state's population.

In mid-March, just to be sure he was touching all bases, Cy wrote to Frank Page in North Carolina again revisiting the January meeting in Chicago. He reminded Page that the committee had "discussed at length" the question of giving additional mileage to Kentucky and that they had voted to leave U.S. Route 60 as it was and give U.S. Route 62 from Springfield to Newport News through Kentucky. "Some weeks ago I heard that Route 60 had been changed to 62. The State of Oklahoma, and myself as a member of the Executive Committee, strenuously object to any change of U.S. Route 60. We have prepared our markers and have them ready to put up. Missouri has done the same thing. I do not see why Kentucky at this time, after the map having been approved by the Joint Board, have [sic] the right to come in and have a change made in alignment that affects the entire United States." The crux of his letter though was in the final paragraph: "Now I know Kansas and Kentucky have been making some charges against me in reference to U.S. Route 60 and representing that I have been unfair to their States. The highway department of Kansas does not say so and are [sic] satisfied with the map as it is today."[28]

In fact, it was not just Kentucky. The zero roads were causing problems everywhere. In Colorado the issue was whether U.S. 40 South would run west from Manhattan, Kansas, to Colorado Springs and Leadville or if the road would get some lesser number. If it turned out to be only a byway, then traffic would be pulled to Denver instead. The secretary of the Colorado Springs chamber wrote to Avery: "We believe we are entitled to a through number [i.e., zero] but as this is out of the question now, we ask that South 40 be extended from Limon to Grand Junction and join North 40 there."

Cy, with his many friends in Colorado Springs from the Albert Pike days, promised to get in touch with James and speak on behalf of their cause, and within a few weeks reported back to them that the committee had voted to extend U.S. 40 as requested.[29]

By this time, patience was wearing thin in the BPR office. More to the point, Congress was getting restive. On March 30, Chief MacDonald wrote Avery a long letter that was part philosophizing and part thinly veiled threat. More than once, he owned up, he worried that Congress would become involved and defeat the whole plan, which was the situation at the time of an earlier letter. "Even when I wrote you there were so many complaints reaching Congress and we were having so many objections raised by both Congressmen and Senators that I seriously believed the sentiment at that time would have turned against the plan. By exerting every possible effort the situation has been reasonably composed in all the states except New York at this time." He went on then to the purpose of his letter: the situation regarding the highway number 60.

MacDonald wrote:

Personally, I think that more time has been spent on this matter than it deserves. I do not feel that it makes one bit of difference to the States along the route from Chicago to Los Angeles whether it is Route no 60 or 62 or any other number so long as the number is carried continuously, and that has been conceded. . . .

I do not have in the whole scheme of numbering one pet project. I do feel that the State of Oklahoma has been very well treated in the matter and I hope you do. I appreciate your desire to hold for Oklahoma all the advantage possible, but it seems to me that Route 60 with an outlet to Chicago and to the east coast is a greater advantage to Oklahoma than either one alone, inasmuch as there will be no difference whatsoever in the State of Oklahoma.

I am writing you at this length because I personally desire you personally to feel right about this matter, and to take some position that will allow us to adjust the matter without any strong arm methods. I am sure you will see that this is the tenor of this letter.

Sincerely yours, THM Chief of Bureau[30]

And so matters stood. On April 3, Piepmeier wrote to James. The Missouri Highway Department would be receiving bids for U.S. highway markers within a week, he said, but "I am at a loss to know what to do in marking U.S. Highway 60 from Chicago to Los Angeles."[31]

On April 6, Cy began to take the matter in hand. He sent a conciliatory letter to MacDonald. "I recognize the difficulty you have in placating the different political interests when they get together in Washington." And he added the first glimmer of hope for MacDonald that something might be able to be worked out: "I will take this matter up with Mr. Piepmeier and see what I can arrange that is satisfactory to him if 60 from Chicago to Los Angeles be left as U.S. 60 and the highway from Springfield East through Kentucky be called U.S. 60 South. . . . Inasmuch as a part of the route from Springfield is not east directly and the balance is north, I believe it will be less confusing to have it that way and I believe I can get Mr. Piepmeier to concede to this."[32]

MacDonald wrote back to Cy on April 14, discussing several other of his highway numbering headaches besides those involving Cy's road. "I appreciate your helpful attitude," he said, adding that he believed Cy's suggestion would be acceptable to the Kentuckians. He went on to describe an issue he was having with southeast Kansas that would involve a road into Vinita. He also mentioned again that he was getting very worried about Congress's interest in the national highway project. He was fielding a lot of questions from members, which he believed were instigated by the trails people, and Florida senator Park Trammell (D) had even introduced a resolution that would prohibit any markings that did not include trails names. The chief added that he had spoken with Trammel and managed to get the resolution stopped at least temporarily. "Evidently there is a great deal of false and mischievous propaganda working to defeat the whole project." He was hesitant, he said, to

FATHER OF ROUTE 66

print any maps until the whole executive committee was on board and all questions cleared up, most specifically the question of Route 60.[33]

In the meantime, Markham sent a letter to Kentucky state engineer Todd, assuring him that the powers-that-be in Washington had pulled out all stops in trying to get Avery and Piepmeier to agree to Kentucky getting number sixty, but at the same time chiding Todd, saying that he had agreed to number sixty-two "at the time the system was laid out" and it was "very clear" that the Kentucky officials had been fully informed of the decision long before the governor and congressional delegation descended on the Bureau of Public Roads to protest what they felt was an unfair decision.[34]

The change requests continued to roll in to the AASHO office. In late April, Markham sent a ballot to the executive committee for a mail vote, primarily to finalize requests taken up in January—or those easily handled. It did not include the issue of the highway from Springfield to Newport News.[35]

As Cy had promised Chief MacDonald, he traveled to Missouri at the end of April to meet with Piepmeier and he took Oklahoma state highway engineer John Page with him. The three men got together in Springfield at the hometown of Avery's friend and fellow highway supporter John T. Woodruff. Most likely, the men met in Woodruff's Colonial Hotel.

By this time, Cy was critically aware that the whole highway numbering system was in peril. It had always been far more important to him to have his highway through Tulsa than the number it carried. He had been upset by the high-handed manner in which the number had been changed and distraught over money expended for now-useless signage and maps, but it was Piepmeier more than Cy who was truly wrought up over the situation.

After quite some discussion, Cy led the conversation around to the possibility of adopting one of the alternative numbers that had not yet been considered. He asked Page to look into the numbers that were left over. There were not many; with the way the numbering system had come down, after the major east-west highways ending with zero and the major north-south highways ending with one or five, the joint board had quickly given other numbers to bypasses, alternative routes, and the rest of the selected primary roads: odd numbers for north/south roads and even numbers for east/west roads.

Page went back through his records to a report by Markham that listed unused numbers. Out of the twenty-four unused single- and double-digit numbers, Page suggested that sixty-six might work.

Sixty-six.

To Avery that sounded like it might be a good choice. It may have been that he realized how easily the number sixty-six rolls off the tongue. With his promotional bent, he may have seen design possibilities in the rounded back of the double sixes. And it is not unlikely, given the era's interest in the occult and spiritual, that at least one of the three men recognized the double sixes as a master number. In numerology, this particular master number was known to bring material pleasures and success. By mid-afternoon Piepmeier was on board and the decision was made.

At four o'clock in the afternoon of April 30, 1926, Avery sent a brief telegram to MacDonald: "Regarding Chicago Los Angeles Road, if California, Arizona, New Mexico, Texas and Illinois will accept Sixty Six instead of Sixty we are willing to agree to this change. We prefer Sixty Six to Sixty Two." The telegram was signed Avery and Piepmeier.[36]

In Washington, D.C., MacDonald and James surely received the telegram with elation. No doubt they held some sort of impromptu celebration—war had been averted, Congress was still largely caged, and the national highway system would indeed come to pass. The long siege was over. The BPR's chief engineer, Capt. P. St. John Wilson, sent a telegram to Markham, who was visiting his friends and family in Kansas: "Have joint telegram from Avery and Piepmeier saying they will agree to change of number on Chicago to Los Angeles road from sixty to sixty-six if other states traversed will agree." Unlike the others, however, Wilson's orderly engineering mind was not comfortable with the new arrangement. His telegram to Markham continued: "This would make two zero numbers—sixty and seventy—as branches of sixty six and upset the general theory of numbering."[37]

Not surprisingly, no one else cared about the niceties of the theory, at least not enough to stop the highway system's newfound momentum.

There were still issues outstanding and would be for another year or more, but overall, the biggest problem had been addressed. Or so they hoped; still ahead was to get agreement from the rest of the executive committee and the Kentucky faction. Since it took time to get the word out, the rest of the world was still offering up opinions on the matter. On May 3, for example, Virginia highway commissioner H. G. Shirley cast his lot squarely with Kentucky governor Fields and announced that Virginia was opposed to adding "any letter or word to the route number."[38]

Kentucky's Todd, apparently oblivious to the concerns of his governor, never mind the Virginia highway people, wrote to Markham on May 5: "I believe our officials will accept 60-East if it is the best the Executive Committee can arrange for this state, but I am sure they feel they are being discriminated against. Of course we could not expect four transcontinental roads through Kentucky as we did not have four roads open east and west but we did have one east and west road in excellent condition for carrying traffic, and it hardly seems just that it should be ignored."[39]

Not everyone, however, was sympathetic to the Kentucky demands. F. R. White, Iowa's chief highway engineer and also a member of the executive committee, wrote to Markham in response to the April ballot, which had been sent out before the number sixty-six was selected for Avery's highway. "I have not voted on the avalanche of changes and recommendations with respect to the Kentucky Routes. . . . It appears to me from an examination . . . that Kentucky is rather suggesting changes all over the southeastern part of the U.S. which changes very considerably affect the routes in a number of the other states."[40]

Although he later changed his mind, Markham decided that the situation was still too volatile to be approved by a mail ballot. "There has been objection developed against the change of numbers on the north and south routes and while it appears reasonably certain that an adjustment can be made to give Kentucky U.S. Number 60 the whole situation will have to be very carefully considered before it can be definitely closed."[41]

Markham, Frank Page, and probably James wanted to be absolutely sure that the altercation was really settled and would not reappear around the next bend in the road. With this in mind, Markham wrote to Cy a few weeks later reporting on a conversation he had with Page regarding the uniform highway markings. "It appears advisable, and Mr. Page insists, that cases involving interstate connections should be held for discussion at a meeting of the Executive Committee and should not be handled further by letter ballot. I think you will agree with me that Mr. Page's attitude in this matter is conservative and sound. Some of the cases are very perplexing and will need careful handling."

Ever prudent, Markham also knew that Avery and Piepmeier were ready to order new signs and maps and claim their highway but urged them to hold off. "I suggest therefore that in proceeding with your marking you omit for the time being the route markers on the route which will be affected by the Kentucky adjustment."[42]

By the end of July, things were truly falling into place. James wrote first to Avery and then to Piepmeier that Kentucky had agreed with the U.S. 60 from Springfield to Newport News and U.S. 66 for Chicago to Los Angeles. Given that the key players had assented, he also told them to expect a letter ballot to the executive committee and to hold off making signage until after that. "I will notify you as soon as Mr. Markham has received a majority of votes from the committee."[43]

On July 26, Cy wrote back to James, sealing the deal:

> I wish to especially thank you for your interest in this matter and assure you that the only object we, of Oklahoma, have had, was to have a continuous route number from Chicago to Los Angeles without any branches.
>
> We assure you that it will be a road through Oklahoma that the U.S. Government will be proud of.[44]

From there, it was a matter of arranging details and finalizing decisions. By August 4, the executive committee members had also given their approval to the U.S. 66 and 60 deal.

Cy had put about a third of the markers up on Oklahoma's other national highways and was anxious to number "his" road. He was not above reminding James that he had quite a lot of now-useless U.S. 60 shields in hand and would have to junk them. He also wrote to

Markham that manufacture of Oklahoma's U.S. 66 signs was under-way.[45]

Markham, however, was not yet ready to be done with Avery and Piepmeier. He wrote back reminding Avery that his (Avery's) vote on the Kentucky-Missouri agreement had not yet been received by AASHO nor had he, Markham, received enough other executive committee votes to consider the case closed.[46]

During the first week in August, the last of the executive committee members assented to the U.S. 66 and 60 deal. Chief MacDonald wrote to Cy that he was ready to declare the end. But the war over the national highway system was still not finished. Among others, the chief had another headache concerning Oklahoma roads, one from Kansas into northeast Oklahoma and for U.S. 54 southwest from Liberal, Kansas. "The people along the way have been very insistent, and have carried the case of 54 to the Secretary and have also beseeched Senator Curtis to help them with 73. These are relatively unimportant matters to you, but in the interests of harmony and since you have the remainder of your system now practically as you desired it, I am hoping you will agree to this."[47]

Cy agreed. He also sent his thanks to Markham. "I know this matter has been rather a trying one for you and appreciate the difficulty you have experienced in harmonizing all the different States on this inter-state road map." He also sent Markham a heads-up that Elmer Thomas had won the Oklahoma Democratic primary and was on his way to becoming the next U.S. senator from Oklahoma. This would be good news for Markham as well as for the BPR and the nation's highways.[48]

But still it dragged on. Near the end of August, Markham sent out one more ballot, this time regarding New Mexico, which had no single continuous highway number for any north-south road across the state, and about finalizing adjustments agreed on between Pennsylvania and Ohio. The executive committee approved.

In November, the AASHO members, BPR officials, and Kentucky's governor Fields, as a special guest, gathered for their annual meeting, this time at Pinehurst, a resort in AASHO president Frank Page's home state of North Carolina. A year before in Detroit, James had praised the cooperation and unity of spirit that had driven the joint board's work to designate a national highway system. This year he spoke again, but his tone was significantly different: "While I have no authority from the Executive Committee to recommend the adoption of the adjustments made in the system of U.S. Highways, I wish to state my personal opinion. I urge the immediate adoption of the system as now laid out. It is not perfect. After 18 months almost continuous experience with the work I am convinced that to leave the case for further consideration will not improve it."[49]

AASHO members agreed, and on November 11, 1926, they voted to accept the work of the joint board and the executive committee. The United States now had a 96,626-mile numbered highway system. The only thing left was confirmation by the states. Maps and ballots were mailed to every state highway department in the country to secure final approval.

Three and a half weeks later, on a rainy December 7 in Oklahoma City, Cy met with Roy Johnson and E. Bee Guthrey to do the Oklahoma Highway Commission's business. French Gentry was sick at home in Enid. They approved a survey for Custer County, a $1,500 appropriation for ditches in Muskogee County, $7,400 to complete a drainage structure and grading for Mayes County, and they also resolved to accept the work of the joint board and adopt the nine sections of the Oklahoma state highway system that had been selected to be included in the new national highway system.

It was also moved by Avery and seconded by Johnson to immediately mark the newly designated U.S. highways. One of these roads was U.S. Route 66.

The minutes of that meeting describe Cy's highway in Oklahoma as "beginning at a point on the Kansas state line south of Baxter Springs. Follows State Route 39 to the junction with State Highway No. 7 at the town of Commerce, thence follows Route 7 through Miami, Vinita, Tulsa, Chandler, Oklahoma City, thence follows State Highway No. 3 to El Reno, Bridgeport, Clinton, Sayer to the Texas State line near Texola."

The highway commissioners also voted on U.S. Route 64—the Albert Pike Highway—U.S. route 70, the byway U.S. Route 266 to Oklahoma

City, U.S. Route 73, U.S. Route 75, and U.S. Route 77. Sidney Suggs's old Meridian Highway became U.S. Route 81. Guthrey recorded that both Avery and Johnson voted "Aye."[50]

And so it was done. When it was mostly all over, the *Tulsa Tribune* wrote an adulatory article praising Cy's role in the process. The joint board, the article said, "acted favorably on Avery's suggestion that Oklahoma be the intersecting point for transcontinental travel."[51]

TEN

Ousted!

What is the basis of the fight on the state highway
commission and fight for reinstatement of the old county
commissioner system of building public roads? That's easy.
It's the old, old contest over the right to spend money.

—*Chicago Examiner*, 1926

For Cy, 1926 was one of those years. He reached a pinnacle of political prominence. Thanks to his charm, political skills, and dogged enthusiasm for all things involving roads, he headed a national trails association and was president of the Associated Highways of America (AHA); he had been elected county commissioner, named Oklahoma highway commissioner, and appointed by the Secretary of Agriculture to a twenty-one-man joint board to select, layout, and choose a marking scheme for a national system of U.S. highways. From there he had been named to a committee of five to decide the numbers and designations for those same national highways, and then to the executive committee of American Association of State Highway Officials (AASHO). During his term as highway commissioner, Oklahoma saw unparalleled progress in road improvement. Because of his involvement with the national highway project he managed to bring three cross-country roads through Tulsa, and he would see his great diagonal highway enrolled in the national system. By January 1927, however, he was out of a job. Both his successes and his ouster were the result of his political dealings—shrewd in one case, misjudged in the other.

Cy's participation in the national highway project kept him out of Oklahoma a good portion of 1925 and 1926. As a result, even though his highway department had unqualified success at improving the state's roads, he badly misjudged his popularity and political abilities when he took a stand in the 1926 governor's race.

The problems stemmed from the simmering animosity between the state highway department and the commissioners from Oklahoma's seventy-seven counties. For Cy, it was an old story. In February 1925, before he had been in state office for a whole year, the State Commissioners Association had induced a legislative investigative committee to look into the operation of the state highway commission. In a panic, Roy Johnson telephoned the Bureau of Public Roads' (BPR) A. R. Losh in Fort Worth urging him to come to Oklahoma City and appear before the committee. Losh sent a frantic telegram to Chief MacDonald seeking permission to testify, noting "evidently situation serious."[1] Nothing came of the hearings except a warning to Avery, Gentry, and Johnson that their path to better Oklahoma roads was going to be a rough one.

Near the beginning of 1926, the three highway commissioners were charged with corruption when the Osage tribal attorney received an anonymous letter concerning the misuse of road funds in Osage County. Once more, the ensuing investigation exonerated the highway men but not before it involved the commissioner of Indian Affairs, Charles H. Burke, in Washington, D.C. Afterward, Burke wrote to Chief MacDonald, "We are glad to know the charges have proved to be without foundation."[2]

Particularly difficult was Cy's relationship with the commissioners in his own home county. One of the Tulsa commissioners, W. L. North, was especially outspoken in his condemnation of Avery's highway construction methods, especially his penchant for using concrete as a road surface instead of asphalt, which was less expensive.

Besides harassment inside the state, Cy's department also faced continuing disparagement from Losh, who was, after all, a good BPR soldier and not subject to the constraints of day-to-day working relationships or the realities of state politics.

Probably because of Cy's travels, Oklahoma road construction contracts were often extended without new bids, and requirements were sometimes changed after a job had begun—a situation that went against BPR regulations. Since the bureau had to approve any plans that involved federal funds, on more than one occasion Losh appealed to MacDonald for help. Losh's most significant concern was the way Cy, Johnson, and Gentry shuffled funds in order to get roads built in Oklahoma's various counties, even though these shuffles generally coincided with the passage of bond issues. Losh deplored Cy's practices, but as he wrote to MacDonald, "Mr. Avery stated very frankly that he was entirely in sympathy with the attitude and policy of the Bureau . . . but that it was necessary for the Oklahoma Highway Commission to work on a cooperative basis with the various counties and to do this successfully it becomes necessary at times to make substantial concessions to the county authorities as was true in this case."

On another occasion Losh complained that John Page, the state highway engineer, had received bids on various types of pavement but selected rock asphalt on a concrete base because the county wanted that particular surface. Losh's concern was that the base selected was more expensive than a concrete surface. He admitted that the county involved was paying the difference, but he opposed the practice of taking bids and then not honoring the low bid submitted. He wrote to BPR's chief engineer, "We have made it plain to all the states in this district that this practice does not meet with our approval."[3]

Another issue that worried Losh was Cy's relationship with the Lock Joint Pipe Company. Cy had begun working with the New Jersey–based company on the Spavinaw project, and theirs had grown into a compatible and long-term relationship, with Lock Joint supplying pipe for culverts and low-water bridges on many highway jobs. In one case, although Losh recommended against it, Cy, with concurring votes from Gentry and Johnson, extended a Lock Joint contract without new bids. After Losh complained to his higher-ups in Washington, D.C., the chief of BPR's division of construction wrote back, presumably after consulting a bureau attorney, that "while the procedure may not be illegal it is certainly inadvisable. . . . It is not desirable to renew such a contract without the formality of receiving competitive bids."[4]

Besides his wrangles with the county commissioners and issues with the BPR, Cy made a bad political decision when he took a stand in the 1926 governor's race. Even worse, he backed the wrong horse. So at the end of the year, when he wrapped up his national highway duties and came home to refocus his attention on paving Oklahoma's highways, he found himself working for a new governor, but not the man to whom he had thrown his support. And even before he was sworn into office, the new governor wanted Cy out.

When Martin Trapp was ruled ineligible to run for a full term by the Oklahoma Supreme Court, Cy, who still had two more years to serve as state highway commissioner, came out in support of the Republican candidate, who happened to be a Tulsan. He declared that "Omer Benedict, the Republican candidate for governor, has publicly announced his satisfaction with the present highway law and the present personnel of the Commission. Henry S. Johnston, the Democratic candidate for governor, suggests numerous changes in the highway law and declines to give to the public, any intimation as to what his attitude will be regarding the personnel."

Noting that Republican state highway commissioner Roy Johnson's term had actually expired several months before, in March, and that Gentry was quite ill, Cy went on to discuss the options afforded to whichever man would be elected governor. "There are a great many voters in Oklahoma who would really like to know whether a vote for Henry S. Johnston for governor is a vote against Roy M. Johnson as a member of the State Highway Commission, and Henry S. Johnston is the only man who can answer this question."[5]

It did not take long to know he had made a big mistake. For the rest of his life he kept an original copy of an editorial written later in the campaign by his friends at the *Tulsa Tribune*. Cy, the editorial noted, had pushed for and gotten a highway law that gave specific terms to highway commissioners, thus taking the highway department at least a step away from politics. "Avery got, in this respect, all he wanted, as he deserved. It is all the more unfortunate, therefore, that he has himself been largely responsible for throwing the highway commission into the thick of the first campaign that has arisen since the new law became effective."[6]

Both the Democratic and Republican parties passed resolutions condemning Avery's highway commission. While it wasn't surprising

FATHER OF ROUTE 66

to have opposition from the Republicans, the Democratic opposition stung. Still it wasn't totally unexpected. Not only had he publicly spoken out against Johnston, he was still facing those long-running difficulties with the county commissioners.

Originally the Democratic Party's resolution had been particularly positive concerning the cooperative working relationship in road construction between counties and the state. However, the County Commissioners Association wouldn't have it. They had already gone to court and been knocked down over the constitutionality of the state highway department's spending, but they demanded their say in the party's platform. By the time the resolution was revised and publicized, it included a statement that the "various counties be permitted to choose the material of which the state commission shall build its roads"—even though that meant that different counties might choose different materials.[7] It was really a call to diminish the power of the state highway department.

Before Cy's tenure, legislators and friends of the governor would send requests and recommendations regarding employment of constituents or friends. Cy, for the most part, hired professionals. The newly elected governor Johnston saw more value in granting political favors than in having a professional highway department.

Democrat Henry S. Johnston was an attorney and longtime Oklahoma political figure who had taken part in Oklahoma's constitutional convention in 1907. He was also a Prohibitionist and a supporter, if not a member, of the Oklahoma Klan. As soon as the votes were counted that elected him governor, Johnston set out to get rid of Cy.

Even before his January 10 inauguration, Johnston sent word to Cy that it would be best for him to resign. Cy refused—and he made his refusal very public. Gentry also refused to step down. Department secretary E. Bee Guthrey, on the other hand, bid the highway department adieu and acknowledged how much he had enjoyed his job.

As Cy told a *Tulsa Tribune* reporter:

> The highway commissioners are appointed for definite terms. It was not the intention of the legislators to make the commissioners subject to the whims of the governors or they would have made the terms expire with each governor.

If Mr. Johnston wants to get us out let him induce the legislature to change the law. That would be the logical way for him to proceed. I do not believe that the legislature would change the law, which would show that the governor's position is not sound. It was the legislature's ideal to take the highway commission out of politics. . . . We don't intend to resign, but rather to keep on building highways for Oklahoma.[8]

With that, Cy left town for a national road builders convention in Chicago. It was a bad move.

One of Governor Johnston's first acts after being sworn in was to call for a new highway law. He said he wanted to realign the state highway commission from three to five members. Unfortunately, there were enough state legislators already fuming over Cy's ability to spread jobs and money without their oversight that he and the highway department were fairly easy targets. As the governor requested, a highway bill was introduced that called for a new highway commission. Particularly pointed was the bill's so-called Otjen Amendment, which cited political activity as a cause for removing a commissioner.

As the law worked its way through the legislature, it captured statewide attention. Newspapers in pro–highway department communities went to bat for Cy and the commission. In Commissioner Roy Johnson's home town, the *Ardmore Statesman* pointed out that the Oklahoma highway system had been copied by a number of other states and that Cy's team had "built more hard-surfaced roads in the past three years than was built in the preceding nearly seventeen, has built them better, and at less cost."[9]

Farther west, the *Frederick Leader* noted that "it may be that Governor Johnston and his supporters in the present war raging over the highway department have some amendments to the law which will improve it. It is certain, however, that the governor's personal aspersions upon the members of the present highway commission do not shed any light, add any argument, elucidate any point, nor serve any good purpose in the controversy."[10]

French Gentry's hometown newspaper, the *Enid News* said that "road building in Oklahoma is now conducted outside the stockade of petty political bickering and horse trading; and the very personal quarrel which has brought the thunders of the administration down on the commission is proof of the political freedom possible to its members under the present law."[11]

The *Daily Oklahoman* printed a form people could fill out and mail to their state senators to show their support or opposition to the new highway bill. When hearings were held on the highway bill, more than one hundred good roads people descended on the legislature to show their support for Cy and display their opposition to the bill.

Even with all that, the outcome of Johnston's highway law was never really in question. After it passed the house, but before the senate vote, state engineer Page wrote to Losh at the BPR predicting its passage. He foresaw the elimination of Avery's highway commission "after which my tenure in office as State Highway Engineer will be very brief."[12]

Actually, the bill was passed in a great hurry one day in late January when word got out that Cy, along with Johnson and Guthrey, were on their way to hold a highway commission meeting in Enid to vote on $1 million worth of highway contracts. Gentry, who had been laid up for months, was needed to vote, and Cy wanted the contracts let before any action was taken regarding his job. The legislature was in such a hurry to get the bill passed for Governor Johnston that Cy's friends did manage to keep the Otjen Amendment out of the final bill, but that was all. As soon as the bill was passed, it was rushed to the governor who signed it and fired the highway commissioners that very evening—thereby maintaining control over the unlet contracts.[13]

Johnston had won. The new law called for a new, five-person commission. The governor also gloated that getting rid of Cy was the whole purpose of the legislation. He called Cy an "unbanished Kaiser." Immediately he appointed five new men for the highway commission. This time, the governor erred; none of his appointees was known to the BPR—and none of them was approved by the Oklahoma Senate.

Cy acknowledged to a *Tulsa Tribune* reporter that he had been "retired to the position of a private citizen. . . . It had been my object to give Tulsa 100 miles of paved road leading in every direction but now I will have to leave that worthy object to other men."[14] Privately he wrote to his friend

Charley Thomas in Colorado Springs, "The Kluxers pitched me out on my head although they had to change the law and create a Commission of five instead of three and changed the length of terms. . . . Although every paper in the state and every Chamber of Commerce and Road Association was for us we went the way of the 'Whang Doodle.'"[15]

As the news spread, Cy heard from his supporters. Losh wrote that he not only enjoyed their working relationship but "very much appreciate the personal connections which I have formed with you."[16] From Washington, D.C., Markham wrote, "I am quite sure you realize there are a great many people who regret that politics has made this change."[17] A friend from New York telegrammed, "I still think you know more about building roads in a minute than Johnston will know about being governor in a lifetime."[18]

There were those who pointed out that Cy's activities during the primary and general election had rendered any working relationship with Johnston nil and that would have hampered highway building even with no change in the law. And there were also those who believed that Cy's focus on Tulsa had shortchanged other areas. And then there were the people like F. S. Howard, a businessman from Baron, Oklahoma, who foretold that Cy should become a candidate for governor himself.

Gentry and Johnson, also out of jobs, commiserated. In mid-February, Johnson wrote to Gentry that "in the three years you, Cy and I have been associated we have learned to love each other like brothers. Though we may have differed at times in matters of judgment, yet our aims and purposes were always the same. . . . Each was giving the best in himself for the interest in the state." Johnson, an oil mogul, also commented that "Cy has devoted more time and thought to the work than either you or I . . . at a greater financial sacrifice. . . . Cy's business interests need closer personal attention to assure their successful operation than is true with the respective businesses owned by yourself and myself."[19]

As soon as Avery, Gentry, and Johnson were gone from the highway commission, Johnston ousted a number of other department employees, including seven district maintenance superintendents. Then, as predicted, he took aim at the state highway engineer, John Page.

Johnston's vendetta against Page essentially had the same backstory as the Avery saga. Page had asked the commission to fire A. P. Carmichael, a highway department employee who was caught requesting an expense reimbursement for gasoline and motor oil that was not delivered to the state but instead used by him personally. The commission fired Carmichael. Unfortunately for Page—and Cy—Carmichael's brother Frank was a member of the Oklahoma House of Representatives. Frank Carmichael successfully prevailed on Johnston to ask for Page's resignation.

Page later said that "the governor apparently in an unreasoning passion of venomous hatred of me, inspired by certain individuals in whom he seems to have confidence, demanded of the Commission that I be removed. His wish was promptly carried out by the Commission."

Page considered resigning, especially, he said because he had no issues with the members of the new highway commission, but "I could not in justice to myself resign." He may have had no quarrels with the new five-man commission, but Page described the first month of meetings as "resembling a mob scene. Crooks and grifters with pet schemes, old matters previously rejected, hoards of job seekers and politicians" all descended on the commission. "I stood by and advised, informed and counseled. I jealously guarded the interests of the commission and the state of Oklahoma. . . . During Governor Trapp's administration, the highway department was never involved in politics. Democrats and Republicans, Catholics and Protestants were employed and no discrimination whatsoever was shown." The results, he pointed out, were "efficiency and loyalty."[20] Page's high regard for the way Cy conducted highway department business made Cy's active involvement in the 1926 governor's race even more mystifying.

In mid-February, Governor Johnston summoned BPR's Losh to Oklahoma City for a meeting and offered him the state highway engineer job. Aghast, Losh pointed out that Page was not only well qualified for his position and had been successful but also had worked closely with the BPR. Further, Losh told Johnston, Cy Avery's department had done excellent maintenance work, which he hoped the state would continue. Page lasted until May. Then he was out. At that time he told a reporter that he was sure that another engineer could ably perform the state engineer duties but "from my own experience with the administration they will be handicapped from the start."[21]

In his dismissal, Johnston said Page had cost the state hundreds of thousands of dollars in road maintenance and charged him with being unreasonably biased in favor of concrete hard surfacing. Johnston also called Page "a consummate ass."[22]

John Page spent his whole life building highways. Born in Baltimore, he was graduated from the Baltimore Polytechnic Institute there and began his career with the Maryland and Delaware highway departments. Following a stint in the army during World War I, he joined the BPR under Chief MacDonald and became a highway engineer in Fort Worth working with highway officials in Texas, Louisiana, and Oklahoma. That made him a perfect choice to become Cy's state highway engineer. Later, after he lost his job in Oklahoma, he returned to the fold, and served the BPR until his retirement in the mid-1950s, earning a Silver Medal for Meritorious Service from the Department of Commerce. He suffered a stroke in 1960 and died August 19, 1969.

Just weeks after Page's firing, the *Oklahoman* came out strongly in defense of "A Great Department Wrecked," and the *Tulsa Tribune* pointed out that the general population doesn't "care who gets the business. What they want is roads." The *Tribune* went on to note that during Cy's and Page's firings, "much was said about the subserviency of the old commission to the cement trust. Hints of collusion between commission, contractors and the trust, which according to those hints cost the state many thousands of dollars. But the new commission finds, as did the old, that concrete roads cost less, despite the trust, than any other kind of so-called permanent pavements."[23] In one matter at least, Cy was vindicated.

In July 1927, Losh wrote to MacDonald that the engineering organization in Oklahoma was demoralized over Page's firing. MacDonald in turn wrote back that as near as he could tell pretty much everything was deteriorating rapidly in Oklahoma so far as road building and maintenance were concerned. A week later, the *Tulsa Tribune* carried an editorial to the same point: "The dirt roads of Oklahoma are each day going from bad to worse. If Johnston goes on as he is, by the time his administration is over, Oklahoma is going to be hub deep in dust in dry weather and wheel deep in mud in wet weather everywhere, except where the highway commission headed by Cyrus Avery had put the state on hard foundation before Johnston mussed the whole thing up with the smallest kind of petty politics."[24]

Even for Oklahoma, Johnston was an astoundingly unsuccessful governor. He was also something of an eccentric. He was deeply interested in the occult, and practiced astrology, numerology, and hypnosis. He hired a fellow believer in the supernatural, a Mrs. O. O. Hammonds, as his private secretary and before long, there were rumors that she was hypnotizing him and that she was the person who made appointments and signed and decided on various pieces of legislation. To make matters worse, the governor took on Mrs. Hammonds's uncle as his political advisor and word was that the uncle's counsel was based on astrology.

Even though the state senate had supported him in passing a new highway law, before the year was out, the senators had had enough. With articles of impeachment on their mind, the legislature called itself into a special session. Like Jack Walton before him, Johnston called in the Oklahoma National Guard and invoked the courts.

Locked out of the capitol, the legislators moved to the nearby Huckins Hotel and voted to impeach Johnston. Just for good measure they also voted to impeach the chief justice of the Oklahoma Supreme Court and the chair of the Board of Agriculture. The senate agreed with the charges, but before they adjourned, cooler heads prevailed. Since both the Supreme Court and the Oklahoma City District Court had already ruled once against the constitutionality of the session, on December 29 the legislators voted to drop impeachment charges and went home.

The situation festered until the following June, when Johnston was a delegate to the National Democratic Convention in Houston. As a voting delegate he endorsed Al Smith, a Catholic and a "wet." Not a good idea. Once he returned home, this governor who had been elected by Prohibitionists and the religious right spent months campaigning for Smith in all parts of the state. His constituency was not impressed. Smith lost Oklahoma by a wide margin and Republicans swept into the legislature.

As soon as the new legislature was sworn in, the house voted on thirteen articles of impeachment against Johnston. During the trial, which lasted six weeks, the governor was suspended from office. On March 20, 1929, the Oklahoma Senate convicted Governor Johnston of general incompetence and removed him from office.

Johnston's lieutenant governor, William Judson Holloway, became the state's eighth governor. One of Governor Holloway's first acts was to dismiss the five highway commissioners. He reinstated a three-member board and named Ponca City oil millionaire Lew Wentz to be chair of the Oklahoma Highway Commission. Wentz was a good pick; he resumed Cy's successful focus on road building across the state.

ELEVEN

U.S. 66 Highway Association

The appellation "Mainstreet" to the important federal highway which passes east and west through El Reno is scarcely appropriate yet, but at the rate of recent growth it will be unrivalled. Probably the most aggressive campaign ever launched to popularize a motor highway is now working upon this particular artery of traffic.

—*El Reno (Oklahoma) American*

By July 1926, the worst of the highway-numbering headaches were behind Cy, and the real headaches in Oklahoma had yet to begin, so when his friend and fellow highway promoter John Woodruff invited him to the grand opening of his posh new Kentwood Arms Hotel in Springfield, Cy jumped at the chance. He told Essie to pack a ball gown and prepared to drive his comfortable touring car over the road that now certainly would become a main artery of American travel.

Cy piloted his Packard down the highway—still rarely more than a dirt and gravel track in Oklahoma—from Tulsa through Claremore, Miami, Joplin and into Springfield. In Springfield, he followed soon-to-be U.S. 66 through town and around the central square. About a half-mile east of the square, he turned right onto a long tree-shaded drive that led to an imposing brick hotel set back from the road on a wide green lawn. Built to be a regional showplace, Woodruff's latest project boasted an immense ballroom on the top floor and open promenades at either end, plus all the conveniences that a hotel could offer.[1] As Woodruff's guests, the Averys spend three days visiting with other dignitaries and many members of the state and local media. A one point Cy drove out with Woodruff to look over the construction of newly designated U.S. 66 around Springfield. He was delighted with the progress that had been made since his historic visit three months earlier.

Like Cy, Woodruff was a veteran leader in the good roads movement. Cy had met him when both were involved with the Ozarks Trails. Later, Woodruff had been instrumental in organizing the White River Trails Association and bringing that group into the Associated Highways of America (AHA). As the two men studied the highway construction that was in progress around Springfield, their conversation naturally enough turned toward how they could promote U.S. Highway 66. Important as the highway would be to Tulsa, it would even more valuable to Springfield, which was only about a third of the size of the great oil city.

Years later, Woodruff remembered that afternoon. "He [Avery] was particularly impressed with the importance of Highway 66. I suggested that we should organize a 66 Highway Association to promote the early completion and permanent maintenance of this great highway, but we did not perfect plans at that time."[2] The two chatted about the possibility and then went back to the celebration of the Kentwood Arms.

In October, about the time that the final map of the national highway system was being drawn up to send to American Association of State Highway Officials (AASHO) members, Cy was back at the Kentwood Arms, this time without Essie, to meet with Woodruff and a handful of other local diehard road promoters. Their purpose: to see that U.S. 66 was the first cross-country highway paved from end to end. These veteran highway men were all well aware that even with federal aid funds and the public's relentless determination to have hard-surfaced roads, U.S. 66 would not become a national highway in the public's eye without their help. At least not on their time schedule.

Never one to do it with a few people if he could get a larger group involved, Cy floated the idea that the Springfield and Tulsa Chambers of Commerce should join in sending invitations to all the towns along the highway route. This would include Chicago and Los Angeles, although realistically he understood the two big cities would have less interest in promoting Route 66 than the smaller highway communities. The other men attending the meeting agreed enthusiastically. Ever the visionary, he promised five thousand cars a day on Route 66 once it was paved. "We designed Route 66 as the most important highway in the U.S. and it will carry more traffic than any other road in America," he told the eager group.[3]

Invitations to organize a highway association were duly sent out and well received. Towns along the gravel and dirt track to Los Angeles jumped at the chance to do something concrete for U.S. 66. In February Cy, by now out of a job, and the Tulsa chamber hosted a much larger-than-expected and very upbeat gathering of community representatives from five of the seven Route 66 states (California, Arizona, and Illinois were absent). Many, probably most, of the delegates were men whom he had known and worked with for years, and they had all journeyed to Tulsa with a common goal: to talk pavement.

And so the U.S. 66 Highway Association was born. Together, these promotion-minded business leaders wrote bylaws that allowed for a general membership with an annual five-dollar fee for individuals. An annual meeting would be held the second week of March. They elected John Woodruff as the first president of the U.S. 66 Highway Association, and Cy was selected as the state vice president from Oklahoma.

Cy was in fine form. He simply exuded enthusiasm for his great diagonal highway. As soon as Woodruff was elected and took the podium, Cy jumped up and presented a five-dollar bill to the secretary. "I would like the honor of being Member Number 1," he told the surprised and delighted audience. No doubt he upstaged the new president but it was probably not the first time—or the last.

Later, when the board met in executive session, they hired E. Bee Guthrey, also out of an Oklahoma state job, as executive secretary at the sum of $400 per month with "all expenses" and an automobile. They named *The Nation's Highways* as the official publication of U.S. 66 and voted to allow Guthrey to continue publishing it.

The board also instructed Woodruff to search around for a half-time corresponding secretary, suggesting he choose someone near Springfield. He selected a local public relations and promotion man named Lon Scott. The choice proved fortuitous, at least in the short term: as the result of a promotional luncheon in Oklahoma City, Scott ultimately may have been almost as responsible for Route 66's international fame as was Cy.[4]

The U.S. 66 Highway Association became a Missouri corporation on April 2, 1927. Even the legal documents were eloquent, reflecting the organizers' passion for their cause:

> The association is formed to promote the early completion and secure permanent maintenance of U.S. Highway No. 66 between Chicago and Los Angeles, commonly called "the main street of america" [sic] and to encourage the people at large to use the same, it being the shortest and most direct route between the Great Lakes and the Pacific Coast, traversing as it does the prairies of Illinois, the scenic beauties of the Missouri Ozark Region, the lead and zinc section of the Joplin-Miami district, the oil fields of Oklahoma and the Texas panhandle, the south foot hills [sic] of the Rocky Mountains in New Mexico, the Grand Canyon area, Arizona and Southern California, and to these objects and purposes we dedicate our best efforts and pledge our united support.[5]

Many years later, Woodruff wrote, "We went to work diligently and for the next few years carried on an aggressive campaign to speed up construction, popularize the highway and promote travel activity of many kinds. . . . I make no claim that the Highway 66 Association is responsible for the popularity of that highway, but I do contend that the efforts of the Association advanced its completion by several years. I have assisted in many other highway projects, but none this far as interesting as U.S. Highway 66, 'The Main Street of America.'"[6]

A gala two-day meeting in May brought hundreds of road enthusiasts to Springfield to confirm the existence of the Route 66 Association, as the U.S. 66 Highway Association became commonly known. Cy drove over with Essie and their daughter, Helen, to join the revelers at the Kentwood Arms. Hugh Stevens, vice president of the Missouri State Highway Commission, was a dinner speaker. Losh drove in from Fort Worth. Springfield's Boy Scout Band and Girls Drum Corps provided musical entertainment for the road fans and the local paper welcomed the throng to the "Main Street Conference."

Across the state, however, another road association took issue with what Cy had done. The *Kansas City Journal-Post* reported that the old Roosevelt Midland Trail had called itself the "Main Street of America" and that the new U.S. Highway 40 Association had printed all its maps and literature with the slogan, "Main Street of America." They objected vociferously to Cy's usurpation of their slogan.[7] Both associations probably had taken the phrase from early day Lincoln Highway promotion, but neither the Lincoln Highway nor the Highway 40 Association turned out to be any match for Route 66 or Cy Avery.

The Route 66 Association purchased magazine ads and put up billboards. It held meetings in as many towns along U.S. 66 as would host the meetings. Cy gave speeches at the drop of an invitation. And as soon as they had enough money in the coffers, they began printing and distributing maps—which only included the names of towns that actually paid dues to the association.

Boosterism and ballyhoo were one aspect of the Route 66 Association's work, backroom dealings was another. Men like Avery and Woodruff were always busy behind the scenes, working with city and county officials to get bond issues proposed and passed so that paving could happen. By February 1928, when Cy welcomed 150 delegates to Oklahoma City, including his sister-in-law and her husband who had driven from Joplin to represent Missouri's interests, he was able to report good results for road bonds in Oklahoma counties. When he gave his report as Oklahoma vice president, he announced, "Since this association was organized thirteen months ago, we have been instrumental in getting the hard surfacing of the road in every Oklahoma county financed except one."[8]

Finance was the beginning, but it would take ten more years before all 2,400 miles of U.S. 66 would be paved with Oklahoma being the last state to have pavement from one border to the other. Nonetheless, Cy's great diagonal highway quickly captured the nation's attention. By the end of 1928 people all along U.S. 66 were waking up to the great possibilities surrounding that mostly unpaved road that ran through the centers of their towns, that road the Route 66 Association was calling the Main Street of America.

The year 1928, in fact, was the year that made the highway famous. That was the year of C. C. Pyle's one-of-a-kind, great "International-Trans-Continental Foot Race" on Route 66. Later there were other things: migrants in the 1930s, millions of soldiers during World War II, postwar vacationers, novelist John Steinbeck, songwriter Bobby Troup, and legendary crooner Nat King Cole all added to the cachet of Route 66. After that, there was a long-running television show starring Martin Milner and George Maharis. But nothing ever matched the sheer audacity of the race that was conceived in Oklahoma City at a civic luncheon in early 1927.

After Cy stepped down from his Oklahoma state highway commissioner job, he must have gone back to work. As Roy Johnson had noted in his letter to French Gentry, Cy's business needed attention. He had a wife and daughter to support, not to mention a home, a farm, and at least one automobile. He did own the gas station, restaurant, and tourist cabins out on a section of Eleventh Street that would soon become U.S. 66, and he had two reliable business partners in his sons, Leighton and Gordon. He must have continued to buy and sell real estate during the months that he was shepherding the U.S. 66 Highway Association into being, but no matter. Business was never Cy's first concern. As soon as the Route 66 Association became a reality, he was off, traveling his highway to confer with local dignitaries or make a speech to any two people who would take the time to listen. Reporters loved him because he treated them like his special friends, and he was quick to drop everything when they called.

Throughout 1927 and 1928 the new Route 66 Association met regularly, and it met in a different 66 town every time. Sometimes Cy, Woodruff, Guthrey, Scott, and the rest would hold actual meetings, but often Scott or Guthrey would roll into town, give a speech or two, press the flesh with leading businessmen, and conduct press interviews arranged to ramp up enthusiasm for paving the highway. There was also the issue of collecting donations, which would pay for maps, signage, and more promotion. All of the officers of the association were involved in this, but for Scott and Guthrey it was personal. This was the source of their incomes.

One of Guthrey's trips to Rolla, Missouri, is a good example of the Route 66 Association at work. He met with the Chamber of Commerce board and other businessmen along with a reporter from the

Rolla Herald. His message was that this highway had the potential to become America's main street but that wouldn't happen without dollars to pay for maps and promotions. Guthrey had a vested interest in raising money, but he was also a roads booster of the first order.[9]

Scott traveled with a prepared article on the history of the highway and the Route 66 Association, complete with an alluring map of the route. The map featured line drawings of the highway's highlights, from farms in Illinois, Missouri, and Kansas to oil wells in Oklahoma and Texas, covered wagons and cactus in New Mexico, pueblos in Arizona, and palm trees on the other side of mountains in California. Both the map and article were widely reprinted in the newspapers of those remote Route 66 towns.

It was neither Guthrey nor Avery, nor Scott's clever map, however, that really made Route 66 larger-than-life in the public imagination. It was something that didn't even involve automobiles. It was a foot race. Almost as soon as Scott was hired 1927, he was at a civic dinner in Oklahoma City when someone raised the question of big-time publicity for the highway. One of the attendees, most likely Avery's friend Alec Singletary of the Oklahoma Chamber of Commerce, shouted out, "Put on a foot race!"

Scott later told his family, "So many were flabbergasted and so utterly stunned with mirth they were guffawing, 'Foot race, foot race, foot race,' and laughing as they walked out of the banquet hall. There were dozens of them—the finest gentlemen in Oklahoma, Missouri, Kansas and a few from Texas. Our business, political, and religious leaders, our civic leaders, yes our best citizens were red in the face from laughing."[10] Afterward, several reporters confronted Scott and suggested he should get in touch with a character and sports promoter named C. C. Pyle.

Everyone had heard of C. C. Pyle. He was a twentieth-century P. T. Barnum and then some. He had come out of nowhere to make a name and fortune for himself when he persuaded University of Illinois football hero Red Grange to turn pro. By the time Scott was convinced to get in touch, "Cash and Carry" Pyle as he was known, had made headlines not only with Grange but also with six-time Wimbledon winner Suzanne Leglen, whom he also persuaded to defect to professional sports. He dallied in fight promotions and the movies, married three times, wore a Charlie Chaplin mustache, and sported a flashy wardrobe that included pearl buttons on his spats. For sportswriters, Pyle never disappointed—he was always quotable and always newsworthy.

Given Pyle's reputation and his thirst for publicity, he probably didn't spend a lot of time pondering whether to take on a footrace along Highway 66. The idea was first-rate: it would be a one-of-a-kind event that would capture attention around the globe.

This was an era that was pushing the limits in all directions. Men and women engaged in outlandish stunts and extreme challenges on a national and international scale. During the 1920s Gertrude Ederle swam the English Channel. Naval officer Richard Byrd piloted a plane over the North Pole. Charles Lindbergh and Amelia Earhart both flew over the Atlantic. Women shortened their skirts and cut their hair. Flagpole sitters and dance marathons took place on a regular basis. Cross-country car trips were still a novelty, hearkening back to pioneer days when stalwarts fought their way across North America in covered wagons, but automobile, motorcycle, bicycle, and airplane races were in the news daily. Combine that national restlessness with the birth of radio, newsreels, and billboard advertising, and Pyle didn't have to think twice.

After receiving the invitation, Pyle got in touch with Scott at the association's office in Springfield, and they struck a deal: the Route 66 Association would pay C. C. Pyle $60,000 to manage the race, payable when the runners reached Chicago. Scott would sign on to do publicity.

In August 1927, the association announced that the race route had been set from Los Angeles to Chicago. That was all that mattered to Cy and John Woodruff, but that was only part of Pyle's concern. Pyle's race stretched from Los Angeles to Chicago on U.S. 66 and then went east to New York City and Madison Square Garden.

Right away, the Route 66 people commenced spreading the word. Scott and Guthrey traveled from St. Louis to California stopping at towns along the way to tout the marvels of the highway and the huge benefit to be gained from U.S. 66's Great Transcontinental Foot Race. At the Route 66 Association's annual meeting in Oklahoma City in February 1928 the upcoming race was a major agenda item.

In early January, Scott had been in Winslow, Arizona, accompanied by a couple of Pyle's representatives from New York and Chicago. At the regional Route 66 Association organization meeting, Scott talked highway talk then Pyle's men waxed eloquent on the fabulous opportunity offered by the great race. They did a good job; before the meeting even began Pyle's men had raised a $500 pledge from local businessmen to support the race to end all races.

For his part, Scott made it clear why the association was supporting the wacky event and the benefit that would accrue to local businessmen. As the *Winslow Daily Mail* put it: "The real thought . . . behind the scheme is to do some service in bringing to the attention of the motoring public of America some of the delightful features of driving, living and doing business on the Main Street of America." And whether it came from Scott or the pen of the local newspaper reporter, the end of the *Daily Mail* article said it best for all concerned: "U.S. 66 serves the greatest undeveloped areas in America and whatever the cost the men of 66 want more neighbors."[11]

Those "greatest undeveloped areas" almost were the downfall of Mr. Pyle. He was in the business of making money and counted on the small towns to ante up funds to bring the runners into their communities. He also envisioned huge crowds all along the way, despite the dearth of people in America's great Southwest.

Pyle sent out a worldwide call for athletes to compete in the race that would cross deserts, mountains, plains, and prairies, small towns and big cities—more than 3,400 grueling miles from the Pacific Ocean to the Atlantic Ocean, and expected 1,000 runners to start. The entry fee was $125—a week's wages for a factory worker—with the promise that $100 would be returned to pay for their way home when runners dropped out or the race ended. He offered $25,000 first prize, $10,000 second prize, and $48,000 more to be split among the rest of the top ten finishers. He was fascinated by the idea of such a race and he believed everyone else would be also.

He was right: the world was fascinated. Thousands of spectators, plus dozens and dozens of writers, photographers, newsreel cameramen, radio announcers, and other members of the media were crowded into

Los Angeles's Ascot Speedway on Sunday, March 4, when Red Grange lit a bomb to start the race. At the boom, 199 runners from fifteen different countries set out running east.

The runners were a motley and infinitely press-worthy lot. Among the multitudes was Arthur Newton, a forty-four-year-old British native and resident of Rhodesia, who was an ultramarathoner. Juri Lossman of Estonia was an Olympic silver medalist. Marathon winners Englishman Peter Gavuzzi, and Finns Gunnar Nilson and Willie Kolehmainen had signed on, as had Nicholas Quamawahu, a Hopi Indian from northeast Arizona. Jamaican Phillip Granville, who lived in Canada and held many Canadian distance records, wanted to add the transcontinental footrace to his roster. Dozens of college athletes had come out. Lucian Frost, an actor with a flowing beard who had played Moses in Hollywood productions, ran in long robes reminiscent of Biblical times. There was a chanting Hindu philosopher, an Alaskan mailman, and an Italian who sang operatic arias as he ran. One man played the ukulele while his two hound dogs trotted alongside. Among the crowd of runners was a young Cherokee man from northeast Oklahoma named Andy Payne, who believed if he could win the $25,000 prize money, he could buy a house and marry his sweetheart.

The Route 66 Association's idea was that with the world watching, the great race would bear a U.S. 66 imprint and garner publicity for the highway and the towns along the way. Pyle, on the other hand, probably never had any intention of sharing the spotlight. From the beginning it was "C. C. Pyle's Great Transcontinental Footrace"—until then sportswriter Westbrook Pegler dubbed it the "Bunion Derby."

Bunion Derby stuck. And Bunion Derby fit the grueling conditions that the runners had to contend with. Pyle had set distances for each day at upward from fifty miles—hard enough under optimal conditions but difficult in the extreme when the route covered a desert, prairie, or mountainous terrain. Part of the way, runners ran on newly poured cement and the promise of the highways that were to come. The rest of the way, they ran through dust, gravel, and mud.

Seventy-five runners dropped out the first day. By the time the race reached the western edge of the Mojave Desert at Victorville, California, about a third of the starters had gone home. Within weeks, the numbers declined further. At the end of every day, Pyle would send a bus back to pick up injured or exhausted runners. All in all, it was a pretty dismal event. Because of the distances, crowds were sparse and, except for Pyle's traveling radio station (whose owners later sued him for back rent), the members of the media dwindled.

Fortunately, the romance of the race plus Pyle's sheer audacity had captured the interest of a number of the nation's top sportswriters, including the likes of Pegler and Paul Gallico. They kept the world apprised of the race and of Pyle's goings on with their eloquent and acerbic commentary. Some of the commentary involved a luxurious $25,000 red bus, where Pyle and Red Grange slept and hosted dignitaries. The splashy bus contrasted sadly with the runners' mostly Spartan sleeping facilities and humdrum food.

Besides the red bus, the racers were accompanied by a miscellaneous procession of trucks, buses, and automobiles. Pyle had put together a Great Transcontinental Footrace carnival that arrived early in towns and set up before the runners came through. The caravan also boasted a traveling three-hundred-gallon Maxwell House Coffee pot that dispensed free coffee, the radio truck, and a portable hospital manned by a doctor. Runners' families drove their own cars and trucks so they could be on hand to tend to them at day's end. A millionaire in a Pierce Arrow roadster brought along a sleeping bus and two trainers for his son, who was one of the runners.

But all was not well. Pyle had assumed the towns along the way would compete for the opportunity to feed and bed the runners, but he overestimated the size and wealth of the communities along U.S. 66. The small towns in America's great outback weren't equipped to handle the crowds or, in many cases, to pay Pyle. Runners often slept on the floor of an Elks Lodge or a high school gymnasium. They ate a lot of ham and eggs and free peanut butter sandwiches from the Maxwell House Coffee wagon. Plus, to save on expenses, Pyle was routing the race over very long distances. Worst of all, there simply weren't very many people in most of the towns along Route 66. By April, news of the race itself had pretty much fallen to small articles on the sports pages.

On the other hand, the Bunion Derby remained a very big deal for the men, women, and children in those "greatest undeveloped areas" of Arizona, New Mexico, Oklahoma, and Missouri. Many of those places did their best to treat the runners like heroes. Schools closed. Police escorts accompanied the runners into and through town. Whole populations lined Highway 66 to watch the runners shoot past.

Andy Payne would have been a hero in that part of the country simply because he was an Oklahoman, but about the time that the runners reached Oklahoma, he took the lead. That was big news for the local press, and Payne was a big draw for Pyle's race. Throughout the state, crowds lined the race route to cheer him on. More than one of the towns gave a banquet for the runners, some gave them money and one of the towns commissioned Payne as police captain.

When the runners reached Oklahoma City, more than a thousand cars followed them into town and huge crowds lined the streets to welcome the athletes. At the state fairgrounds a special tent was set up for the runners, bands played, and the governor gave a prize to the first man into town. Despite the hoopla, however, Pyle's race left a bad taste in the mouths of Oklahoma City's leaders. The Chamber of Commerce had paid Pyle $5,000 to bring the competitors in on Highway 66. Pyle took the money, but the runners came in on a different road. That was bad enough, but the city had also expected a huge crowd to pay admission to greet runners at the fairgrounds and defray their payment to Pyle—and the gate only brought in $800. The *Ada (Okla.) Evening News* editorialized on the situation, noting, "If other cities were as easy marks as Oklahoma City the promoter is in a fair way to make a nice little fortune above the money paid in prizes."[12] In Claremore, things were more upbeat. Will Rogers offered his own prize to the first runner into his hometown. Into and through Tulsa thousands of people and cars lined the route to cheer the runners as they ran past. In Miami, the streets were roped off.

Schools in many towns along the way were closed so the children could watch the great race. Hugh Davis, who grew up to run the Tulsa Zoo, remembered he was eighteen or nineteen when the Bunion Derby came through his town. "They were the biggest athletes in the world. We perched up on a wall for hours and watched the runners come along." In the small town of Stroud, Eldred Condry was a schoolboy. "I remember . . . I was standing right on the curb when Andy Payne came by and all the rest of the boys. You couldn't hardly get along the main street of Stroud that day. It was something!"[13]

In Missouri, John Hulston was one of the kids let out of school to see what he remembered as

the zaniest sporting event of all times . . . which I saw come through . . . on old U.S. Highway 66 in April, 1928. By the time they got to Missouri, three-fourths of the runners had dropped out. Our favorite runner was Andy Payne, a lean 20-year-old part-Cherokee farm boy from near Claremore . . . who they said used to run against horses on Sunday afternoons. His closest rival on the day we saw them was an Englishman with a black beard who complained that motorists tried to run him down because he gained in total time on Payne. This night they stayed in Springfield, where Pyle set up a carnival-like show where people could buy souvenirs, see "Red" Grange and the runners, all for a quarter.[14]

From Oklahoma on, it was pretty much of a three-way race among Payne, the English marathoner Peter Gavuzzi, and a New Jersey merchant marine veteran named John Salo.

The runners followed U.S. 66 across the Mississippi River at St. Louis then plodded north through the Illinois cornfields into Chicago. When they reached the Windy City, there were only sixty-nine left of the 199 who had begun the race in California. And the Route 66 Association was very unhappy.

Woodruff and Avery were irate over Pyle's failure to properly emphasize U.S. Highway 66. Added to that was a string of negative publicity following Pyle himself: former business partners, former wives, and at least one girlfriend filed lawsuits for money they believed he owed them. Pyle's various amorous and financial problems seemed to be front and center in any of the newsreels or stories that mentioned the highway.

Pyle biographer Jim Reisler put it this way: "For starters, adverse publicity about Pyle's money troubles had embarrassed association officials. And not only had Pyle hogged most of the publicity—he had named the race after himself, for goodness sakes, but he had also done next to nothing to drum up attention to the wonders of traveling Route 66. Hadn't one of the major goals been to extol the joys of motor camping in the wilds of Arizona and Oklahoma?"[15]

Pyle had counted on receiving the $60,000 promised by the 66 Association as soon as he reached the windy city, but Avery and Woodruff refused to pay him. Yet as he had with every other of the many calamities that befell him during the long race, Pyle weathered his abandonment by the association with aplomb. The runners continued east from Chicago.

As the footsore group struggled on toward the East Coast, John Salo the merchant marine veteran from New Jersey, moved into second place behind Payne. This was another stroke of much-needed luck for Pyle. When the runners reached Salo's home town of Passaic with Salo in second place they were greeted by a police motorcycle escort. Banner and flags lined the highway. Thousands turned out to cheer on the runners. The town threw a parade, held a banquet, and offered Salo a job as a patrolman in the police department.

If only the runners' entrance into New York had been as welcoming. Instead of a cheering crowd of thousands, only a few dozen people were on hand to greet the fifty-five bedraggled, emaciated, exhausted men who slogged into Madison Square Garden on the evening of May 26. They jogged a final twenty miles inside the Garden—two hundred laps around the one-tenth mile track. One of them, Wildfire Thompson of Bear Hollow, Arkansas, ran around the track backward. Salo was the first to actually finish the 3,422-mile race. His time was 588 hours 40 minutes. Payne, who arrived just behind Salo, was the overall winner at 573 hours 4 minutes.

Pyle strung the runners along for an extra week before he could put his hands on prize money. Neither the income from towns along the way nor the crowds for his carnival had materialized as he expected. Before the race was over, even his shiny, red luxury bus was repossessed, although he did manage to get it back. It took Pyle several press conferences, a host of negative publicity, and a wire transfer from his California bank before he had the cash in hand. Finally, at nine o'clock at night on Friday, June 1, 1928, Pyle rewarded the ten top runners—and immediately began making plans for the following year.

Payne returned to Oklahoma richer by $25,000, married his sweetheart and as a side benefit, in November 1934 was elected and then re-elected many times throughout his life to be clerk of the Oklahoma Supreme Court. Lon Scott was not so fortunate. Even before the race began, Cy had found himself in the not-unusual position of problem solver for his highway. Scott, the highway promoter, and Pyle, the great self-promoter, were at odds.

Pyle wrote to Cy a month before the start of the race complaining mightily about Scott, who had been detached from the Route 66 Association to go on the road with the Great Transcontinental Foot Race. Scott, it seems, was spending far more time promoting the highway than the race. Pyle was beside himself, never mind that within a couple of weeks Cy and John Woodruff would believe that U.S. 66 was being shortchanged.

Not one to mince words, Pyle wrote a long letter to Cy on stationary headed "C. C. Pyle's International Trans-Continental Foot Race, Los Angeles to New York." The letterhead did not mention Highway 66. Pyle expected the association to return some of the $1,000 that he had paid Scott because he felt "we have been the victims of a plot by Scott to build up the Highway on my sporting event. . . . I am going to run the Foot Race over your Highway and I am going to give everything I promised to give this year," but he added that as far as Springfield was concerned, "the Home of the President of the Highway and the residence of the Corresponding Secretary, unless we receive our quota without any percentage proposition whatsoever, I shall not have my contestants run through and shall have them go around instead of through Springfield. . . . I shall camp them in the country and then go clear around it if it takes us fifty miles out of the route, because I think a fair deal is coming to me and I certainly am going to have it in Mr. Woodruff's and Mr. Scott's town or I will not go through it." On the other hand, he seemed to have a good relationship with Cy, thanking him for his involvement and "constructive" attitude, and adding a compliment for Guthrey, who "has done everything it is possible for a man to do, and is entitled to great credit."[16] It took all of Cy's finesse to cajole Pyle into keeping the race route through Springfield.

Regardless of who paid or did not pay whom, negative publicity, and multiple lawsuits, the Bunion Derby did bring Route 66 to the nation's attention. It became known as a highway to be reckoned with, a road of romance, and the thoroughfare that connected humdrum middle America with golden and glowing southern California. Later U.S. 66 would become a road of flight, a military road, and conduit for America's first real family vacations. In the meantime, though, the Bunion Derby moved Route 66 out of the category of being just "some highway." It was a budding symbol for twentieth-century America.

Of course, budding symbol or not, a lot of the 2,400-mile highway still needed to be paved. In mid-June, only days after Andy Payne collected his $25,000 prize money, John Woodruff suffered through his own version of the Bunion Derby to get to a Route 66 Association meeting in Flagstaff. Woodruff planned a three-day drive west in his Pierce-Arrow roadster with overnight stops in Oklahoma City and Amarillo. He was accompanied by his fifteen-year-old son, Tom, who came along for the adventure and to do some of the driving. The first day of their journey went as planned and the two reached Oklahoma City in good time. However, the next morning they ran into a rainstorm, which got worse as they drove west. By five o'clock, they were still in the rain and forty miles short of Amarillo. Other travelers warned them that Highway 66 was under repair, flooded, and impassable and told them to take a detour that would add thirty additional miles. Even on the detour, the roads were terrible, and the mud was the worst Woodruff said he had ever encountered. A few miles after a car in front of them went into a ditch, the Woodruffs' roadster slid off the road as well and would not budge. Woodruff described the rest of the trip:

> We were cold, wet and hungry but there we stayed until dawn. Even then, casting about we found no means of relief. At daylight we saw the top of a windmill about a mile ahead. We concluded there must be habitation, so Tom took the muddy road toward it. About an hour later he brought back

a farmer with two small ponies and a heavy chain. With difficulty the car was pulled back to the road, but the mud was too deep for it to go forward on its own power. I engaged the farmer to pull us into Panhandle, 15 miles distant. We arrived there around 11:00. Then we headed for Amarillo but did not arrive until after 4:00. The day was lost but we hoped we might drive on a paved highway leading west from Amarillo and reach Tucumcari during the night. We hurried on but at the New Mexico line halted to find out the road conditions on west.

A man coming out of New Mexico told me, "My God man, if it's not a matter of life and death, don't tackle it." . . . At that we turned around and went back to Amarillo. Tom remained there and I took a night train for Flagstaff arriving in time for the meeting on Tuesday morning.

In Flagstaff, Woodruff found a good crowd of highway boosters from Arizona and New Mexico waiting for him, plus a sizeable delegation from California. As he remarked, "Rain and floods may come, mud abound, but none of them now retard travel on Highway 66."[17]

At the meeting, Woodruff reported on the various successful road bond issues supported by the association—$41 million worth—and announced that the highway was completely financed from Chicago to Vega, Texas, through parts of New Mexico and Arizona and all of California. Delegates enthusiastically pledged funds to carry on the association's work, especially after they heard that the traffic increase over the past year—thanks largely to the association's promotion and advertising—was between 400 and 600 percent. The 1928–29 budget included two field men for $10,000 each, a director of publicity at $12,000 (Scott), an executive secretary (Guthrey) to assist the road bond campaigns, and a field secretary to work on airway transportation matters and raise money for maps, logs, booklets, and other advertising.[18]

The 1929 meeting of the association was held in Miami, Oklahoma, and after two years as the organization's vice president, Cy, who wasn't even present—he was in Brownsville, Texas, to celebrate the inception of airmail—was swept in as president. His supporters, only too aware of the Henry Johnston impeachment trial going on in Oklahoma City, repeatedly noted that "Cyrus Avery is the man who knows more about road conditions in this state and highway construction in general than does any other man available for the leadership of this organization."[19]

It was an interesting meeting. The Missouri and Texas delegations campaigned vigorously for Woodruff but the specter of publicist Lon Scott's issues with C. C. Pyle left some question as to whether Woodruff might also be a detriment to the association. Cy's supporters won the day. Scott was fired. Perhaps equally significant as the ouster of Woodruff and election of Cy was the related vote to move the national headquarters of the Route 66 Association from Springfield to Tulsa. It was, after all, Cy's road.

State reports at the Miami meeting confirmed good progress on hardsurfacing U.S. 66. All but one of Oklahoma's Route 66 counties had voted bond issues, Missouri lacked only ninety miles of pavement, Texas promised a good road within three years, and New Mexico reported that oiled surfaces worked better in dry climates. The highway was long-since concreted across Illinois, except for a few places that were brick.

The one hundred delegates at the Miami meeting also voted a budget of $47,300, most of which would be used to promote the road. Any town that did not pay its share would be omitted from maps and promotional literature. For the towns represented at the meeting, this threat was a strong incentive to ante up. For the 110 towns not represented (primarily from Illinois and California where U.S. 66 would never be as important as in the places in between), no contributions were expected.

For Cy, it was a season of vindication. Once again he was at the helm of a national highway organization. Moreover, the Oklahoma legislature impeached and voted Governor Johnston out of office. The charge was general ineptitude, but below the surface were two other issues. The ongoing battle between Oklahoma's Klan and anti-Klan factions was one. The other was the hash Johnston had made of the state highway department.

For the next few years, Cy continued to lead the Route 66 Association specifically and to promote highway building in general, especially for roads that would pass through Tulsa. He began to be seen as an elder statesman of the national highway system.

Ever the politician, he never turned his back on old friends and allies. Route 66 wasn't the only one of the national highways that had a booster club; in the tradition of the trails organizations, many of the towns along the cross-country highways banded together to promote "their way" west. One of particular interest to Cy was U.S. 64, the core of which was his old Albert Pike Highway and Kansas's Old Santa Fe Trail Association highway. As president of the Route 66 Association, he was invited to keynote the U.S. 64 group's convention in 1930.

Like most of his speeches, this one played to his audience and ginned up support for highway construction. First he outlined some highway history, then pointed out that the national highway system included less than half of the 7 percent of the federal aid highways, "so you can realize how fortunate you are here in Ft. Smith [where the meeting was being held] when you have two of the dominant U.S. highways, i.e., U.S. 64 and 71, on a system so restricted as the U.S. system is." He also presented his talk in such a way as to impress upon the audience his role in making that happen. Of course.

But like any preaching, that speech also involved a certain amount of discussion about money. Guthrey, who at that juncture was earning his living as a promotions man for various highway organizations, offered this bit of advice before Cy took the podium:

> No association of this character can be a success unless it maintains at least one full-time, paid man to look after its interests, and you could very forcefully and effectively say to that convention . . . they are going to utilize at least half of this paid man's time in raising his salary, that by such procedure they will necessarily reduce his effectiveness at least fifty percent. . . . Each town should have sufficient interest in the welfare of the association to look after their local finances and cooperate with the paid man in such a manner as to protect his time for association work instead of association financing. If you can in some manner work this thought into your speech you will be rendering a real service.[20]

That Fort Smith convention was a large gathering but Cy was equally likely to be seen spreading the word at a county picnic or a small town Chamber of Commerce luncheon, as he did one day in Miami when he was in town to serve as a federal juror.

After the Bunion Derby, probably the next biggest event on Route 66 was the 1931 St. Patrick's Day party in Rolla to celebrate the completion of pavement through Missouri. By this time, thanks initially to the Bunion Derby, the highway was as well known for its entertainment value as it was for being a conduit to the West Coast. The Rolla celebration just reconfirmed that image, and Cy was in the thick of it.

Rolla, a small college town midway between St. Louis and Springfield, was in a perfect location to draw people from all over the state of Missouri. St. Patrick's Day had been set as the day for the event because the local college, the Missouri School of Mines and Metallurgy, already held an annual and relatively rowdy celebration to honor Patrick, the patron saint of engineers. As the planning got down to business, Cy attended at least one meeting to give his input and gain assurance that the Route 66 Association would receive a large part of the credit for the beautiful new pavement—credit that might otherwise go only to Missouri's state highway department.

When the time came, Cyrus, Essie, and fifteen-year-old Helen motored up from Tulsa and spent the night in Joplin with Mr. and Mrs. Dolph Shaner, Essie's sister and her highway-booster husband. The next morning, all five piled into the Avery car and drove 170 miles on the fine paved highway between Joplin and Rolla.

Huge crowds poured into Rolla for the celebration, possibly as many as ten thousand people. The event headquarters was the newly completed Hotel Edwin Long, a $150,000 showplace on the edge of the highway. Parties and receptions were scheduled end to end—it was a welcome respite from the harsh realities of the nation's deep depression.

The centerpiece of the celebration was the giant parade. Cy waited on the reviewing stand with Woodruff, Missouri governor Henry S. Caulfield, and other officials as more than a hundred floats made their way slowly up the newly paved highway. The parade was a sight to behold. Two miles long, it showcased elaborate floats interspersed with high school marching bands, beauty queens, and politicians, all smiling and waving at the festive crowd from the back of shiny automobiles. On the reviewing stand, Cy was probably trying to figure out how he could pick the best float when a flatbed truck decked out with a log cabin and an old man dressed as Daniel Boone broke down right smack in front of the dignitaries.

The driver of the float with the convenient engine trouble was Lester Dill, a loose-jointed Ozarker who owned Meramac Caverns just up U.S. 66 in Stanton, Missouri. Dill was cut from the same cloth as Avery, and it was no accident that his float stopped when and where it did. "I was going to win first prize or nothing," Dill recalled years later, long after his antics had caused the national press to nickname him Missouri's Cave Man (one stunt involved a pelt-clad actor running amok in the Empire State Building). "We dressed my dad up as Daniel Boone and took a log cabin and cut it down so it would fit on the back of a truck. I drove that truck right up to the governor's reviewing stand—there were more people in Rolla than I ever saw before or since. Anyway, I stopped the truck in front of the reviewing stand and couldn't get it started again." He laughed. That gave Dill the opportunity to shake hands with Avery, the governor, and the other officials of the Route 66 Association. He won the blue ribbon.[21]

Cy was a keynote speaker that day. He told the cheering throng, "This 65 mile section of Highway 66 represents the latest and best type of concrete paving. It's completion gives 66 a continuously paved highway from Chicago to the Oklahoma line." He noted that the national highway system, now numbered and marked, "is an outgrowth and result of all the work done by the former trail associations of the Southwest."

He pointed out that the 1916 Federal Aid Highway Act, the one that essentially kicked off America's national road-building activities, had been known as the Shackelford Bill after Missouri congressman Dorsey Shackelford of St. Louis. He told the audience about a 1920 gathering of the U.S. Good Roads Association, the Bankhead Highway Association, and the Albert Pike Association, where delegates passed a resolution asking for a restriction on federal aid so as to focus on building a national system of highways. He concluded, "In the past we have spent the bulk of our time in securing construction and pavement. In the future, we expect to devote our time and attention to securing for the main street of america the proper publicity, to the end that we may best serve the traveling public to and fro over this great highway."[22] His comments were a bit premature as Oklahoma would still be laying down pavement until 1936. At the time of the celebration, however, most of Route 66 between Oklahoma City northeast to the Kansas border had been paved.

Four weeks after the Rolla extravaganza, Cy welcomed fifteen thousand delegates to the annual U.S. 66 Highway Association meeting in Elk City, Oklahoma, and presided over an announcement that all that was left to pave of U.S. 66 in Oklahoma was a seven-mile strip in Ottawa County, eleven miles in Craig County, and a one-hundred-plus-mile gap west of Oklahoma City between Clinton and El Reno. In addition to highway business, attendees at the meeting were treated to a parade, a speech by the governor's wife, and a war dance by Arapaho and Cheyenne Indians. During this extravaganza, Cy stepped down as president, ending his official highway activities on both a state and national level.

A state study that year confirmed what Cy had predicted and known all along. Between 1929 and 1930, the Oklahoma State Highway Department showed an increase of more than five hundred cars per day on U.S. 66 between the Missouri and Texas borders.[23]

In late 1930, Governor William J. Holloway, who had replaced Henry Johnston, and the state highway commission chair Lew H. Wentz officially opened the last segment of new cement pavement between Tulsa and Oklahoma City, making a three-hour trip between the state's two major cities possible, compared to a six-hour journey only a year before.

In August 1933 the last section of asphalt was put down on a stretch of highway in Craig County near Cy's old hometown of Vinita. Cy, the keynote speaker at the celebration, gave credit to the early visionaries who saw trails associations as the first step in cross-country highway building, and to the men and women who gave their dollars and time to make those roads a reality. In particular he singled out Coin Harvey, the eccentric economist who had dreamed up the idea of an Ozark Trail highway in the first place, and those days "when we built our roads with a paint brush and the enthusiasm of citizens along the way."[24]

He remained actively involved with the Route 66 Association for several years and was a ready speaker on highways in general and U.S. 66 in particular for the rest of his life. But by 1933, when he was elected president of the Tulsa Chamber of Commerce, his formal relationship with his highway had come to an end.

TWELVE

Citizen Servant

The Post-Highway Years

> The test of a man is the fight he makes.
> The grit that he daily shows;
> The Way he stands on his feet and takes
> Fate's numerous bumps and blows.
> A coward can smile when there's naught to fear
> When nothing his progress bars:
> But it takes a man to stand and cheer
> While the other fellow stars . . .
>
> — Carlyle Straub, "The Test of a Man"

Before the stock market crashed in 1929, Tulsa was a place all its own. Part frontier city, part staid midwestern community with its churches, schools, and civic organizations, but all oil town. Tulsa's character developed out of an extravagance that could only be afforded with oil riches: opulent mansions, huge automobiles, hired movie stars and opera divas, and dozens of direct connections to Washington, D.C. Tulsa even could boast being the home of Miss America, when Cherokee beauty Norma Smallwood was crowned in 1926. Not everyone was impressed.

Edna Ferber came to town in 1929 doing research for a novel about Oklahoma's early days. Tulsa's leadership welcomed her with open arms. In her whirlwind visit, she was taken to the oil fields, feted at dinners, and saw the best that the town had to offer. Oilman and philanthropist Waite Phillips threw a lavish banquet in her honor at his seventy-two-room mansion.

When Ferber returned to the East Coast, she wrote about her visit—a scathing magazine article that was dismissive of almost everything about Tulsa. The opinions she had formed about that part of the country were further reflected in *Cimarron*, the story of a thinly disguised oil boomtown on the frontier, and still later, in *Giant*, her prize-winning novel about Texas oil.

Ferber's article caused quite some consternation among Tulsans, but not for long. The big little metropolis at the confluence of the Midwest and the Great Plains went on growing, building, and bringing the world to visit. Cy, as a product of a staid eastern village, a frontier farm, and the region's early oil days, loved everything about Tulsa. He embraced it all, from the city's water problems to its bad roads to the great need for better education, and he always saw himself as a person who could make those things better for his fellow Tulsans.

Once he left the national scene, Cy refocused on his beloved city. Leadership in the Chamber of Commerce, the First Baptist Church, Rotary and the Masons were among his extracurricular activities. He purchased a DeSoto agency which he operated briefly, but closed during the Depression, and turned again to his land business.

Just months before the great crash, the *Tulsa Tribune* described Cy as "an oil man who thinks of the transportation phase of the matter and has an enviable record behind him as both a producer of petroleum and a builder of roads."[1] His oil production, they said, was in the shallow areas, and for the most part, his oil business involved the buying and selling of leases, not owning oil wells. As far as his family remembered, he had only one long-producing well. His real business was in investments and banking, and both of those were focused on real estate. Because he had grown up in Indian Territory, had lived in Vinita, and had helped build Tulsa, he probably knew more people in northeast Oklahoma and knew more about the land and land values there than anyone else. His real estate, farming, and roadwork kept him in close touch with that "home base."

His various business interests never seemed to be the real focus of his life. The promise of new technology and new ideas fed him and kept him involved in the larger political world long after most of his contemporaries had retired to long afternoons of sipping iced tea on shady porches. Cy kept working into his eighties. He also kept talking to anyone who would listen.

More than once he remarked, "I got into politics and that ruins a fellow because he gets so busy doing business for other people he neglects his own."[2]

In 1926, he wrote an article for a national real estate publication. The piece, "How to Create a Farm Land Market through Construction of Paved Highways," combined his two loves.[3]

In 1927, in the wake of founding the U.S. 66 Highway Association, he added another dimension to his vision for the future, and that was the so-called highways of the air. Aviation, after all, was already a big user of oil products, which was very good for Tulsa. And for a city on the edge of the Great Plains, aviation, like highways, offered those all-important connections to the rest of the world.

Across America, air races and feats of stamina were front-page news. Pilots were American heroes, and none more so than the handsome young aviator named Charles Lindbergh, who had made his famous flight across the Atlantic in May 1927. That was just after the Route 66 Association was incorporated, and two months before Cy, the chamber, and Tulsa decided to embrace aviation as they had embraced highways.

One of the biggest and most popular air promotions of the era was the competitive Ford Reliability Tour, a Ford Motor Company–sponsored barnstorming air competition of top aviators who raced each other from city to city for prizes. Once they landed in the target cities they put on grand air shows performing gravity-defying stunts, staging mock aerial combat, and giving plane rides to the adventurous. In July 1927, they came to Tulsa. Cy was among the dignitaries and ten thousand spectators who watched in awe as fourteen planes appeared above the horizon, circled, and landed at privately owned McIntyre Airport.

That night at a celebratory banquet on the roof of the Mayo Hotel, Cy stepped into the breach for an absent Patrick Hurley and, according to the local press, "he astonished Tulsans who have heard him speak on other occasions by barely mentioning his favorite topic of 'roads and more roads.'" Instead, he told the crowd that aerial transportation would mean more to Oklahoma than any other industrial development. Within a year, he predicted, Tulsa would have a municipal airport.[4]

Cy's speech was something of a bluff. That afternoon the manager of the Ford Reliability Tour had let the city know that Tulsa was behind the curve as far as landing fields were concerned. There were small private airfields aplenty in Tulsa, but he told the city fathers that the Reliability Tour would not return until the pilots could touch down at an honest-to-goodness municipal airport.

The Reliability Tour manager's pronouncement must have come as an embarrassment to Tulsa's leaders. However, this was Tulsa. Before or during the banquet, Cy no doubt had already had some conversation with his fellow chamber board members, and he knew as well as anyone that if Tulsa's leaders decided something should happen, it generally did. So when he stood up after the dinner that evening, his promise of an airport within a year may have been a challenge, but he knew it did not ring hollow.

After the last of the Ford tour planes roared away, the chamber's Aviation Committee set to work. Their first step was already in place, thanks to chamber president, oilman William G. Skelly. A major aviation promoter, Skelly had already invited Charles Lindbergh to Tulsa as a special guest of the upcoming International Petroleum Exhibition.

Nothing could have been planned much better. Always an over-the-top event, the 1927 exposition opened when President Coolidge pressed a button in Washington, D.C., that set off a "gusher" on the exposition grounds. Following the president's kick-off, Skelly, Avery, and thousands of other cheered and waved as America's hero came out of the sky and landed his modified Ryan M-2, the *Spirit of St. Louis*, at McIntyre Airport.[5]

Given that this was the international oil industry's confab, Lindbergh was not the only person who flew in. At least a dozen oilmen and exhibitors also arrived by air. The *Oklahoman* took note that Standard Oil of Indiana's chairman and several vice presidents winged their way in on a "giant tri-motored monoplane," as did executives of the Texas Company (later Texaco). A couple of Phillips Petroleum executives flew in from Bartlesville, a Joplin lead company, Memphis coffee firm, and a typewriter company also sent their teams to Tulsa by air.[6]

During the exposition, the Mid-Continent Oil and Gas Association held a gala banquet at the Mayo Hotel for six hundred people, including an assistant secretary of commerce and assistant secretary of the navy for aviation. Lindbergh was there as Skelly's special guest. Lindbergh spoke briefly, complimenting the city's interest in aviation, but he, too, made an observation about the city's lack of a real airport.

As a chamber vice president and an always popular speaker, Cy closed the banquet: "It's been a long time since Washington Irving came down the Arkansas River to this section of the country—almost 100 years ago in 1832 . . . and it has been a long time since our government started construction of the first road west from Boston. . . . Now civilization has stepped higher—onto the ladder of aviation. . . . Air travel means more to the state of Oklahoma than to any other in the union . . . in developing the wonderful resources of this state." He again predicted that the city would have a first-class municipal airport within a year.[7]

Cy, Skelly, and several others from the chamber formed a committee to select an airport site. In January 1928, they recommended a location in northeast Tulsa, the part of town where Cy was a leading dealer in undeveloped real estate.

The next step was pure Tulsa. Cy later recalled that a few weeks after their initial report, the committee decided to get a group of citizens together to underwrite the cost of acquiring the land and developing the airport. It was the Tulsa way of doing things.

Skelly invited potential investors to his grand home for dinner and discussion. By the time the brandy had been drunk and cigars smoked, a handful of the city's leaders pledged $200,000 toward the project.

In early May 1928, the Tulsa Airport Corporation, made up of Cy, Skelly, Waite Phillips, and a handful of other Tulsa millionaires, agreed to underwrite the purchase of 405 acres that would become the new airport. Cy's share was $10,000. Their investment was made with what was known as the "Stud Horse Note," in the tradition of groups of horse breeders who would pool funds to purchase a stallion with the expectation that their share of the expenses would be paid back out of the stallion's stud fees. Similarly, Tulsa's city fathers put up the money for a commercial airport on the expectation that they would be able to recoup their investments.

Cy observed, "The Tulsa Chamber of Commerce has been promoting paved highways in and out of Tulsa for the past ten years as one of the vital links in transportation which is so necessary to the building of a City or State. Now the Chamber . . . is backing what will be 'The Highways of Tomorrow,' namely, Transportation by Air. In no section of the United States is time of more value than to those who are in the oil business. Our natural climatic conditions and our long distances make transportation by air both feasible and economical for Tulsa and its trade territory. . . . Air transportation from the Northeast to the Southwest and West is bound to pick out the most practical route for all year flying the same as was done in selecting U.S. 66 as the most feasible and direct all year route." He was a fervent airport supporter, but his heart and interests were with roads, always. So it wasn't surprising that one of his recommendations for the new airport was that it be "south of the center of Mohawk Park and is accessible by more paved, oiled and graveled roads than any other tract of land within the vicinity of Tulsa."[8]

That was in May. Those civic leaders who were backing the new airport were in a sweat, according to Cy, to get enough of the airport developed by July to welcome the 1928 Ford Reliability air tour. But this was Tulsa. On July 3, 1928, when the Ford tour planes roared in, the airport was ready for them and the pilots helped kick off a three-day celebration.[9]

The Tulsa Municipal Airport was dedicated on July 5 and immediately opened for business. At five o'clock that afternoon, the city's first airmail flight took off carrying a 186-pound load of letters and packages. Not only did airmail represent the most up-to-date way to deliver written communication, it would also provide a vital and reliable income stream for the young airport.[10]

Less than a year later, Tulsa voters approved $650,000 in airport bonds, and in late 1930 the underwriters turned the airport over to the city to be managed by the Park Board. The deal was completed in July 1931, when Erv Deputy, assistant trust officer at Exchange Trust Company, wrote to Cy and forty-five others, who had eventually become part of the airport corporation, that "405 acres have been purchased and the city has accepted the deeds and all debts are paid in full."[11]

FATHER OF ROUTE 66

Charles Short, a World War I aviator, was the airport's first and longtime manager. Over the years he brought in many famous pilots—people like Amelia Earhart, Jimmy Doolittle, and Wiley Post, in addition to Lindbergh—and oversaw a growth in passenger traffic to rival airports in the world's largest cities.

When Short retired in 1954, Cy sent him a brief note of congratulations, noting: "Charley . . . It has always been disappointing to me and my associates who first conceived the idea of the Airport to find in all the publicity . . . the Airport began under the jurisdiction of the Park Board when in fact, as you well know better than anyone else, a bunch of us worked long and hard to produce the setup which the Park Board inherited. However, the greatest service any citizen can render to his community is to be able to initiate those faculties [*sic*] which endure to the benefit of the whole city."

Short agreed. He wrote back to Cy, "I have had a hard time getting over to the Park Board that this airport was started by the Tulsa Airport Corp., and operated two years very successfully."[12]

In 1929, thanks to Short, Tulsa was a stop on the first women's air race, the Powder Puff Derby, so nicknamed by Oklahoman Will Rogers. The Powder Puff Derby brought another group of famous aviators to Tulsa, including Earhart, Louise Thaden, Mary Haizlip, Blanche Noyes, and Phoebe Omlie.[13]

That same year, Cy and his longtime friend hotel man C. A. Mayo were passengers on a pioneering flight to Brownsville to dedicate the Brownsville International Airport and inaugurate the Mexico City to Brownsville to New York airmail route. They saw Lindbergh land in Brownsville with the first airmail from Mexico City to Brownsville and watched the city's celebratory airshow with a crowd of aviation supporters. Although Cy had been in a plane a number of times, the trip to Brownsville was his first long plane ride. "This was a wonderful trip—950 miles in one day. Some flight for us," Cy wrote later on his souvenir program from the day.[14]

During 1929, Cy moved into the public spotlight once more. While he was in Brownsville celebrating airmail, he was elected president of the U.S. 66 Highway Association, and that put him back on the road championing highway paving and travel. In Tulsa he was busy reviving his role as an advocate of agriculture. And with Governor Johnston's exodus, he was once again in demand as a "citizen servant."

Gov. William Holloway, who succeeded Johnston, named Cy to an honorary survey commission to study problems with the state's educational system and make recommendations to the state's board of education. Eight years before, he had been on another top-level educational panel, which studied the effectiveness of Oklahoma's state-supported schools. That panel's study resulted in the closing of many schools. This time, the concern focused on funding. Cy and his colleagues ultimately recommended the state make special allocations of property, income, and sales taxes to help equalize the wide variety of education programs in Oklahoma.

The next year, things began to change for Cy, and also for Tulsa. In 1930, his adored mother, Ruie Rebecca Stevens Avery, died. All his life, Ruie was Cy's touchstone. She had taught him early to love learning and to cast his nets broadly. Because of her influence and encouragement he was well versed in classic literature, but he was also a student of science and technology developments as they happened. She had taught him to be virtuous—her letters to him reflected her pride in him and his character—and she instilled in him the concept of being a "citizen servant," something he took to heart and lived most of his life. He laid Ruie Rebecca to rest next to his father in Tulsa's Rose Hill Cemetery. When the time came, he and Essie joined his parents there.

Also, in 1930, the year after the stock market crashed, the Daisy Bradford gusher in east Texas opened the country's largest oil field. Rather than being good news, the field glutted the market and drove oil prices to record lows. Agriculture had been on the ropes for years but without the underpinning of oil and other commerce, Oklahoma was left without resources to respond to the growing needs of her citizens. Cy's own business was suffering, but as a member of the chamber's board, he spent a good portion of his time and effort helping lead the city's fruitless attempts to provide relief. Will Rogers gave benefit concerts and private agencies did what they could, but it was never enough.

As the months passed, the drought and Great Depression ground deeper and deeper into the Oklahoma economy. Farmers in eastern Oklahoma were hurting. As a farmer himself, Cy knew only too well the problems of dried-up stock ponds, parched feed crops, and hungry livestock. He created and then became chair of a chamber committee aimed at supporting agriculture in northeast Oklahoma. That put him on the speakers' circuit for real, and he combined his highway promotion talks with talks on agriculture, the other subject close to his heart.

Mostly when he went out in those days he talked about grasses. In February 1931 he traveled to his friend Will Rogers's hometown of Claremore to keynote a twenty-one-county gathering on the farm situation. Nearly two hundred people listened as he traced the history of farming in northeastern Oklahoma from the days when local Indians did what he called "ranch farming" to tenant farming and then statehood, when he declared—for the moment ignoring the ruinous drought—that "this has become one of the best agricultural sections of the great Southwest."

When he did finally acknowledge the disastrous agricultural economy he said, "My answer to that is the answer made by the old farmer when asked one time during a long continuous wet spell if he thought it would ever quit raining. His laconic reply was, 'it always has.' We are more prone to listen to good advice when conditions are bad than when they are good. . . . If in the next ten years we can be assured of even twenty-five percent of our tillable land being put into meadow grasses, alfalfa and red clover, and on each farm we can find a dozen dairy cows, 100 good laying chickens and four or five brood sows, we will double the taxable wealth of farms in these twenty-one counties."[15]

In June, he was in Eufala, talking again about tame grass meadows. In August, he was guest speaker when the Chelsea Chamber of Commerce and the high school's vocational agriculture department held a meeting to encourage tame grass meadows and pastures for the depleted farmland in that area.

The *Miami News Record* described him as "a successful businessman, a man who has adopted the same sound, practical policies to agriculture and livestock raising that he has always followed in other lines of business." The paper asked him to write a letter to the farmers of the region. He of course complied and repeated his message: "If every farmer would only learn that we cannot produce livestock (cattle, sheep, hogs, horses and chickens) without good hay meadows we would have a more prosperous set of farmers and a better class of livestock. . . . I maintain that you can grow Kentucky bluegrass, timothy, red clover, alfalfa, all the legumes and all the meadow grasses on every bit of either the prairie or river bottom land in your county."[16]

When the Oklahoma City packinghouses warned about a dearth of choice beef cattle, Cy suggested farmers raise "dual purpose cows," like the Milking Short Horn or the Brown Swiss, and used that recommendation as an opportunity to encourage farmers to plant good pastures. He saw livestock and pasture as a profitable combination for any farmer—as it was for him.

Throughout the dry years he continued to write and lecture on the value of planting grasses, whether in hilly, green eastern Oklahoma or in the Great Plains country around Enid and Elk City. Orchard grass, sweet clover, and Kentucky bluegrass were the trinity that he would invoke at every opportunity. In 1933 the Tulsa chamber published the first of two monographs that he wrote on the subject.

By the winter of 1932, tenant farmers were working more than half the state's 1.5 million farms and more than 300,000 urban Oklahomans were out of work. In the national election that fall, every county in the state voted for Franklin Roosevelt. The New Deal kicked in by mid-1933 with federal relief programs, bringing at least some respite to desperate people. Thousands of unemployed Tulsans found a lifeline in jobs with the Civilian Conservation Corps if they were young or the Work Progress Administration (WPA) if they were adults.

During this time, Cy got involved in a long shot, an ultimately unsuccessful effort to bring money and jobs to northeast Oklahoma. Working with the Isaac Walton League, he petitioned the U.S. Forest Service to develop a 65,000-acre hardwood forest in northeastern Oklahoma, in his old stomping grounds in Delaware and Mayes Counties south of Spavinaw.[17] Later, he worked with better success to convince Tulsa to build a stockyard.

In 1933, having been a board member, vice president, and chair of the agriculture and aviation committees of the Tulsa chamber, Cy was elected president. While it did not carry the weight it had a decade before, and the budget was minimized so as to funnel chamber funds into local relief efforts, that august organization was still the most important civic group in town. From the vantage of chamber president, he threw his hat in the ring as a Democratic candidate for governor in the 1934 election.

He had been active in party politics all his life. In 1919, when Pres. Woodrow Wilson came to Tulsa, he was a member of the welcoming committee. When Oklahoma made a bid for the 1928 National Democratic Convention, Cy was one of a select group that went to bat for the event. The group included a former national committee man, president of the University of Oklahoma, former attorney general, and Tulsa's mayor. Ultimately, the convention was held in Houston and selected Al Smith as party standard-bearer. Given Oklahoma's dry laws and Klan history it was probably best the convention was not held in Tulsa.

As the 1933 governor's race began to take shape, a local newspaper columnist opined: "As usual, this gubernatorial campaign will be the most torrid in history. They always are."[18]

If not torrid, the campaign was at least crowded. When Cy did announce his intention to run for governor he was one of nearly a dozen Democrats in a diverse field including former governor Jack Walton, who had been impeached. As always in Oklahoma, it was the Democrats who mattered. Cy was described as one of the conservatives running.

Despite his Democratic activities and service as highway commissioner under a Democratic governor, Cy's campaign was not a success. That was due, at least in part because his past came back to haunt him. A letter to the *Oklahoman* had pointed out that "if my memory serves correctly, in the campaign of 1926 he electioneered and did everything in his power for his brother Tulsan, the late Mr. Benedict, Republican nominee for governor against the Democratic nominee, Henry S. Johnston of Perry . . . in the last campaign got out and worked for a Republican and against a Democrat after a vote of the people had nominated the Democrat. He also came to Garfield County and campaigned for an Independent. I did not think Mr. Avery would have the nerve, after bolting his party nominee, to come before the Democrats and ask for their support."[19]

Cy's platform was one geared to the times with planks that would appeal to people with economic woes and the elderly. He was sixty-two that year and, like most Americans, worried about money. He called for a reduction in the cost of government, reduced taxes, adequate old-age pensions, and homestead exemptions. True to his passion for road building, he also called for repeal of a law that had diverted gasoline tax from highway department funds.

Cy did what he could to drum up votes, even pandering to two hundred state peace officers who were meeting in Tulsa. In his speech to them he called for a statewide police system. "A state force properly officered and chosen on merit, protected in their jobs by civil service and aided by sheriffs and city police systems, could rid the state of robbers and petty thieves in a short time," he orated.[20] It didn't help.

In fact, he never had a chance for the Democratic nomination. He got lost in the crowded field, polling less than 3,000 votes in a race where Congressman E. W. Marland, who ultimately won the governorship, received 111,301. Even former governor Walton brought in more than 60,000 votes in the primary.

Cy was disappointed but as usual, he carried on. Four years later he worked long and hard on his friend W. S. Key's also-unsuccessful Democratic campaign for governor. And before he was finished, Cy took one more crack at electoral politics. In 1944, he ran for a third term as Tulsa county commissioner. He lost. "I polled 4,000 votes," he later wrote on his certificate of nomination. "More than President Roosevelt and lost by 4,000 to the Republican."[21]

Politics of various kinds and a career in real estate are not the best way to weather the nation's worst depression. Cy's fortune dwindled. Avery and Sons Real Estate, which had dealt primarily in land rather than improved property, was dissolved during or immediately after the Great Depression.

"In a business like that, there would have been an extensive use of leveraging," pointed out Cy's grandson and namesake, Cyrus Stevens Avery II, known as Stevens, a Washington, D.C., finance executive.

"That sort of business is great when prices are rising and times are good, but it works as drastically against you in reverse."[22]

Cy's daughter-in-law, Ruth Sigler Avery, was of the same opinion. "He bought a lot of land on the margin in the twenties and thirties. This cost him the loss of several fortunes when the depression hit Tulsa hard in the mid-thirties."[23]

The chamber gave him free use of an empty office.

Most of Cy's dealings in the oil and gas world were in leases as a broker, another profession that could not withstand the ravages of the Depression. Fortunately, at least one of his oil wells continued to produce—although at Depression oil prices it provided a meager income at best—and he still had the gasoline station and other businesses on the edge of U.S. 66. Because of the kind of man he was, he was able to maintain friendships and longtime business connections, and he remained active in public life. Cy's economic situation, however, was never again as comfortable as it had been before the Depression, and never again would the media refer to him as one of Tulsa's millionaires.

Probably worse than any actual loss of income, Cy had to tell his beloved Helen, who was a student at the University of Oklahoma, that he could no longer afford her tuition, room, and board. Helen returned to Tulsa and moved back into her room in the house on Owasso Street. But Cy never faltered. His grandson Stevens remembered, "He had a sense of self that kept him going. He was a real optimist who lived in the present and looked to the future."[24]

Cy regularly advised others always to live "so you have good health, and have ants in your pants!" Personally, he adopted a philosophy based on a quote from English poet and philosopher Joseph Addison. It was a more formal version of the same sentiment, and one that stood him in good stead for many years: "The secret of happiness is having someone to love, something worthwhile to do and something to hope for.." For Cy, that quote seemed to serve as his life philosophy: He was a strong family man, always busy with a project that he deemed useful to the larger society, and he was always looking to the future.[25]

As he once told the Pryor Chamber of Commerce, "Money isn't enough for each person to give if the community is to progress. Each person must be willing to give his time and his effort. That makes the community."[26]

Another thing that kept Cy going was Spavinaw. All his life he would slip away to the country where he had grown up, sometimes to hunt or fish, sometimes to bring friends to one of the various places he owned, or to visit his sisters who lived nearby.

Years later, he wrote about his Spavinaw connection to Mary C. Boudinot, a descendant of Elias Boudinot and distant relative of Stand Watie. She had written to the mayor of Tulsa inquiring about the original Watie homestead, and the letter eventually found its way to Cy. The house, he told her, had burned during the Civil War, and his father had built a new one around one of the standing chimneys. Cy and A.J. lived on the Watie homestead for about four years, he wrote to Ms. Boudinot, but after his mother and sisters arrived, his father purchased a farm on the Elk River near Noel, Missouri, and they left Indian Territory.

Sometime later, Cy bought the Watie property along with forty-five acres of land. For several years he operated it as a free-range ranch and used the house, which he had fixed up a bit, as a retreat for hunting and fishing trips. The house and land eventually passed out of his possession, and later the property was incorporated into Tulsa's Spavinaw water project.[27]

After he sold the Watie property, his trips to Spavinaw were either with friends, to a family cabin owned by his sister Bertha, who had married a local physician, or to Rockwood, the cabin of a distant cousin. Cy's grandniece Rose Stauber remembered his visits during the years she was a girl growing up on the Elk River farm. Cy would come by the farm for a quick visit, then take her grandmother Carrie to pick up Bertha, and the three siblings would go to the Spavinaw cabin for a day or so.

Back then, Rose remembered the adults talking among themselves that "Cy always needed money." Given that his basic business was a constant gamble, that's probably true. Nonetheless, he remained undaunted.[28]

His Democratic connections came through for Cy in 1935. General William Key, his old friend from the Trapp administration, World War I veteran, former prison superintendent, and former National Democratic Committeeman, was head of the Oklahoma WPA. Key appointed Cy to be WPA director for the thirteen-county First District in eastern Oklahoma.

Cy's WPA appointment was greeted with strong support in Oklahoma, generally because, as one letter of congratulations put it, "You are richly qualified for the job, but also because of the splendid part you have played in the furtherance of highways throughout the state and your great and continued interest in the farmer and his agricultural problems."[29]

"We need men like yourself in these positions," wrote a grocer in Vinita named G. H. Martin. "We have so much politics in our state and Federal business that it is very difficult to accomplish much. But I feel you will try and do some good. If you can get your local appointees outside of our political setup I believe we will accomplish more."[30]

Martin's letter was all too prescient. Cy and his WPA teams accomplished a great deal while he was a WPA director, but ultimately politics got in the way—again.

Governor Marland, who had trounced Cy in the Democratic primary just a year before, was against Cy's nomination, although he didn't file any official opposition. WPA field representative M. J. Miller, on the other hand, had also been against the Avery appointment and let General Key know it. He wrote to Key from his office in New Orleans: "You will recall that Mr. Avery was discussed at the Dallas meeting and in view of the facts presented then we do not feel that Mr. Avery is especially qualified for this position and we are therefore not inclined to approve him. Our suggestion is that some other person better suited and qualified for the position be selected and submitted to this office."[31]

Despite the opposition, Cy was in, and he undertook the new assignment with his typical enthusiasm and equally typical effectiveness. He hired unemployed people to build roads, civic buildings, and schools. He worked with the state health department on community sanitation and malaria control. He was also contacted by the Oklahoma Historical Society regarding putting up markers along the roads in the places where Oklahoma joined other states. He began with a marker at the Oklahoma-Missouri-Kansas junction.

Given the drought across the Midwest, he and his team built small dams to conserve what water was available. At one point Cy put his crews to work on dam sites approved in eight counties of the thirteen in his region.

In April 1937, he drove over to Pryor to dedicate the new WPA school building. He was well liked there and had a lot of old friends from his days in nearby Vinita and his work on the Spavinaw project. As Oklahoma highway commissioner he had seen to the paving of Pryor's Main Street. As regional WPA director, Cy had sent work crews across Mayes County to construct better roads, stock pond dams, schools, community buildings, bridges, and school gymnasiums. He even oversaw building a new water works plant in Pryor.[32]

In May 1937 Key stepped down from his WPA position to accept an appointment as major general in the Oklahoma National Guard and commanding officer of the U.S. Army's Forty-Fifth division. Without Key's support, things changed drastically for Cy. In much the same way they had helped usher him out of his highway commission position, newspapers reported on his WPA tenure in excruciating and misleading detail. Among the low-water dams his WPA crews built on various farms was one on property Cy held title to in Nowata County, just northeast of Vinita. When he purchased the property another relief organization, the Civic Works Administration (CWA), was half finished building that low-water dam. Given the situation, he concluded that he was justified in using the WPA crew to finish the job and even did it over the winter when no other work was available. The dam was the momentum that Miller, the WPA official in New Orleans, needed to justify pushing Cy out. He charged that Cy had co-opted his WPA crews to build the pond on his own farm and moreover that Cy's crews had also paved a road past E. Bee Guthrey's farm. What Miller didn't mention was that during his tenure Cy had employed as many as eighteen thousand people at one time and his WPA crews built $6 million worth of roads, dams, school buildings, disposal plants, city halls, court houses, armories, and various other projects.[33]

The charge against Cy was infuriating. E. L. Heiser, who had been head of the Nowata County Civil Works Administration and had overseen the beginning of the low-water dam project, wrote an open letter in the *Ada (Okla.) Evening News* "for the benefit of any investigators and also for the information of the virtuous (?) [*sic*] citizens bringing the charges." Heiser went on to list, step by step, his role in developing the Nowata County farm pond program to benefit local livestock. When he discovered that Cy's property was not locally owned, he called Cy to get his approval to build the dam. When Heiser resigned in June 1935, the job was about three-quarters complete.[34] This was about the time of Cy's WPA appointment. Even the *Tulsa Tribune*, which published an article about all of this, noted that formerly accepted activities were now being used against Avery.[35]

News of the brouhaha brought Cy's supporters out in force. Oklahoma's Democratic National Committee man Scott Farris sent a telegram to DNC chair James Farley in Washington, D.C., that "a very unfair fight is being waged against our long time acquaintance Cyrus S. Avery. His removal is being sought and charges are being made against him on ground that a pond was constructed on an obscure worthless 160 acres of land in northern Nowata County. . . . I hope you will see that no harm comes to Mr. Avery on this unjust charge."[36]

In Washington, D.C., Sen. Elmer Thomas asked WPA head Harry Hopkins to look into the situation. Former governor Trapp wrote to Oklahoma's other senator, Josh Lee, that the WPA regional office head was not only not sympathetic to Trapp's and Avery's brand of conservative Democrats but in the last election "had appeared to favor the other side."[37]

Other letters poured into congressional offices but to no avail. By the end of the month, Cy and his old sidekick Guthrey, whom Cy had hired as project statistician, were once more out of office.

Cy's public response was befitting a man who had been called "a stormy petrel" when he was highway commissioner. "I may be a damned fool," he said of the farm pond project, "but I'm not a crook."[38]

Not long afterward General Key wrote to Guthrey that it had been an unfortunate situation, adding, "You realized that the Regional Office was unfriendly to you both. My feeble efforts together with the fine work which you have both accomplished forestalled any drastic actions until I severed my connection with the program."[39]

The whole messy situation was "just politics," a game that Cy knew all too well, but it stung nonetheless. Especially since he needed the job.

Guthrey wrote as much to Ron Stephens, the man who succeeded Key at WPA. A real injustice had been done to Avery, who had produced results in excess of any pay he received, Guthrey wrote. "Our political enemies have achieved a temporary victory but they have neither dented our honor nor diminished even in the slightest degree our loyalty to the administration."[40]

Guthrey wrote to Cy that same day. "A fellow can't play tag all his life without being 'it' once in a while. We know and most of our friends know that we have been poked with the dirty end of the stick, but we also know that we got along fairly well before the WPA came into existence and that in all human probability we will continue to rock along without taking out a work card or looking out for the commodity truck."

And like the loyal lieutenant that he was, Guthrey finished his letter with advice to Cy: "Take a good rest. You need it. Call any time you need me."[41]

Key also wrote, remarking that Cy "faced many problems in the Tulsa District that did not exist in other areas. When you get rested up I hope that you will bring your good wife and spend a weekend with Mrs. Key and me. We number you among our closest friends, and would feel honored to have you visit us often."[42]

Despite the way it turned out, his WPA experience was not all bad for Cy. In 1945, when Key was head of the Allied Command in Hungary, Cy wrote the general that he periodically ran into people from the old WPA days. "I do not know just what it was about that organization but they are always as glad to see each other as old college chums would be."[43] Cy and Key stayed in close touch until 1959, when Key died at the age of sixty-nine.

By the late 1930s, the worst of the Great Depression was easing, but life was still difficult in Oklahoma, a land that depended on farming, which was barely surviving, and oil, which was seeing a glut and the lowest prices in many years.

For the next several years, Cy immersed himself in his business, his farm, and his family. During this period his real estate company, Avery and Sons, was disbanded, with Gordon and Leighton each going their own way, and Cy working on his own. The much-loved house on Owasso Street was sold; Cy and Essie moved several times, finally settling into a two-bedroom apartment in a building in the same general neighborhood.

Daughter Helen was married to a young Douglas Aircraft executive, and Gordon produced two grandchildren for Cy and Essie, both boys. Not long afterward, Leighton and his wife, Ruth, would give them two granddaughters. Cy was thrilled. His family was always important to him and he was especially proud of his grandchildren, taking pains to spend time with them as they grew up.

A few years later, he suffered what was probably the worst blow of his life. In December 1943 his son Gordon died, leaving a wife and two young sons. In a letter to his friend Key, Cy reported that it was "quick pneumonia. . . . He had been very successful the last year and was just beginning to be self-sustaining. His death complicated my affairs considerably."[44] The close-knit family faced another separation of sorts in 1945, when Helen's husband, R. C. Berghell, who had been general manager of the Tulsa Douglas Aircraft Company plant, was transferred back to the home office in southern California. Not long thereafter, they gave him another grandson named Bob, after his father.

Around 1940, Cy acquired several hundred acres of land west of Tulsa. "Six hundred acres of grasses and two dogs" was how he described Lucky Ranch on Coyote Trail near Sand Springs. Here, he raised cattle and continued his longtime study of various kinds of grasses. The farm was described by a reporter as "The lushest grass I have ever seen." and Cy was described as a "nature lover, conservationist and lazy" in the best sort of way with a philosophy that boiled down to "let the cows do the work."

Cy remained convinced that "if on every farm in Oklahoma, one-fourth of the land was devoted to meadows, clover, alfalfa and sweet clover fields, we would have less chattel mortgages on our livestock as well as our own farms. Forty acres of meadow, a few hogs, and a few milk cows will make of every farm an institution which pays and one which will be good every year regardless of dry weather or the boll weevil"[45] He was a proponent of this philosophy throughout his life, and never tired of bringing friends and business acquaintances to his farms to see the results of his work, share a barbecue meal, and tell stories into the night.

The Coyote Trail property had a little house, not more than a shack actually, and good land for cattle and grasses. At the time he said that his ambition for the ranch was "to prove you can put every known tame pasture plant into a native meadow, and never plow the land or use mechanical planting."[46]

It was also a place, like his old farm on Route 66, by now subdivided and sold, where he could bring friends and cronies and where he hosted his grandchildren. Granddaughter Joy Avery remembered those days. "The ranch had cattle and horses. The house there, it was more of a log cabin, had three steps up to the front door, then a big room with a fire-place and a bedroom with a four poster iron bed. It had a big wood stove. All the furnishings were leftovers and seconds that had been given to him. It was a place where kids could run around, ride horses and fish. He made sure we didn't get bit by snakes, or get poison ivy or drown in the pond. He'd cook for us. It was a wonderful way to grow up."[47]

Gordon's son Stevens, who was a decade older than Joy, also relished his visits to the ranch. "We would spend the night. He'd do the cook-ing. I'd get to ride horses, swim in the pond au natural. He'd tell sto-ries, especially about his hunting trips in Colorado. He'd tell us what they hunted, and he'd go into great detail." Stevens and his brother Allen hung onto every word.[48] Bob Berghell, the youngest of the grandchil-dren, often spent whole summers in Tulsa with Cy and Essie. The best part of those vacations, he remembered, were the days he spent at "The Ranch."

It was not unusual for Cy to leave a business dinner or a family gather-ing and drive out to the ranch for the night or a couple of days. All his life he needed to stay in touch with the land.

By the mid-1940s prosperity had come back to Tulsa. During the war years, Tulsa had grown to the point that people were even beginning to talk about enlarging the water system. This time there was no contro-versy; they went back to Spavinaw. The second Spavinaw project began in 1948 without much fanfare, and water began running out of Tulsa faucets in 1952. Like the first Spavinaw project, this endeavor called for a dam on Spavinaw Creek—this one upstream from the original—laying a second pipeline to Tulsa and enlarging the reservoirs in Mohawk Park. Because technology had advanced, the engineers also installed pumps to speed water flow along the way.

Just like the first time, Tulsa called on Cy, by now in his late seventies, to head the negotiating team that would secure right-of-way for a second fifty-five-mile water line. His rich dark hair had thinned considerably and turned white, and he wore thick glasses now, but he was still energetic and full of enthusiasm. Cy accepted the challenge.

He began work at a salary of $500 per month plus a car and expenses. As with the original Spavinaw project, part of the job involved buying and moving a whole town. This time the town was the little Cherokee community of Eucha, for which the second lake was named. Unlike the project to move the village of Spavinaw, relocating Eucha involved relocating a cemetery, where Union Civil War hero and Cherokee chief Oochalata, or Charles Thompson, was buried. During the negotiations about moving the cemetery, the city reassured the tribe that all proper steps would be taken and that no one would be reburied in water. The city even agreed to work with the tribe's cemetery committee and dig several test graves, which they could watch to make sure none filled with water. But, as the local paper reported, "the question no one at the pow-wow could answer came from an old Cherokee woman, wrinkled and stooped with her years: 'When the government moved our people from Georgia in 1830, they said we would not be bothered again as long as the grass grows and the river flows. Why are they moving us now?'"[49] The rest of the project was unremarkable.

The Spavinaw job brought Cy back in contact with his old friends at the Lock Joint Pipe Company. He had met the Lock Joint people nearly thirty years before when they had fabricated the huge pipes for the original Spavinaw flow line. While he was Oklahoma highway commissioner, Lock Joint supplied many of the pipes for highway culverts and other roadwork. They got along well. He appreciated their products, and they appreciated the projects in which he was involved.

In mid-1949, Cy had a chance to visit Lock Joint president Allen Hirsch and tour the company's headquarters and plant in New Jersey. After he returned home, he wrote a letter to Hirsch with a suggestion. Why not build a fabrication plant in Oklahoma? Not a temporary plant like the one that had been built at Verdigris in the twenties to turn out the pipe for Tulsa's water system but a permanent, regional fabrication site? Concrete, by this time, had found uses not just for pipe and road construction but also for building blocks and even for whole buildings. He outlined opportunities that he foresaw in Tulsa and Oklahoma City, noting that he and Leighton were currently embarked in a fourteen-unit apartment house that would be built 90 percent of concrete blocks, that in his WPA days he had used concrete in sewer tile for thirteen counties, and that the need for concrete tile in road construction was still on the increase.

He suggested to Hirsch that "with my background and the many years interested in the city, county and state construction I am in a position, together with the assistance of my son, to get our share of the sale of all these products." He wondered further whether Lock Joint would be "interested in joining me in the manufacturing of these materials."[50] The suggestion was met favorably in New Jersey. After some negotiation, part of which involved a narrower definition of what Cy's role would be and part of which involved a request for sales commissions on top of a salary, the deal was done.

In 1950, when the second Spavinaw project was well under construction and Cy's part in it was winding up, he resigned from the water assignment to take a position with Lock Joint. In his letter of resignation he wrote that he had been offered a position, "which is greatly to my advantage financially."[51] In fact, the job was a godsend; he really needed the money.

Shortly after Cy joined Lock Joint, he invited the city fathers of Oklahoma City to come to Pryor and Spavinaw to inspect Tulsa's water supply and no doubt consider doing business with the company. Cy was in top form, and as was his style, he entertained the visitors at a fish dinner with plenty of good conversation and storytelling. Regardless of what other drinks were served that night, it's a sure bet there was plenty of clear fresh Spavinaw water for the Oklahoma City leadership.

As Cy had suggested, Lock Joint built a major concrete fabrication plant just outside Tulsa, in Sand Springs. When the new plant was finished, he and plant manager Thomas Nelson sponsored an open house and barbecue for friends and potential clients. For Cy, this was business as usual, and even at his advanced age he was a natural. He loved to talk but he also loved to listen, and he was always interested in learning what was about to happen. He was Lock Joint's Oklahoma sales manager for eight years.

His yearly trips to attend the company's annual meeting in New Jersey also offered an opportunity to visit family on the East Coast. Once, he took time to stop by West Point where his grandson Stevens was a cadet at the U.S. Military Academy. Another year, he went back to Stevensville and to Camptown, where his father had been born. On returning home, he wrote to a cousin in Pennsylvania, "I felt a little like Rip Van Winkle walking around there after all these years. I also visited the place where Dwight [another cousin] and I built a splash dam and he installed an undershot wheel so that we could operate a small sawmill."[52] Water projects, it seems, were part of Cy's life practically from the beginning.

In 1958, at the age of eighty-seven, Cy finally retired. By this time, as one of Tulsa's elder statesmen he was regularly sought out by members of the media for his perspective on days gone by. Almost yearly, someone would come to talk with Cy about one of his three favorite subjects: agriculture, highways, or water. When he began to answer their questions and share his memories, he would lean back in his chair or better yet invite the reporter out to the ranch for a really good conversation.

The subject of water for Tulsa continued to be important to him, and like his views on agriculture, his opinions about Tulsa's water supply foreshadowed early twenty-first-century thinking. For one thing, Cy did not believe that the authorities were taking the issue nearly seriously enough. In 1956 he wrote to Tulsa attorney John R. Woodward that "there is a lot of misinformation going around now days. . . . One thing interesting is we manufacture everything in the State of Oklahoma but do not have any plans for making water."[53] He also noted in that letter the arrival of Cyrus Stevens Avery III, his first great-grandson. The baby's father was Gordon's son and his namesake. Stevens.

On Cy's ninetieth birthday, back from daughter Helen's home in Los Angeles to attend a birthday party thrown by some of his old friends, he told a reporter it was past time to build a dam on the Illinois River. "We shouldn't wait for an emergency. We've always done that. If I were in on it I'd immediately get a bond issue before the people and proceed to build the Illinois dam. Quit worrying about water for industry. . . . We don't want industry that uses billions of gallons of water . . . We need to get those small, growing electronics and missile industries. They're all over the west. It's a jet age we're living in now, not a water age. We've got to make Tulsa a place where the average man can live."[54] The reporters marveled at Cy: here, they wrote, was a person still looking to the future at an age when most men spend their time satisfied with memories.

There were memories too, of course, plenty of them. As one of the prices of a long life, Cy watched as his old friends died off. In 1949, when hotel impresario Cass Mayo died at seventy-one, Cy was one of six active pallbearers. There were more than thirty honorary ones.

In 1950 when the Tulsa Historical Society unveiled an oil portrait to commemorate his newspaperman friend Eugene Lorton, Cy made the presentation. In 1951 former governor Trapp, his friend and political benefactor, was buried in Oklahoma City with a funeral that, according to the press, was held "with the state political leaders of the twenties paying final respects." The news report praised Trapp for being the "father of state highway building,"[55] but the real father of state highway building was an honorary pallbearer. In 1952 R. A. Singletary, who along with Cy had been an early and important highway supporter, passed away. In 1957 architect Charley Thomas of Albert Pike Highway days died in Colorado Springs.

Despite the milestones that are inevitable for those who live many years, Cy's life was far from dismal. In 1958, more than forty years after he began building roads in Tulsa County, he received news that the county commission had changed the name of River Road to Avery Drive. When he heard the news, he observed, "Forty years is a long time but it only goes to show that anyone interested in roads should never quit."[56] Cy Avery never did. He never even slowed down.

Avery Drive and, more than fifty years after that, Tulsa's Cyrus Avery Centennial Plaza, were nice touches, but when he died in 1963 just short of his ninety-second birthday, Cy already had his monuments. One was water for Tulsa. The other was something he created himself out of whole cloth and a belief that the road to Tulsa's future should be a highway that went through the middle of town and stretched from the shores of Lake Michigan on the northeast to the shores of the Pacific Ocean on the west.

Today, generations of people around the world know Cy Avery. If not by name, they know him by his legacy because, more than anything else, he was the father of U.S. Highway 66.

Notes

Abbreviations

AASHO   American Association of State Highway Officials

Avery Papers   Cyrus Stevens Avery Papers, Department of Special Collections and Archives, Oklahoma State University, Tulsa Campus Library, Archives and Special Collections

BHP   B. H. Piepmeier, Missouri State Highway Engineer

BPR   Federal Bureau of Public Roads

CSA   Cyrus Stevens Avery

EWJ   E. W. James, chief of design, Federal Bureau of Public Roads

NACP   National Archives at College Park, Maryland. Records of the Bureau of Public Roads 1920–39, Record Group 30

THM   Thomas H. MacDonald, chief, Federal Bureau of Public Roads

WCM   William C. Markham, executive director, American Association of State Highway Officials (AASHO)

Chapter 1

1. Troup, "Get Your Kicks on Route 66."
2. *Oklahoma*, 35.
3. Harlow, *Oklahoma Leaders*, 154.
4. Parins, *Elias Cornelius Boudinot*, 191–92.
5. Goble, *Tulsa!*, 30–31.
6. Stauber, "You Could Take Cyrus Avery Away from His Roots," 2.
7. Wallace, *Pennsylvania*, 164.
8. Wallace, *Pennsylvania*, 167.
9. "1867–1900—The Eads Bridge," *Riverweb*, accessed August 21, 2011.
10. CSA to Mary Boudinot, letter, January 23, 1956. Cyrus Stevens Avery Papers, Department of Special Collections and Archives, Oklahoma State University, Tulsa Campus Library, hereafter Avery Papers.
11. Joy Avery interview.
12. CSA, speech to Sheriff & Peace Officers Association of Oklahoma, typed manuscript, January 8, 1934, Avery Papers.
13. Ibid.
14. Stauber, "You Could Take Cyrus Avery Away from His Roots," 4.

15. Ruth Avery interview.

16. Stevens Avery interview.

17. Harlow, *Oklahoma Leaders*, 158.

18. "28 Years Ago in Pryor Creek, IT," *Pryor Creek Review*, 1897, n.d., Avery Papers.

19. CSA to Ruie Rebecca Avery, letter, n.d., Avery Papers.

20. "Stag Party for Mr. Brooks," *Daily Oklahoman*, January 3, 1904.

21. *The Man Who Never Disappoints, Fred Emerson Brooks*, flyer, accessed August 7, 2013.

22. CSA, quoted in Harlow, *Oklahoma Leaders*, 158.

23. Avery was an active fraternity alumnus for most of his life. Sinclair information from "Fijis in the Spotlight," 14.

24. "Then/Now," *Tulsa Tribune*, February 6, 1957.

Chapter 2

1. "Education (1880–1941)," in *Tulsa History*, Tulsa Preservation Commission website, accessed May 5, 2011.

2. Goble, *Tulsa!*, 68

3. "Who Is Cyrus S. Avery?," typed manuscript, November 16, 1967, Avery Papers.

4. *Tulsa World*, August 29, 1912.

5. Harlow, *Oklahoma Leaders*, 159.

6. Yvonne Litchfield, "Historical Society Retrieving Story of 'Tulsey Town'," *Tulsa World*, n.d., Avery Papers; and Joy Avery interview.

7. Minutes, Tulsa Commercial Club, December 22, 1911, Tulsa Area Chamber of Commerce archives.

8. "Dry Farming Congress," *Montreal Gazette*, October 25, 1912; and "Farming Learning Business Methods," *New York Times*, November 16, 1913.

9. Minutes, Commercial Club, Tulsa Oklahoma, December 4, 1913, Tulsa Area Chamber of Commerce archives.

10. *Oklahoma, a Guide to the Sooner State*, 20.

11. *Tulsa Spirit*, January 1918, Tulsa Area Chamber of Commerce archives.

12. Ford et al., *Historic Tulsa*, 25.

13. *Tulsa Spirit*, 1916, Tulsa Area Chamber of Commerce archives.

14. Potter, *The Gospel of Good Roads*.

15. Weingroff, "Milestones for U.S. Highway Transportation," last updated April 8, 2011.

16. Rhea, *The Battle of the Wilderness*, 238.

17. Eldridge, "The Office of Public Road Inquiries," 174.

18. Weingroff, "Milestones for U.S. Highway Transportation."

19. Roosevelt, "Address to the National and International Good Roads Convention," 168.

20. Peters, "The Good-Roads Movement," 20.

Chapter 3

1. Sidney Suggs to William Howard Taft, quoted in "The Drive for Good Roads," in "Spans of Time," Oklahoma Department of Transportation, accessed May 8, 2011.

2. "Oklahoma," 608.

3. Corbett, "Oklahoma's Highways," 155–56.

4. Kaszynski, *The American Highway*, 27.

5. Ibid., 35.

6. Ibid., 32.

7. "Good Roads Association," *Oklahoma Encyclopedia of History and Culture*, accessed April 18, 2011.

8. Ibid.

9. "The Drive for Good Roads," in "Spans of Time," Oklahoma State Highway Department, accessed May 8, 2011.

10. Corbett, "Oklahoma's Highways," 198.

11. Sidney Suggs to William Howard Taft, in "The Drive for Good Roads," in "Spans of Time," accessed May 8, 2011.

12. "Meeting of Good Roads in Tulsa," *Tulsa World*, June 10, 1912.

13. "Mid-Continent Pike is Reality," *Tulsa World*, June 29, 1912.

14. "Cyrus S. Avery," *Oklahoma*, 36.

15. Joy Avery interview.

16. Burton, "Missouri's Good Road Campaign," 49–54.

17. Leighton Avery interview, Avery Papers.

18. "Who Is Cyrus S. Avery?," typed manuscript, Avery Papers.

19. "Good Roads Movement," *Durant (Okla.) Weekly News*, September 19, 1913.

20. Gene Curtis, "This Day in History" *Tulsa World*, December 12, 2011.

21. "Launch Statewide Good Roads Movement," *Tulsa World*, December 15, 1915.

22. Burke, *ODOT*, 10.

23. "Bridge Committee Report," February 2, 1915, *Commercial Club Meetings* (bound book), Tulsa Area Chamber of Commerce archives.

24. CSA, "The Arkansas River Bridge," in "Tulsa Chamber of Commerce—Activity in Highway Development," typed manuscript, 1952, Avery Papers.

25. "Way Back When—Today in History," *Tulsa World*, September 18, 2011.

26. CSA, "Establishment of Highway Department of Chamber of Commerce," in "Tulsa Chamber of Commerce—Activity in Highway Development," typed manuscript, 1952, Avery Papers.

27. CSA, "Bond Issue for Paving County Highway System," in "Tulsa Chamber of Commerce—Activity in Highway Development," typed manuscript, 1952, Avery Papers.

28. "Snippits from Tulsa Spirit #5," *Tulsa Spirit*, January 1918, Welcome to Tulsa County OK, website, accessed December 12, 2013.

Chapter 4

Epigraph: Elbert Hubbard, *The Notebook of Elbert Hubbard* (New York: William B. Wise, 1927).

1. Harvey acquired his nickname "Coin" from his staunch support of the late nineteenth-century Populist push for free coinage of silver for currency. When William Jennings Bryan ran for president in 1896 under the Free Silver banner, Harvey was his campaign manager.

2. Minutes, Commercial Club, November 4, 1913, in Tulsa Area Chamber of Commerce archives.

3. "Meet in Evening," *Oklahoman*, April 19, 1915.

4. "Highway A-7 Ditch No. 6 Bridge, Tyronza, Poinsett County, Summary," Arkansas Historic Preservation Program, accessed August 7, 2013.

5. *Oklahoma City Times*, November 20–22, 1916, and *Daily Oklahoman*, November 20–23, 1916, quoted in Lawler, "The Ozark Trails Association," 33.

6. Lawler, "The Ozark Trails Association," 29.

7. "The Ozark Trails, New Mexico—Spread of the Ozarks," Drive the Old Spanish Trail, accessed July 10, 2011.

8. CSA, "Organization of Ozark Trail Association," Tulsa Chamber of Commerce—Activity in Highway Development, typed manuscript, 1952, Avery Papers.

9. "Good Roads Meet to Be an Epoch," *Daily Oklahoman*, December 31, 1916.

10. Joy, "Transcontinental Trails," 162.

11. CSA, speech to U.S. Highway 64 Association, Fort Smith, Arkansas, January 1930, typed manuscript, Avery Papers.

12. *Amarillo Daily News*, June 28, 1917.

13. "2000 Expected at Convention," *Daily Oklahoman*, June 21, 1917. Sen. Robert K. Owen of Oklahoma had introduced a resolution in Congress to have Ozark Trails designated as an official route from St. Louis to the West Coast and also to have it designated as a military highway.

14. "Military Touch Adds Interest in Ozark Trail," *Daily Oklahoman*, June 24, 1917.

15. CSA, speech to U.S. Highway 64 Association, Avery Papers.

16. CSA, "The Albert Pike Highway," *Nation's Highways*, April 1921, 8.

17. "The Associated Highways of America," *Municipal Journal*, February 15, 1919, 140–41. Quoted in American Roads website, accessed June 15, 2012.

Chapter 5

Epigraph: C. H. Lamb, secretary, Gilcrease Oil Company, to Cy Avery at the Mayo Clinic, August 14, 1922.

1. C. O. (no further name) to CSA, letter. November 11, 1919, Avery Papers.

2. "Rotary Members to Help on War Bonds," *Tulsa World*, October 21, 1918.

3. Cralle, "Social Change and Isolation," 121.

4. Swift, *The Big Roads*, 56-58.

5. Corbett, "Oklahoma's Highways," 218.

6. THM, paper presented at seventeenth annual convention of the American Road Builders' Association, Louisville, February 9–13, 1920, reprinted in *Good Roads*, April 14, 1920.

7. CSA, "History of U.S. Roads," typed document, Avery Papers.

8. C. Thomas to CSA, letter, May 17, 1924, Avery Papers.

9. Leighton Avery interview by Quinta Scott, June 12, 1982, typed transcription of taped interview, Avery Papers.

10. Ruth Avery interview.

Old English Inn Dinner Rolls

(Two days to prepare. Serves 10 people)

- 1/2 cup shortening
- 2 eggs, beaten
- 1/2 cup sugar
- 2 cups homogenized milk
- 1 cake of yeast
- 2 Tablespoons warm water
- 1/2 cup mashed potatoes
- 4 cups sifted flour
- 2 teaspoons baking powder
- 1 teaspoon soda
- 2 teaspoons salt
- 2 cups sifted flour for next morning

Warm shortening, sugar, and milk in saucepan until shortening melts. Add mashed potatoes and cool. Dissolve yeast in 2 tablespoons warm water and add to beaten eggs. Add this to potato mixture. Sift 4 cups flour, baking powder, soda and salt together.

Stir liquid mixture into dry ingredients. Put into a large bowl and let rise in warm place until it doubles. This is the sponge. Cover overnight with a light cloth. The next morning add remaining 2 cups of sifted flour to the sponge and knead until satiny. Put dough in greased bowl and let rise in warm surroundings. Knead on lightly floured board. Form into rolls and place on greased pan. Let stand 5 minutes.

Bake in 425-degree oven for 15 minutes.

Recipe from Ruth Sigler Avery; available among the Avery Papers.

11. CSA, "The Albert Pike Highway Association," and "Tulsa County Road System," *Nation's Highways*, April 1921.

12. CSA, "Townsend Bill," *Nation's Highways*, June 1921.

13. "The Lincoln Highway," in *Nation's Highways*, May 1921, 12.

14. CSA to H. O. Cooley, telegram, August 1922, Avery Papers.

15. Fred Kopplin to CSA, letter, August 18, 1922, Avery Papers.

16. Leighton Avery interview, Avery Papers.

17. Ellsworth, *Death in a Promised Land*, 25, 44.

18. "Nab Negro for Attacking Girl in Elevator, *Tulsa Tribune*, May 31, 1921.

19. Leighton Avery interview, Avery Papers.

20. Ibid.

Chapter 6

1. Krehbiel, *Tulsa's "Daily World,"* 9.

2. Ken Neal, "World Leader," *Tulsa World Centennial Supplement*, January 12, 1998, 43.

3. "Need of Water Supply," *Tulsa Daily World*, March 3, 1913, quoted in Krehbiel, *Tulsa's "Daily World,"* 12.

4. *Tulsa Daily World*, July 27, 1915.

5. Rains, "The Spavinaw Water Construction Project," 39.

6. Ibid., 43.

7. Ibid., 44. McFarlin also happened to be the richest man in Tulsa.

8. *Tulsa World*, November 16, 1920, quoted in ibid., 92.

9. Ibid., 109–13.

10. "'Perfect Park' Title Bestowed on Mohawk Park," *Tulsa Tribune*, November 11, 1923.

11. "Tulsans Give Park Land to City," *Tulsa World*, December 21, 1924.

12. Today Mohawk Park and Golf Course is the thirty-fifth largest U.S. city park.

13. Rains, "The Spavinaw Water Construction Project," 127n27.

14. Klein, *Grappling with Demon Rum*, 79.

15. "Creekmore Gives Up 10-Year Fight," *Tulsa Daily World*, February 23, 1917.

16. *Creekmore v. City of Tulsa*, Supreme Court of Oklahoma, decided June 25, 1929, accessed June 4, 2012.

17. CSA interview cited in Rains, "The Spavinaw Water Construction Project," 126n27.

18. Rains, "The Spavinaw Water Construction Project," 139–41.

19. *Tulsa Tribune*, November 2, 1924.

20. Rains, "The Spavinaw Water Construction Project," 147. The second bond issue was so unpopular, in fact, that Lorton and the *World* strongly opposed it and acrimoniously denounced Avery, probably because of his attachment to Governor Trapp whom Lorton had no use for. The first vote failed, but a second election a month later passed. Eventually Lorton and Avery made peace, and Lorton continued his strong support for Avery's highway-building activities.

21. Rains, "The Spavinaw Water Construction Project," 152; *Tulsa World*, June 19, 1925, and July 3, 1925.

22. *Tulsa World*, July 7, 1925.

23. *Tulsa World*, July 15, 1925; July 23, 1925; August 21, 1925; August 22, 1925.

24. CSA to Mary C. Boudinot, personal letter, January 23, 1956, Avery Papers.

Chapter 7

Epigraph: Martin Trapp, governor of Oklahoma, first state of the state address, January 15, 1924, *100 Years of Oklahoma Governors*.

1. Corbett, "Oklahoma's Highways," 215.

2. "Third Annual Report of the State Engineer," Oklahoma State Highway Department, 6–8, quoted in ibid., 208.

3. The 7 percent number was supposedly based on the belief that that was the least amount of pavement it would take to cover one major north-south highway and one intersecting east-west highway in any state.

4. "Walton Barbecue," *Delaware County Chieftain,* January 17, 1923.

5. John F. Hayden to CSA, letter, March 15, 1923, Avery Papers.

6. Oklahoma State Highway Commission, *Session Laws of 1923–24,* ch. 48, SB44, sec. 10, 55.

7. "'Best' Highway Bill Becomes Law Today," *Tulsa Tribune,* March 13, 1924.

8. Roy M. Johnson to CSA. January 9, 1951, Avery Papers.

9. CSA to THM, letter, March 1, 1924, NACP.

10. Riley Wilson, "Those Curves on Old Roads Not 'Errors,'" *Tulsa Daily World,* May 1, 1955.

11. Avery, "Stormy Petrel in Johnston Administration Is Pioneer Road Advocate," *Oklahoma City Times,* January 26, 1927.

12. Corbett, "Oklahoma's Highways," 234.

13. Ibid.

14. L. E. Boykin to THM, memo, February 14, 1925, NACP.

15. "Says Board Misused Oklahoma Funds," *New York Times,* n.d., clipping in NACP BPR files from 1925.

16. L. E. Boykin to Philip St. John Wilson, February 24, 1925, NACP.

17. Corbett, "Oklahoma's Highways," 238.

18. Gov. Martin Trapp, "State of the State Address," January 4, 1927, "Governor Martin E. Trapp," *100 Years of Oklahoma Governors,* accessed November 8, 2011.

Chapter 8

Epigraph: "Highways of the Nation Are Now Numbered," *New York Times,* September 27, 1925.

1. "Auto Deaths," *Ardmore Daily Ardmorite,* December 10, 1922; and "Motor Vehicle Traffic Fatalities & Fatality Rate," accessed December 29, 2013.

2. "Four Great Highways from Sea to Sea," *Literary Digest,* May 26, 1923, 61.

3. Calvin Coolidge, first annual message to Congress, December 6, 1923, Calvin Coolidge Memorial Foundation, accessed April 14, 2012.

4. Calvin Coolidge, address at Memorial Continental Hall, January 21, 1924, Calvin Coolidge Memorial Foundation.

5. Oklahoma Highway Commission, *Report of the State Highway Commission for the Years 1925 to 1926 Inclusive,* January 1, 1927, accessed February 9, 2012.

6. Weingroff, "Clearly Vicious as a Matter of Policy."

7. "Action Taken by the Joint Board on Interstate Highways at its First Full Meeting April 21, 1925, Resolution No. 5 Regarding Trail Marking," American Association of State Highway Officials, Bound Records.

8. Weingroff, "From Names to Numbers."

9. Howard H. Gore to Frank F. Rogers, letter, January 8, 1925, NACP.

10. W. C. Markham and CSA, telegram exchange, January 24 1925, Avery Papers.

11. W. C. Markham to Frank Rogers, January 26, 1925, NACP.

12. Howard H. Gore to Hon. Scott Leavitt (R-Montana), circa March 1, 1925, NACP.

13. Series of letters, W. A. Markham to F. Rogers, March 27–April 4, 1925, Joint Board Meetings, 1925, AASHO, Bound Records.

14. "Frank Thomas Sheets—2008, Hall Of Fame Inductees 2008," Route 66 Association of Illinois, posted July 28, 2008—4:22 P.M. by the administration, accessed April 19, 2012.

15. "Digest of First Replies from Members of Joint Board 1925," Avery Papers.

16. Weingroff, "From Names to Numbers."

17. Ibid.

18. "Report of the Six Group Meetings," Minutes, Joint Board Meetings, 1925, AASHO, Bound Records.

19. CSA, speech to members of U.S. 64 Highway Association, January 1930, Avery Papers.

20. "Oklahoma State Highway Number 7 Tentatively Named Part of New National Road," *Tulsa Tribune*, May 31, 1925.

21. "Report of the Six Group Meetings," Minutes, Joint Board Meetings, 1925, AASHO, Bound Records.

22. Ibid.

23. Ibid.

24. CSA to EWJ, letter, June 16, 1925, Avery Papers.

25. A. R. Losh to THM, letter, June 18, 1925, NACP.

26. City of Duncan, Oklahoma, to and from A. S. Wilson, June–July 1925, NACP.

27. CSA, speech to U.S. 64 Highway Association, January 1930, Avery Papers.

28. THM to Hon J. W. Harreld, U.S. Senate, letter, March 24, 1926, NACP.

29. Calvin Coolidge, address at Arlington National Cemetery, May 30, 1925, accessed April 14, 2012.

30. THM, "Memorandum for the Secretary," United States Department of Agriculture, Bureau of Public Roads, August 12, 1925, NACP.

31. A. R. Losh to P. St. J. Wilson, memo, July 2, 1925, NACP.

32. CSA to EWJ, letter, July 6, 1925, Avery Papers.

33. EWJ to CSA, letter, July 10, 1925, Avery Papers.

34. CSA, handwritten notes from August 3, 1925, evening meeting of the joint board, Avery Papers.

35. Ibid.

36. Weingroff, "From Names to Numbers."

37. Richard Weingroff to Arthur Krim, Society for Commercial Archeology, letter, September 18, 1990, document in *Articles and Letters about Route 66*, index section 4, notebook, Oklahoma Department of Transportation, Oklahoma City.

38. "Action Taken by The Joint Board on Interstate Highways at Its Second Full Meeting, August 3, 1925," AASHO, Bound Records.

39. Weingroff, "E. W. James," EWJ to Frederick W. Cron, March 1, 1967, accessed August 3, 2012.

40. Weingroff, "From Names to Numbers."

41. William M. Jardine to THM, November 18, 1925, NACP.

42. EWJ, "Report to AASHO."

Chapter 9

1. James A. French, N.M. highway commissioner, to EWJ, letter, December 7, 1925, NACP.

2. "Minutes, AASHO Executive Committee," January 14, 1926, AASHO, Bound Records.

3. Weingroff, "From Names to Numbers."

4. Ibid.

5. "Minutes, AASHO Executive Committee," January 14, 1926, AASHO, Bound Records.

6. CSA to Elmer Thomas, telegram, February 9, 1926, Avery Papers.

7. CSA to WCM, February 9, 1926, Avery Papers.

8. WCM to CSA, letter, February 9, 1926, Avery Papers.

9. CSA to Elmer Thomas, letter, February 10, 1926, Avery Papers.

10. CSA to THM, telegram, February 10, 1926, 12:41 p.m., NACP.

11. THM to CSA, telegram, February 10, 1926, 4:30 p.m., NACP.

12. CSA to EWJ, telegram, February 10, 1926, 5:54 p.m., NACP.

13. THM to CSA, letter, February 12, 1926, Avery Papers.

14. BHP to CSA, letter, February 13, 1926, Avery Papers.

15. BHP to CSA, telegram, February 15, 1926, Avery Papers.

16. BHP to CSA, letter, February 15, 1926, Avery Papers.

17. AASHO Executive Committee minutes, February 16, 1926, Avery Papers.

18. CSA to THM, letter, February 18, 1926, NACP.

19. EWJ to CSA, letter, February 20, 1926, NACP.

20. CSA to Elmer Thomas, letter, February 22, 1926, Avery Papers.

21. EWJ to CSA, letter, handwritten comment on last page, February 20, 1926, Avery Papers.

22. CSA to EWJ, letter, February 27, 1926, NACP.

23. BHP to Frank Page, letter, March 4, 1926, NACP.

24. Frank Page to WCM, letter, March 11, 1926, NACP.

25. Chairman, Good Roads Committee (John Charles Nicholson?), to Frank Page, February 19, 1926, Avery Papers.

26. EWJ to C. Frank Dunn, letter, March 13, 1926, NACP.

27. EWJ to CSA, March 10, 1926, Avery Papers.

28. CSA to Frank Page, letter, March 17, 1926, AASHO, Bound Records.

29. Series of letters between CSA and E. E. Jackson, Colorado Springs, March 1926, Avery Papers.

30. THM to CSA, letter March 30, 1926, NACP.

31. BHP to EWJ, Letter, April 3, 1926, NACP.

32. CSA to THM, letter, April 6, 1926, NACP.

33. THM to CSA, letter, April 14, 1926, NACP.

34. WCM to E. N. Todd, letter, April 27, 1926, NACP.

35. WCM to AASHO executive committee, letter, April 30, 1926, NACP.

36. CSA and BHP to THM, telegram, April 30, 1926, NACP.

37. P. S. J. Wilson to WCM, telegram, May 3, 1926, NACP.

38. H. G. Shirley to E. N. Todd, letter, May 3, 1926, NACP.

39. E. N. Todd to WCM, letter, May 6, 1926, NACP.

40. F. R. White, chief engineer Iowa Highway Commission, to WCM, letter, June 16, 1926, NACP.

41. WCM to E. N. Todd, Letter, June 16, 1926, NACP.

42. WCM to CSA, letter, July 16, 1926, NACP.

43. EWJ to BHP, letter, July 26, 1926, NACP.

44. CSA to EWJ, letter, July 26, 1926, NACP.

45. CSA to WCM, letter, July 27, 1926, NACP.

46. WCM to CSA, letter, July 31, 1926, Avery Papers.

47. THM to CSA, letter, August 4, 1926, NACP.

48. CSA to WCM, letter, July 27, 1926, NACP.

49. EWJ, "Executive Committee Report on Numbering of United States Highways," January 1927, reprinted as James, "Report to AASHO," 14.

50. "Minutes of the Meeting of the State Highway Commission Held at the Office of the Commission in the State Capitol Building at Oklahoma City, December 7, 1926," includes notation by hand: "Original Commission Action on U.S. 66," Avery Papers.

51. "State Helped by National Road System Nine Federal Routes Join in Oklahoma," *Tulsa Tribune*, January 30, 1927.

Chapter 10

1. A. R. Losh to THM, telegram, February 17, 1925, NACP.

2. Commissioner of Indian Affairs Charles H. Burke to THM, letter, n.d., NACP.

3. A. R. Losh to THM, letter, September 9, 1926, and August 25, 1926, NACP.

4. H. K. Bishop to A. R. Losh, letter, August 30, 1926, NACP.

5. CSA, "The Oklahoma Road Program," speech, typed manuscript, n.d., Avery Papers.

6. *Tulsa Tribune* draft editorial about Avery, Trapp, and the 1926 election, n.d., Avery Papers.

7. R. M. McClintock, "Blows at Highway Commission Seen in Platform Planks Adopted by Both Parties," *Oklahoma Daily News*, September 8, 1926.

8. "Avery Refuses to Relinquish Highway Post," *Tulsa Tribune*, January 7, 1927.

9. *Ardmore Statesman*, *Fredrick Leader*, and *Enid News* all quoted in "Highway Bill Is Opposed by State Press," unidentified newspaper clipping, January 28, 1927, NACP.

10. Ibid.

11. Ibid.

12. John Page to A. R. Losh, letter, January 1927, Avery Papers.

13. "Highway Bill Signed; Avery Is Given Gate," *Daily Oklahoman*, January 28, 1927.

14. "Close of Road Row to Speed Up Assembly," *Tulsa Tribune*, January 27, 1927.

15. CSA to Charles Thomas, letter, February 24, 1927, Avery Papers.

16. A. R. Losh to CSA, letter, January 27, 1927, Avery Papers.

17. CWM to CSA, letter, February 1, 1927, Avery Papers.

18. L. E. Abbott to CSA, telegram, January 31, 1917, Avery Papers.

19. Roy Johnson to French Gentry, letter, February 15, 1927, Avery Papers.

20. "Statement of J. M. Page," typed document in ODOT notebook: *Articles and Letters about Route 66*, index section 4, Oklahoma Department of Transportation.

21. "Mandigo Will Succeed Page," *Blackwell Morning Tribune*, May 17, 1927.

22. No headline. *Daily Oklahoman*, May 19, 1927.

23. "Consider Oklahoma," *Tulsa Tribune*, May 1, 1927.

24. "A Highway Convention," *Tulsa Tribune*, July 23, 1927.

Chapter 11

1. Woodruff, *Reminiscences of an Ozarkian*, 143.

2. "John T. Woodruff and Missouri Road Building," accessed August 7, 2013.

3. January 9, 1927, meeting in Springfield of businessmen from Springfield and Tulsa. Clipping, no headline, n.d., Avery Papers.

4. "Organization Meeting of the U.S. 66 Highway Association, Held at Tulsa, Oklahoma, February 4th, 1927," Avery Papers.

5. *Articles of Agreement the U.S. 66 Highway Association*, filed April 2, 1927, Springfield, Mo., Avery Papers.

6. Woodruff, *Reminiscences of an Ozarkian*, 112.

7. No title, *Kansas City Journal-Post*, April 17, 1927, Avery Papers.

8. "Highway 66 Convention Opens," *Miami News-Record*, February 27, 1928.

9. *Rolla Herald*, May 19, 1927.

10. Leslie Lon Scott, quoted in Wallis, *Route 66*, 12.

11. *Winslow Daily Mail*, January 8, 1928.

12. "Bunion Derby," *Ada Evening News*, April 16, 1928.

13. Davis and Condry quoted in Kelly, *Route 66*, 35.

14. Hulston, *An Ozark Boy's Story*, 100.

15. Reisler, *Cash and Carry*, 166, and especially 156–81. This book gives a terrific blow-by-blow account of the Bunion Derby.

16. C. C. Pyle to CSA, letter, February 19, 1928, Avery Papers.

17. Woodruff, *Reminiscences of an Ozarkian*, 114.

18. *Winslow Daily Mail*, June 12, 1928.

19. "Tulsan Is Named Head of Highway 66 Association," *Joplin Globe*, March 12, 1929.

20. E. Bee Guthrey to CSA, note regarding speech to U.S. 64 Association, April 30, 1930, typed manuscript, Avery Papers.

21. Kelly, *Route 66*, 165.

22. CSA, speech at Route 66 Rolla celebration on March 15, 1931, typed manuscript, March 1931, Avery Papers.

23. "HWY U.S. 66," CSA speech, typed manuscript, Tulsa 1931, Avery Papers.

24. CSA, "Speech at the Celebration to Commemorate the Paving of U.S. 66 in Vinita, August 24, 1933," typed manuscript, Avery Papers.

Chapter 12

Epigraph: Carlyle Straub, "The Test of a Man," in *Retail Clerks International Advocate*, May 1922. Cy kept a framed copy of this poem until he died.

1. "Who's Who in Oil and Why," *Tulsa Tribune*, January 18, 1929.

2. "Then and Now," *Tulsa World*, February 6, 1957, Avery Papers.

3. CSA, "How to Create a Farm Land Market through Construction of Paved Highways."

4. "Air Tour Banquet," July 10, 1927, unidentified clipping, Avery Archive.

5. Cantrell, "Lucky Lindy Lands and Tulsa Airport Takes Off." *GTR News* Web site, updated May 14, 2007, accessed August 15, 2012.

6. "Air Program Rivals Crude at Oil Show," *Oklahoman*, September 18, 1927.

7. Carol E. Gregory, *Making Lazy Circles in the Sky: A History of Tulsa Aviation, 1897–2000*, spiral bound document, copyright July 15, 2002, Avery Papers.

8. CSA, "Tulsa's Municipal Airport," typed manuscript, May 6, 1928, Avery Papers.

9. "Tulsa's First Big Air Tour May Be Last," *Tulsa Tribune*, July 10, 1927.

10. CSA, "Memorandum Re Plans to Develop the Tulsa Municipal Airport," typed manuscript, March 24, 1932, Avery Papers.

11. Erv Deputy to CSA, letter July 21, 1931, Avery Papers.

12. CSA and Charles Short, manager, Tulsa Airport, letters, September 1954, Avery Papers. The airport was renamed Tulsa International Airport in 1963.

13 "The Golden Age," Tulsa Air and Space Museum & Planetarium website, accessed August 15, 2012.

14. CSA note on Souvenir Program for Dedication of Brownsville International Airport, March 9 & 10, 1929, Avery Papers.

15. "Farm Conditions in Northeastern Oklahoma Analyzed as Key to Planning the Future, *Miami Daily News Record*, February 22, 1931.

16. "Prosperity," *Miami News Record*, August 14, 1932.

17. "Seek Hard-Wood Forest in State," *Miami News Record*, June 16, 1933.

18. "Tom Anglin," *Oklahoman*, January 21, 1934.

19. "Letters from the People: Cy Avery's Politics," letter to the editor from A. Haskins, Enid, *Oklahoman*, October 16, 1933.

20. "State Police Force Is Urged by Avery," *Oklahoman*, January 8, 1934.

21. CSA, handwritten note on Certificate of Nomination, Avery Papers.

22. Stevens Avery interview.

23. Ruth Sigler Avery interview.

24. Stevens Avery interview.

25. Ruth Sigler Avery, "Cyrus Stevens Avery," 90.

26. CSA, speech to Pryor Chamber of Commerce, June 28, 1949, reported in *Tulsa Tribune*, clipping, n.d., Avery Archives.

27. CSA to Mary C. Boudinot of Muskogee, letter, January 23, 1956, Avery Papers. In 1907 Cy purchased eighty acres a few miles north of the Watie homestead, possibly incorporating some of the original homestead land.

28. Rose Stauber interview.

29. Peter Cope White to CSA, letter, June 26, 1935, Avery Papers.

30. G. H. Martin to CSA, letter, July 9, 1935, Avery Papers.

31. M. L. Miller to George Key, letter, April 17, 1936, Avery Papers.

32. "A Flower for Cyrus Avery," *Mayes County Democrat*, April 30, 1937.

33. Ruth Sigler Avery, "Cyrus Stevens Avery," 89.

34. E. L. Heiser to CSA, letter June 9, 1937, also *Ada Evening News*, July 9, 1937, Avery Papers.

35. "WPA Practices Once Condoned Threaten Avery," *Tulsa Tribune*, n.d., 1937, Avery Papers.

36. Scott Farris to James A. Farley, telegram, June 7, 1937, Avery Papers.

37. M. E. Trapp to Sen. Josh Lee, letter, June 7, 1937, Avery Papers.

38."Tulsa Works Chief Facing Ouster Move," *Oklahoman*, June 6, 1937.

39. W. S. Key to E. Bee Guthrey, letter, July 16–17, 1937, Avery Papers.

40. E. Bee Guthrey to Ron Stephens, letter, July 13, 1937, Avery Papers.

41. E. Bee Guthrey to CSA, letter, July 13, 1937, Avery Papers.

42. W. S. Key to CSA, letter, July 17, 1937, Avery Papers

43. CSA to W. S. Key, letter, April 10, 1945, Avery Papers.

44. CSA to W. S. Key, letter, April 10, 1945, Avery Papers.

45. Jack Putman, "Agronomy 'Prof without Portfolio' Can Recall Rich, Varied Experiences," *Tulsa Daily World*, July 19, 1959.

46. Ruth Sigler Avery, "Cyrus Stevens Avery," 89.

47. Joy Avery, Stevens Avery, and Bob Berghell interviews with author.

48. Stevens Avery interview.

49. "Older Cherokees Plaintive about Burial Ground Move," *Ada Evening News*, October 19, 1951.

50. CSA to Allen Hirsch, Lock Joint Pipe Company, letter, August 15, 1949, Avery Papers

51. "Avery Resigns as Land Buyer," *Tulsa World*, January 10, 1950.

52. CSA to Mrs. Earnest Hallock, letter, October 15, 1953, Avery Papers.

53. CSA to John Woodward, letter, September 7, 1956, Avery Papers.

54. "Drive for Electronics, Missile Plants Urged," *Tulsa World*, August 1, 1961.

55. "Ex Governor Trapp Buried at Capitol," *Tulsa World*, July 31, 1951.

56. CSA to George O. Straughan, letter, June 11, 1958, letter, Avery Papers.

Bibliography

Libraries, Archives, and Manuscript Collections

American Association of State Highway and Transportation Officials, Washington, D.C. AASHO Bound Records.

Cyrus Stevens Avery Papers, Department of Special Collections and Archives, Oklahoma State University, Tulsa Campus Library.

Delaware County Historical Society and Mariee Wallace Museum, Jay, Okla.

Delaware County Library, Eastern District Library System, Jay, Okla.

Grove Public Library, Grove, Okla.

Lebanon-Laclede County Library, Lebanon, Mo.

National Archives at College Park, Md. Records of the Bureau of Public Roads. 1920–39. Record Group 30, File 481.

Oklahoma Department of Transportation, Oklahoma City.

Springfield-Greene County Library Center, Springfield, Mo.

State Historical Society of Missouri, Columbia and Rolla.

Tulsa Area Chamber of Commerce archives.

Tulsa City-County Library.

Tulsa Historical Society.

Government Publications

Annual Report of First Assistant Postmaster-General Perry S. Heath for the Fiscal Year Ended June 30, 1899. Washington, D.C.: Government Printing Office.

"Highway A-7 Ditch No. 6 Bridge, Tyronza, Poinsett County, Summary." Arkansas Historic Preservation Program. Accessed August 7, 2013. www.arkansaspreservation. com/historic-properties/_search_nomination_popup.aspx?id=2464.

Keane, Melissa, and J. Simon Bruder, contributions by Kenneth M. Euge. *Good Roads Everywhere: A History of Road Building in Arizona.* Prepared for Arizona Department of Transportation, Environmental Planning Section, Phoenix, Ariz. Accessed May 12, 2011. www.azdot.gov/highways/EPG/EPG_Common/PDF/ Technical/Cultural_Good_Roads_Everywhere.pdf.

Oklahoma Conservation Commission, Water Quality Division. "Spavinaw Creek Watershed Implementation Project Final Report." Oklahoma City.

Oklahoma State Highway Commission. *Annual Report of the State Highway Commission for the Years 1919 to 1924, Inclusive.* Oklahoma City: Oklahoma Depatment of Transportation, January 1, 1925. *Oklahoma Digital Pairie,* Oklahoma

Department of Libraries. Accessed February 9, 2012. http://digitalprairie.ok.gov/
cdm/ref/collection/okresources/id/14188.

———. *Report of the State Highway Commission for the Years 1925 to 1926, Inclusive.*
Oklahoma City: Oklahoma Department of Transportation. January 1, 1927.
Oklahoma Digital Prairie, Oklahoma Department of Libraries. Accessed Februarry 9,
2012. http://digitalprairie.ok.gov/cdm/ref/collection/okresources/id/14188.

———. *Report of the State Highway Commission for the Years 1927 to 1928, Inclusive.*
Oklahoma City: Oklahoma Department of Transportation. January 1, 1929.
Oklahoma Digital Prairie, Oklahoma Department of Libraries. Accessed Februarry 9,
2012. http://digitalprairie.ok.gov/cdm/ref/collection/okresources/id/14188.

———. *Session Laws of 1923–24 of the State of Oklahoma.* Oklahoma City: Harlow
Publishing Company, 1926.

Snider, Becky L., and Debbie Sheals, preparers. *Route 66 in Missouri.* Survey and
National Register Project, Project No. S7215msfacg. January 14, 2003. Accessed
September 9, 2012. www.nps.gov/rt66/histsig/missouricontext.htm.

Books and Articles

"The Associated Highways of America." *Municipal Journal,* February 15, 1919,
140–41. Accessed June 15, 2012. www.americanroads.us/articles/Municipal_
Journal_1919_2_15A.html.

Avery, Cyrus S. "The Albert Pike Highway." *Nation's Highways* 1, no. 1 (April 1921): 8.

———. "How to Create a Farm Land Market through Construction of Paved
Highways." *Selling Farm Land Proceedings & Report of the Farm Lands Division
National Association of Real Estate Boards, Annals of Real Estate Practice.* January 1,
1926.

———. "Townsend Bill." *Nation's Highways,* June 1921.

Avery, Ruth Sigler. "Cyrus Stevens Avery." *Chronicles of Oklahoma* 45 (1967): 84–90.

Baird, W. David, and Danney Goble. *The Development of Oklahoma.* Norman:
University of Oklahoma Press. 1994.

Beatty, Jack. *Age of Betrayal.* New York: Alfred A. Knopf, 2007.

Bourne, Jonathan, Jr. "National Aid to Good Roads." *North American Review* 198, no.
694 (September 1913): 320–31.

Burke, Bob. *ODOT 100: Celebrating the First 100 Years of Transportation in Oklahoma.*
Oklahoma City: Oklahoma Heritage Association, 2011.

Burton, C. "Missouri's Good Road Campaign." *Rotarian,* 4, no. 2. (October 1913):
49–54. Reprint from *Motor Age.*

Cantrell, Charles. "Lucky Lindy Lands and Tulsa Airport Takes Off." *GTR News,*
updated May 14, 2007. Accessed August 15, 2012. www.gtrnews.com/greater-tulsa-
reporter/1805/lucky-lindy-lands-and-tulsa-municipal-airport-takes-off.

Clinton, Fred S. "Tulsa's Water Resources—Springs and Spavinaw." *Chronicles of
Oklahoma 1945 #1.* Accessed February 9, 2012. http://digital.library.okstate.edu/
Chronicles/v023/023p59.pdf.

Conover, Ted. *The Routes of Man: How Roads Are Changing the World and the Way We
Live Today.* New York: Alfred A. Knopf, 2010.

Curtis, C. H. "Skip," ed., *Birthplace of Route 66: Springfield, Mo.* Springfield, Mo.: Curtis Enterprises, 2001.

Corbett, William P. "Men, Mud and Mules: The Good Roads Movement in Oklahoma, 1900–1910." *Chronicles of Oklahoma* 58 (Summer 1980): 138–40.

Creekmore vs. City of Tulsa. Supreme Court of Oklahoma, decided June 25, 1929. Justia U.S. Law. Accessed June 4, 2012. http://law.justia.com/cases/oklahoma/supreme-court/1929/45100.html.

Davis, Donald Finlay. *Conspicuous Production.* Philadelphia, Penn.: Temple University Press, 1988.

Debo, Angie. *Prairie City.* Norman: University of Oklahoma Press. 1998.

———. *Tulsa: From Creek Town to Oil Capital.* Norman: University of Oklahoma Press, 1943.

"Early Highway Laws/Washington Irving." *Oklahoma Audio Almanac.* OSU Special Collections and University Archives. October 11, 2000. Accessed March 4, 2010. www.library.okstate.edu/scua/exhibit/oaa/11octoo.htm.

Eldridge, Maurice O. "The Office of Public Road Inquiries." *Good Roads Magazine,* January 1903, 174.

Ellsworth, Scott. *Death in a Promised Land: The Tulsa Race Riot of 1921.* Baton Rouge: Louisiana State University Press, 1982.

"Exceptional Opportunities Are Offered the Homeseeker in the Fertile Sections of Indian Territory in the Vicinity of Vinita, Indian Territory." Flyer. International Bank & Trust Co., Vinita, Okla., 1900.

"Facts and Figures of the Automobile Industry 1920–1930." Rails and Trails.com. Accessed July 8, 2011. www.railsandtrails.com/AutoFacts/.

Federal Works Agency. *Oklahoma: A Guide to the Sooner State.* Norman: University of Oklahoma Press, 1941.

"Fijis in the Spotlight." *Phi Gamma Delta Magazine,* October 1922, 14.

"First Numbering of Route 66 Discovered in Missouri." *Society of Commercial Archaeology (SCA) News Journal,* Summer 1990, 10.

Ford, Beryl, Charles Ford, Rodger Randle, and Bob Burke. *Historic Tulsa, an Illustrated History of Tolsa and Tulsa County.* Sponsored by Oklahoma Heritage Association and Tulsa Historical Society. San Antonio, Tex.: HPN Books, 2006.

"Four Great Highways from Sea to Sea." *Literary Digest,* May 26, 1923, 61.

"Frank Thomas Sheets—2008, Hall of Fame Inductees 2008." Route 66 Association of Illinois. July 28, 2008. Accessed April 19, 2012. www.i166assoc.org/content/frank-thomas-sheets-2008.

Gittinger, Roy. *The Formation of the State of Oklahoma 1803–1906.* Norman: University of Oklahoma Press, 1939.

Goble, Danney. *Tulsa!* Tulsa: Council Oak Books, 1998.

Goddard, Stephen B. *Getting There! The Epic Struggle between Road and Rail in the American Century.* Chicago: University of Chicago Press, 1994.

Harlow, Rex. *Oklahoma Leaders.* Oklahoma City: Harlow Publishing, 1928.

Holt, W. Stull. "The Bureau of Public Roads, Its History, Activities and Organization." In *The Bureau of Public Roads Service Monographs of the United States Government, No. 26.* Baltimore: Johns Hopkins Press, 1923.

Hudson, Mary Lou. "William J. Creekmore—Millionaire Bootlegger 1917." Ancestry rootsweb. Accessed February 10, 2012. http://archiver.rootsweb.ancestry.com/th/read/OUTLAWS-OF-THE-OLD-WEST/2004-03/1078418731.

Hulston, John K. *An Ozarks Boy's Story*. Point Lookout, Mo.: School of the Ozarks Press, 1971.

Irving, Washington. *A Tour on the Prairies*. Paris: Baudry's European Library, 1935.

James, E. W. "Report to AASHO." *American Highways*, January 1926. Reprinted as "The Story of the U.S. Numbered Highway System," *American Highways*, April 1956, 11–15, 31.

"John T. Woodruff and Missouri Road Building." *Ozarks Watch* 7, no. 2 (Fall 1993/Winter 1994): 52–56. Accessed December 30, 2013. http://thelibrary.org/lochist/periodicals/ozarkswatch/ow7020.htm.

Jones, Richard Lloyd, Clyde Gideon Roseberry, Carlton Cole Magee, Joel Heatwole Bixby. *Oklahoma and the Mid-Continent Oil Field*. Tulsa: Oklahoma Biographical Association and James O. Jones, 1930.

Joy, Henry B. "Transcontinental Trails, Their Development and What They Mean to This Country." *Scribners*, February 2014, 160–62.

Kaszynski, William. *The American Highway*. Jefferson, N.C.: McFarland, 2000.

Kelly, Susan Croce, with photographs by Quinta Scott. *Route 66, the Highway and Its People*. Norman: University of Oklahoma Press. 1988.

Kirkendall, Richard S. *1919 to 1953*. Vol. 5 of *A History of Missouri*. Columbia: University of Missouri Press, 1986.

Klein, James Edward. *Grappling with Demon Rum: The Cultural Struggle over Liquor in Early Oklahoma*. Norman: University of Oklahoma Press, 2009.

Krehbiel, Randy. *Tulsa's "Daily World," the Story of a Newspaper and Its Town*. Tulsa: World Publishing, 2007.

Krim, Arthur. *Route 66: Iconography of the American Highway*. Santa Fe, N.Mex.: Center for American Places, 2005.

———. "The Original Mother Road." *SCA Journal*, Spring 1996, 21–26.

League of American Wheelmen. *Good Roads: Devoted to the Construction and Maintenance of Roads and Streets*. Vols. 4 and 5. Kansas City: Burton Publishing, 1903.

"The Lincoln Highway." *Nation's Highways*, May 1921, 12.

MacDonald, T. H. Paper presented at seventeenth annual convention of the American Road Builders' Association, Louisville, Ky., February 9–13, 1920. Reprinted in *Good Roads Magazine*, April 14, 1920, 199–200, 203.

The Man Who Never Disappoints, Fred Emerson Brooks. Flyer. Central Lyceum Bureau of Chicago. Accessed August 7, 2013. http://digital.lib.uiowa.edu/cdm/ref/collection/tc/id/19112.

McReynolds, Edwin C. *Oklahoma: A History of the Sooner State*. Norman: University of Oklahoma Press, 1986.

Missouri: A Guide to the "Show Me" State. Compiled by Writers' Program of the Work Projects Administration in the State of Missouri. New York: Duell, Sloan and Pearce, 1941.

"Motor Vehicle Traffic Fatalities & Fatality Rate: 1899–2003." Based on Historical NHTSA and FHWA Data. Accessed December 29, 2013. http://www.saferoads.org/federal/2004/TrafficFatalities1899-2003.

"Oklahoma." *Good Roads Magazine*, December 1904, 608.

Oklahoma, a Guide to the Sooner State. Compiled by Writers' Program of the Work Projects Administration in the State of Oklahoma. Norman: University of Oklahoma Press, 1941.

Oklahoma Commission to Study the Tulsa Race Riots of 1921. "The Tulsa Race Riot." Spiral bound book. Oklahoma City. February 28, 2001. Copy in author's possession.

Parins, James W. *Elias Cornelius Boudinot: A Life on the Cherokee Border*. Lincoln: University of Nebraska Press, 2006.

Potter, Isaac B. *The Gospel of Good Roads. A Letter to the American Farmer*. New York: League of American Wheelman and National Committee on Improvement of the Highways, 1891.

Proceedings of the Third Annual Road Congress, under the Auspices of the American Highway Association and the American Automobile Association, 1913. American Highway Association, Detroit: Waverly Press, 1914.

Reisler, Jim. *Cash and Carry, the Spectacular Rise and Hard Fall of C. C. Pyle, America's First Sports Agent*. Jefferson, N.C.: McFaarland, 2009.

Rhea, Gordon. *The Battle of the Wilderness*. Baton Rouge: University of Louisiana Press, 2004.

Roosevelt, Theodore. "Address to the National and International Good Roads Convention." April 29, 1903. In *Addresses and Presidential Messages of Theodore Roosevelt, 1902–1904*, 167–171. New York: G. P. Putman's Sons and Knickerbocker Press, 1904.

Rothman, Hal. *Devil's Bargains*. Lawrence: University Press of Kansas, 1998.

Ruth, Kent. *Oklahoma, a Guide to the Sooner State*. Compiled by Kent Ruth and University of Oklahoma Press, arranged by J. Eldon Peek. Norman: University of Oklahoma Press, 1957.

Seitz, Don C. *The Dreadful Decade 1869–1879*. Indianapolis: Bobbs-Merrill, 1926.

Silvey, Larry P., and Douglas S. Drown, eds. *Tulsa Spirit*. Tulsa: Continental Heritage Press. 1979.

Snider, Luther Crocker. *Preliminary Report on the Road Materials and Road Conditions of Oklahoma*. Oklahoma Geological Survey Bulletin, No. 9. Norman: Oklahoma Geological Survey, August 1911.

Sonderman, Joe, "Rolla Celebrates 150 Years." *Show Me Route 66 Magazine* 21, no. 2 (July 2011): 30–34.

Stauber, Rose. "You Could Take Cyrus Avery Away from His Roots, but You Couldn't Take His Roots Away from Cyrus Avery." *Heritage of the Hills Magazine*, Delaware County, Okla., Historical Society, Fall 1990, 2–8.

Swift, Earl. *The Big Roads*. Boston: Houghton Mifflin Harcourt, 2011.

Thoburn, Joseph P. "Cyrus S. Avery." *History of Oklahoma*. Chicago: American Historical Society, 1916.

Troup, Bobby. "Get Your Kicks on Route 66." Recording. Copyright © 1946, copyright assigned © 1974, Londontown Music.

"Tulsa County Road System," *Nation's Highways* 1, no. 1 (April 1921).

Tulsa 1909 Illustrated: The Wonder of the New State. Oklahoma City: Jennings Publishing, 1909.

Tulsa's Water Supply. Online video produced by the City of Tulsa. Accessed July 18, 2012. www.youtube.com/watch?v=tuoCdcm-zOs&lr=1&user=CityofTulsa.

The 22. "The People Who Put Tulsa on the Map." *Tulsa World* Centennial Supplement, January 12, 1998.

Wallace, Paul A. *Pennsylvania, Seat of a Nation*. New York: Harper & Row. 1962.

Wallis, Michael. *Route 66: The Mother Road*. New York: St. Martin's Press, 1990.

Weingroff, Richard. "Clearly Vicious as a Matter of Policy: The Fight against Federal-Aid, Part 2: Unease in the Golden Age." Highway History. Last updated October 15, 2013. www.fhwa.dot.gov/infrastructure/hwyhist05a.cfm.

———. "E. W. James." In *Highway History*, by Federal Highway Administration. Accessed August 3, 2012. http://www.fhwa.dot.gov/infrastructure/ewjames.cfm

———. "From Names to Numbers, the Origins of the U.S. Numbered Highway System." In *Highway History*, by Federal Highway Administration. Last updated October 9, 2013. www.fhwa.dot.gov/infrastructure/history.cfm.

———. "Milestones for U.S. Highway Transportation and the Federal Highway Administration." *Public Roads Magazine* 59, no. 4 (Spring 1996). Updated April 8, 2011. www.fhwa.dot.gov/publications/publicroads/96spring/p96sp44.cfm.

Witzel, Michael Karl, and Gyvel Young-Witzel. *Legendary Route 66*. Saint Paul, Minn.: Voyager Press, 2007.

Woodruff, John Thomas. *Reminiscences of an Ozarkian and Early Tourism Developments*. Springfield: Office of Leisure Research, Southwest Missouri State University, 1994.

Theses, Dissertations, and Miscellaneous

Articles and Letters about Route 66. Three-ring notebook, Oklahoma Department of Transportation, Oklahoma City.

Corbett, William P. "Oklahoma's Highways: Indian Trails to Urban Expressway." Ph.D. dissertation. Oklahoma State University, Stillwater, 1982.

Cralle, Walter Odro. "Social Change and Isolation in the Ozark Mountain Region of Missouri." Ph.D. dissertation, University of Minnesota, 1934.

Hoff, John David, Jr. "A History of Tulsa International Airport." Graduate school thesis. University of Tulsa, 1967.

Lawler, Nan Marie. "The Ozark Trails Association." Master's thesis. University of Arkansas, 1991.

Peters, Kenneth Earl. "The Good-Roads Movement and the Michigan State Highway Department, 1905–1917." Ph.D. dissertation. University of Michigan, 1972.

Rains, Roy. "The Spavinaw Water Construction Project." Master's thesis. University of Tulsa, 1959.

Websites and Digital Collections

Calvin Coolidge Memorial Foundation. http://calvin-coolidge.org.

Chronicles of Oklahoma. Accessed August 7, 2013. http://digital.library.okstate.edu/Chronicles/.

Drive the Old Spanish Trail. "The Ozark Trails, New Mexico—Spread of the Ozarks." Accessed July 10, 2011. www.drivetheost.com/thespreadoftheoz.html.

"The Golden Age." Tulsa Air and Space Museum & Planetarium website. Accessed August 15, 2012. www.tulsaairandspacemuseum.org/goldenage.php?nav=aboutus.

Oklahoma Crossroads. Digital collection in Oklahoma State Archives, Oklahoma City. Accessed April 16, 2012. http://digitalprairie.ok.gov.

Oklahoma Encyclopedia of History and Culture. Oklahoma Historical Society. Accessed April 18, 2011. http://digital.library.okstate.edu/encyclopedia.

Oklahoma State Highway Department. "Spans of Time." Accessed May 8, 2011. www.okladot.state.ok.us/hqdiv/p-r-div/spansoftime/driveforroads.htm.

100 Years of Oklahoma Governors. Accessed April 14, 2012. http://www.odl.state.ok.us/oar/governors/Trapp.htm.

Riverweb. Accessed August 21, 2011. www.riverweb.uiuc.edu/NINETEENTH/TECH/eadsbridge.html.

Tulsa History. "Education (1880–1941)." Tulsa Preservation Commission. Accessed May 5, 2011. www.tulsapreservationcommission.org/history/education/.

———. "Transportation (1850–1945)." Tulsa Preservation Commission. Accessed May 5, 2011. www.tulsapreservationcommission.org/history/transportation/.

Welcome to Tulsa County, OK. "Snippits from Tulsa Spirit #5," *Tulsa Spirit*, January 1918. Accessed December 12, 2013. http://www.tulsaokhistory.com/tulsaspirit/spirit05.html.

Newspapers

Ada Evening News
Amarillo Daily News
(Ardmore, Okla.) Daily Ardmoreite
Blackwell (Okla.) Morning News
Blackwell (Okla.) Morning Tribune
Chicago Times
Delaware County (Okla.) Chieftan
Durant (Okla.) Weekly News
El Reno (Okla.) American
Joplin (Okla.) Globe
Kansas City Journal Post
Kansas City Star
Mayes County Democrat
Miami (Okla.) News Record/Miami Daily News Record
Muskogee Muskotary
New York Times
Oklahoma Daily News

Oklahoman/Daily Oklahoman
Pantograph (Bloomington, Ill.)
Pryor Creek Review (Pryor, Okla.)
Rolla (Mo.) Herald
Springfield (Mo.) Leader
Tulsa Tribune
Tulsa World/Tulsa Daily World
Winslow (Ariz.) Daily Mail

Interviews

Joy Avery, granddaughter of Cy Avery. Tulsa. April 16, 2009.

Ruth Avery, widow of Leighton Avery and daughter-in-law of Cy Avery. Tulsa. September 21, 1984.

Stevens Avery, grandson of Cy Avery, son of Gordon Avery. Telephone interview. May 9, 2011.

Bob Beghell, son of Cy Avery's daughter, Helen. Tulsa. November 2012.

Rose Stauber, grandniece of Cy Avery. Grove, Okla. May 2012.

Index

Page numbers in italics indicate illustrations.

Oklahoma Department of Agriculture, 24

Oklahoma Good Roads Association, 37, 38, 43, 116

Oklahoma Good Roads Federation, 47–48, 117

Oklahoma Highway Commission, 107–108, 112

Oklahoma Highway Department, 115

Oklahoma Highway Law of 1915, 48–49

Oklahoma Highway Law of 1924, 116

Oklahoma Highway Law of 1927, 182–83

Oklahoma–Indian Territory Good Roads Association, 37, 38, 43, 116

Oklahoma National Guard, 187, 228

Oklahoma State Department of Highways, 43, 48

Oklahoma State Highway 1, 62. *See also* roads

Oklahoma State Highway 7, 117, 142. *See also* roads

Oklahoma State Highway 11, 117. *See also* roads

Oklahoma State Highway Commission: and C. Avery, 117, 118–19, 120, 121, 131, 174, 177, 183–84; and Boykin, 121; creation of, 116; and Gentry, 117; and Guthrey, 117; and Holloway, 188; and Johnson, 117; and Johnston, 181–82; and Losh, 119; and MacDonald, 117; and new construction, 121; and Oklahoma State Commissioners Association, 178; purposes of, 116–17, 125–26; and Texas State Highway Department, 124; and U.S. Bureau of Public Roads, 117; and Wentz, 188

Oklahoma State Highway Department, 54, 62

Oklahoma Territory, 16

Old English Inn, 72–73, 74, 82, 243n10

Old Wire Road, 11

Oochalata (Cherokee chief), 233

OPR (Office of Public Roads), 40, 41–42

OPRI (Office of Public Road Inquiry), 37

ORI (Office of Road Inquiry), 33, 34, 39

Osage Indians, 178. *See also* Indians

Otjen Amendment, 182

Owen, Robert K., 242n13

Ozark Sportsmen's Club, 100

Ozark Trails Highway Association (OTA), 53–60, 61; and Owen, 242n13

Page, Charles, 99

Page, Frank, 159, 164, 166, 179

Page, John Marshall, 119, 131, 184–85, 186

Page, Logan Waller, 39, 40, 41–42, 51, 69

Page, Sarah, 77

Panama Canal, 101

Pan American Road Congress, 137

Parker, Isaac, 11

Payne, Andy, 198, 200, 202, 203

Pennsylvania, 6, 10

Peterson, Preston, 136

Phi Gamma Delta fraternity, 14, 240n23

Phillips, Waite, 213, 217

Phillips Petroleum, 216

Piepmeier, B. H., *92*; and C. Avery, 160; and James, 157, 168; and Joint Board, 136, 138, 140–41, and Markham, 158; and Frank Page, 164; and Sheets, 137, and U.S. highway numbering, 136, 138, 150, 157–70

Pike's Peak, 50

Pine, William B., 159–60

populism, 38

Portland cement, 39, 137. *See also* roads

Postal Highway, 54

Powder Puff Derby, 219

Pressey, Harold A., 58–59, 99–100

primary roads, 112. *See also* roads

Pyle, C. C.: adverse publicity for, 201–203; and C. Avery, 203–204; and Grange, 195; and Guthrey, 203–204; and International Trans-Continental Foot Race, 196, 197, 200; and Leglen, 195; and Scott, 203

Pyle, C. C. footrace. *See* International Trans-Continental Foot Race

racism, 48, 76–77. *See also* African Americans

railroads, 7, 8, 9. *See also specific railroads*

U.S. highways: and C. Avery, 128, 144, 165, 180; building of, 128; characteristics of, 149; and Coolidge, 129–30, 146; and Earle, 36; federal aid for, 129, 137; and Gentry, 144; and Gore, 132; and Greene, 156; and James, 153–54, 173–74; and Johnson, 144; and Kentucky, 156–57, 162; maps of, *86–87*, 141–44, 145–46, 147, 150, 151–52, 160, 190; OK-7 as, 142; and Oklahoma, 173; and road markers, 139; routes of, 142; and routing issues in Oklahoma, 145–46; Santa Fe Trail as, 143; and 7 Percent Law, 137; signage of, 140; taxes for, 129; and Trammell, 168; and U.S. Army, 68. *See also* roads; signage; U.S. highway numbering

U.S. Post Office, 34–35

U.S. 66. *See* Route 66

U.S. 66 Highway Association: advertising by, 193, 206; and boosterism, 193, 208; budget for, 206; and C. Avery, 191, 205–206, 210, 211, 219–220; and donations, 194; and Guthrey, 191; headquarters of, 206; incorporation of, 192; and International Trans-Continental Foot Race, 198; meetings of, 194, 197, 204, 205–206, 210; organization of, 190, 191; purposes of, 190; and Scott, 191, 206; and Woodruff, 190, 191, 206. *See also* Route 66

Vandalia, Illinois, 10

Venable, Ross, 120

Victory Highway, 156

Vinita, Oklahoma, 9, 17, 18, 21

Virginia, 171

Walton, John C., 113, 114–15

water: of Arkansas River, 97; and C. Avery,

30, 99, 100–101, 109, 235; bonds for, 101–102; bottling of, 97–98, 99; and Holway, 101; and Hubbard, 99; and Lorton, 98, 99; and McFarlin, 99; nonpartisan committee on, 99; pipelines for, 102–103; and Pressey, 99; pumping stations for, 98; and Spavinaw Water Construction Project, 97; and Taxpayers' Protective League, 100; and Tulsa, 29–30, 97, 98, 99; and Tulsa Chamber of Commerce, 99, 108

water commission. *See* Tulsa Water Commission

Watie, Stand, 7, 8, 12, 226, 251n27

Wayne County, Michigan, 41, 51

Weingroff, Richard, 150–51

wells. *See* oil and oil wells; water

Wentz, Lew H., 188, 210

White, F. R., 171

White River Trails Association, 49, 54, 71, 75, 190

Wiggins Ferry Company, 11

William Jewell (college), 14–15, 141

Williams, Robert Lee, 48, 50

Williams, William F., 136

Wilson, Philip St. John, 123, 170

Wilson, Woodrow, 60, 223

"Wisconsin Plan," 149, 150

Woodruff, John, 71, 189, 190, 191, 206

Works Progress Administration (WPA), 222, 226–30

World's Columbian Exposition, 33

World War I, 61, 65, 66

WPA (Works Progress Administration), 222, 226–30

yeast rolls, 74, 243n10

Yellowstone Trail, 53

Yellowstone Trail Association, 75

Printed in the USA
CPSIA information can be obtained
at www.ICGtesting.com
LVHW040640171223
766606LV00030B/1174/J